Women, Male Violence
and the Law

Women, Male Violence and the Law

Edited by Julie Stubbs

The Institute of Criminology Monograph Series No. 6

Sydney
1994

Institute of Criminology
Monograph Series

Series Editor: **John Braithwaite**

Professor, Research School of Social Sciences
Australian National University

Other titles in the series:

Aboriginal Perspectives on Criminal Justice, edited by Chris Cunneen

Doing Less Time: Penal Reform in Crisis, Janet Chan

Psychiatry in Court: The Use of Psychiatric Reports in Court Proceedings, Peter Shea

The Man in White is Always Right: Cricket and the Law, David Fraser

The Prison and the Home, Ann Aungles

Published by   The Institute of Criminology
Sydney University Law School
173-175 Phillip Street
Sydney NSW 2000, Australia
Ph: (02) 225 9239 Fax (02) 221 5635

Distributed by   Federation Press
Phone (02) 552 2200
Fax (02) 552 1681
PO Box 45 Annandale NSW 2038

ISBN 0 86758 918 3
©1994 The Institute of Criminology and the authors.

Distributed by Federation Press PO Box 45 Annandale NSW 2038, AUSTRALIA
Ph (02) 552 2200 Fax (02) 552 1681

Typeset by Brian Hydesmith, cover design by Melinda May.
Printed and bound by Robert Burton Printers, 63 Carlingford Street, Sefton NSW 2162

Acknowledgments

This collection of essays was first suggested by Mark Findlay, Director of the Institute of Criminology. The Institute of Criminology provided financial and other support for the project, which also received a grant from the N.S.W. Law Foundation Legal Scholarship Support Fund of the Faculty of Law at the University of Sydney. The contributors to this volume also provided their support, energy and ideas.

Research and editorial assistance was provided by Katrina Budrikis, and by Lynda-ann Blanchard. Lynda was also primarily responsible for bibliographic research, word processing and preparation of the manuscript, and for compiling the index, all of which she did with great efficiency and patience. Fiona Wright provided assistance in many ways, and at several stages of the project, and resolved what seemed to be insurmountable problems in computing and with software. Martin de Groot also provided software support in times of crisis. Graeme Coss gave valuable advice and assistance regarding reference issues. Harry provided the coffee.

Contributors

Hilary Astor is an Associate Professor in the Faculty of Law, University of Sydney. She is the co-author, with Professor Christine Chinkin, of *Dispute Resolution in Australia*. She has written widely in the area of mediation and violence against women. She teaches Family Law, Alternative Dispute Resolution and Anti-Discrimination Law.

Ruth Busch is originally from the United States, and has practised law in Canada and in New Zealand. She is now a Senior Lecturer in Law, at the University of Waikato, where she teaches family law, legal system, and women, law, and policy. Her present research involves a multinational study on domestic violence intervention projects (with Neville Robertson and Ellen Pence, the founder of the Duluth Project), the evaluation of the Hamilton Abuse Intervention Pilot Project, and a study of custody/access decision-making in NZ in relationships characterised by domestic violence. She is the principal author, with Neville Robertson, and Hilary Lapsley, of *Protection from Family Violence*, and has also written numerous journal articles on domestic violence.

Hilary Charlesworth is Professor of Law at the University of Adelaide. She teaches and writes in the areas of international law and human rights law. She is also a commissioner of the Australian Law Reform Commission on the reference concerning women's access to the legal system.

Christine Chinkin is Dean and Professor of Law at the University of Southhampton. Her academic interests include dispute resolution, international law and feminist theory. She is the author of *Third parties in international law* and co-author with Hilary Astor of *Dispute resolution in Australia*.

Pam Greer is an Aboriginal consultant who works primarily in training and community development concerning issues of sexual assault, child sexual assault and domestic violence. She is a member of the N.S.W. Child Protection Council, the N.S.W. Domestic Violence Advisory Council, and the N.S.W. Women's Consultative Committee.

Neville Robertson is a community psychologist at the University of Waikato. Much of his work centres on domestic violence, both as a practitioner and as a researcher. As a member of the Men's Action Network, he has worked with abusers for a number of years and he has served as a member of the Professional Practices Committee of the Men for Non-Violence Network. He was a joint author (with Ruth Busch and Hilary Lapsley) of *Protection from Family Violence,* and he is currently working on the evaluation of the Hamilton Abuse Intervention Pilot Project.

Nan Seuffert is a lecturer at the University of Waikato Law School in Hamilton, New Zealand. She has been an activist in the movement to end domestic violence since 1986, and practiced as a lawyer in Boston for two years representing women who had been targets of domestic violence . Her research interests include feminist legal theories, feminist pedagogies and feminist lawyering.

Elizabeth Sheehy is an Associate Professor in the Faculty of Law at the University of Ottawa where she teaches criminal law. Her publications include *Criminal law and Procedure: Cases, context, critique* (with Jennie Abell). She is also a co-editor of the *Canadian Journal of Women and the Law.*

Julie Stubbs is a senior lecturer in the Faculty of Law at the University of Sydney where she teaches courses in criminology, criminological research and policing. She is a member of the management collective of the Domestic Violence Advocacy Service, and the legal sub-committee of the N.S.W. Domestic Violence Advisory Council. She is the co-author (with Diane Powell) of *Domestic violence: The Impact of Legal Reform in New South Wales* and has written widely on issues related to domestic violence, and concerning the battered woman syndrome.

Julia Tolmie is originally from New Zealand, and is a lecturer in the Faculty of Law at the University of Sydney. She teaches criminal law, and litigation. She has published work concerning defences to homicide, the battered woman syndrome, and corporate social responsibility.

Table of Contents

1

Introduction

Julie Stubbs

[The study of woman battering] challenges our deepest aspirations for family life and intimate relations. Battering raises fundamental intellectual and political issues about feminist theory and practice, about law as an instrument of social change, and about the development of and role of legal remedies. Battering also presents important jurisprudential issues, such as the interrelationship between law and social science. It is not only an important subject in and of itself because of the impact it has on society in general, but also because it is a lens for looking at central issues concerning the transformative possibilities and limits of the law.

Elizabeth Schneider[1]

...it is not certain that the law is **incapable** *of introducing some degree of reform in this area [wife abuse].*

Susan Edwards[2]

The underlying theme of *Women, Male Violence and the Law* lies in assessing the possibilities and limits of law(s) in the context of domestic violence.[3] However, each of the issues raised by Elizabeth Schneider in the extract above is reflected within the book. These issues are not straightforward, subject to ready answers or uncontested. The works presented in this collection represent reflections on a range of theoretical and practical issues, and include the findings of recent research concerning legal responses to violence against women in several jurisdictions. The lawyers, social scientists, educators and policy makers who have contributed to this project have diverse backgrounds and experience. However, they share a feminist commitment to the on-going task of challenging the existing social and legal order to recognise women's experiences, and to redress women's disadvantage. They share a genuine concern about the impact of violence on the lives of women and children.

Reforms to law and policy have been central to the state's response to domestic violence in all Australian jurisdictions, and in New Zealand.

Feminists, both within and outside the bureaucracy have struggled to make the law more responsive to women's needs and interests, and successive rounds of reform concerning domestic violence have occurred in most jurisdictions over the past decade. Feminist engagement with the state, and with law reform, has been characterised as fraught with tensions and with contradictions.[4] The outcome of that engagement is by no means certain, and may be the subject of on-going re-negotiation and change. It is important to critically assess the effects of such reforms, however, and in doing so to recognise the limits and the potential of law to bring real change. We need to examine the effects of such reform as situated and specific, and we need to question under what conditions and in what ways such reforms might benefit women. And we need to ask "which women"? It is also necessary to recognise that law is likely to be a limited and insufficient tool with which to bring about broader cultural changes which might render violence genuinely unacceptable in social relations.

Women, Male Violence and the Law draws together a range of recent research material on legal responses to violence against women in Australia and New Zealand. In doing so it addresses some of the most pressing issues for those interested in the further development of law(s) and policies aimed at protecting women and children from such violence. The book does not set out to give an account of the existing laws in the jurisdictions concerned. Nicholas Seddon does a very good job of that with respect to Australian jurisdictions.[5]

The book presents a collection of essays which relate to issues inadequately canvassed in the existing Australian and New Zealand literature concerning domestic violence, or not readily available to readers in those countries. These issues include:

- the attitudes of the judiciary as evident in their decisions in cases concerning domestic violence;
- the experiences of Aboriginal women who seek to utilise the criminal justice system to protect themselves and their children from violence;
- the need for a co-ordinated response by government and non-government agencies in addressing violence against women, and the findings from one city which has adopted such an approach;
- mechanisms for integrating the experiences of academics, workers and those who have otherwise experienced male violence in research which is feminist, ethical and useful; and the
- education of lawyers to better meet their client's needs.

This book also includes evaluations of recent shifts in law(s) and practice in international law (for example in the form of the United Nations Declaration on the Elimination of Violence Against Women), in mediation and in criminal law in the use of the battered woman syndrome (BWS). In reflecting on the jurisprudence concerning the battered woman syndrome, this book also includes a chapter on the Canadian experience subsequent to the ground breaking pro-feminist decision in *Lavallee*,[6] a decision which has been very influential in Australian developments.

This book provides a necessarily partial account of the legal response to domestic violence. There are many additional issues of pressing importance which are not covered here, such as: violence within gay and lesbian relationships; the effects of violence on children; the experiences of women of non-English speaking backgrounds who have experienced violence at the hands of their partners (and perhaps the legal system); and, violence against women in the context of immigration including serial sponsorship. In each of these areas (as with the areas covered in this book) the literature in Australia and New Zealand is not yet well developed. This book is also inevitably partial in presenting only some voices and some perspectives.

A note on language

Throughout the book authors have varied in their choice of language to describe the violence with which they are concerned. Some authors have chosen to use language which acknowledges the gendered nature of the violence (such as "woman battering"), or the criminal nature of the conduct (such as "criminal assault in the home"), over more (gender) neutral expressions (such as "family violence", "domestic violence", or "spouse assault"). Some have adopted the terminology most commonly used in their own jurisdiction. As editor I have not imposed any uniformity in the use of language recognising the inadequacy of any of the alternatives to convey the range of physical, psychological, social and economic abuse which occurs within intimate relationships.[7] The book is confined to dealing with such abuse as it occurs between adults, typically in the context of a current or previous intimate relationship.

Embracing diversity

Much of the work on domestic violence has been implicitly or explicitly essentialist.[8] In part this reflects the deliberate choice of political strategies which have been used historically to highlight the importance of the issue and to mobilise resources in response.[9] Much of the feminist scholarship is very deliberately essentialist[10] highlighting the gendered nature of the violence, and reacting against gender neutral accounts which de-politicise and de-contextualise the violence.

In part however, this gender essentialism reflects a failure in some feminist work to pay sufficient attention to the different experiences of women.[11] A vast literature now exists debating the limitations of gender essentialism and the

universalising claims which have been made in the name of feminist scholarship.[12] Such universal accounts have been challenged by Aboriginal women,
women in the Third World, minority women generally, and working class
women who find that their own experiences are not always (or ever) adequately reflected in feminist discourses and in the development of policy.[13]

Domestic violence is gendered violence and this needs to be acknowledged
and understood. The recognition of the violence as gendered, however, need
not preclude an examination of the specific contexts in which the violence
occurs, nor of the manner in which race, class or sexual identity (or indeed
other social categories) might intersect with gender. Seeing domestic violence
as gendered violence allows us to begin to ask important questions about the
construction of gender, the potential to transform damaging forms of masculinity associated with that violence and about social and cultural factors which
permit men to resort to violence.

The challenge of recognising difference should not be seen as negating the
tremendous gains by feminists in recent decades. However, whilst acknowledging these gains, feminist scholars, policy makers, and others concerned with
domestic violence, need to re-examine the theoretical bases of our work and its
underlying assumptions. We need to recognise the challenge to acknowledge
difference.[14] We need to consider how best to think about the shared experiences we have as women in a way which does not present women's oppression
as natural, immutable, incontestable or beyond amelioration. We also need to
recognise the value of a shared political stance as women in challenging the
violence perpetrated against us, in a manner that acknowledges the differences
amongst women.[15] In Australia this task is particularly pressing.

Arguably, recent decades have seen some considerable improvements in the
provision of legal protection against violence in the home. However the women
most able to mobilise that protection are still those who are most informed,
most financially privileged, those in large urban settings, and those who belong
to dominant cultural groups.[16] Aboriginal women, women in rural areas and
those from non-English speaking backgrounds remain the least protected. The
challenge in re-thinking both theoretical and policy considerations in family
violence in Australia, is to do so in a way which is adequate to the task of
acknowledging difference in experience, difference in perspective, difference in
need, and in developing policy which is responsive to those differences. Those
working in the area need to include the voices of Aboriginal women, and
women from backgrounds other than the dominant culture to test and challenge the dominant assumptions and to be creative in providing responses to
the issue.

Pam Greer's contribution to this volume provides an insight into the value of
an intersectional analysis which recognises the specificity of the positioning of
Aboriginal women, a specificity not adequately addressed by either universal

feminist accounts nor by anti-racist discourse. She demonstrates how dominant and singular constructions and representations of Aboriginal people have rendered the concerns of Aboriginal women subordinate to the (presumed) larger community interest. She also argues that the failure to recognise the differences between and among Aboriginal peoples and communities has been associated with the inappropriate application of research findings from some communities and some jurisdictions to other places. She describes recent attempts by Aboriginal women and some communities to voice their concerns about violence in those communities, and to challenge Aboriginal and non-Aboriginal organisations and the legal system in particular to be responsive to their needs.

Julia Tomie and myself have also begun to examine the benefits of an intersectional approach which acknowledges both race and gender in analysing the use of battered woman syndrome in Australia.

Nan Seuffert's chapter discusses the implications of taking seriously feminist approaches to epistemology, and the criticisms of traditional research methods offered by Maori people. She describes her attempts to develop a research strategy which draws on the insights of feminist interventions in the social sciences, and which provides recognition of the experiences of Maori women in a way which does not appropriate those experiences.

Crossing boundaries: theory and practice, academics, bureaucrats and the community

Recent work in Australia has commenced the task of examining the relationships between bureaucrats (femocrats) and activists in the "movement against domestic violence".[17] The contributions of academics and professionals to the development of responses to domestic violence has, as yet, been given much less attention. The genuine tensions which exist between these roles, and for individuals occupying one or more of these roles, and the related debates about commitment and experience, practice and theory, and the production and ownership of knowledge need to be acknowledged and engaged constructively.[18] The relationship between femocrats and activists outside the bureaucracy has been found to be complex, and at times strained. However, in some contexts the relationships have been productive and supportive. For instance, Heather McGregor and Andrew Hopkins found that the engagement of the women's movement with the state had gone further in Australia than in other countries, and attributed this in part to a sympathetic femocracy.[19]

In this volume Nan Seuffert addresses the relationships between academics, professionals and activists very directly in the context of undertaking research which is feminist, ethical and responsive to the concerns of activists. She draws on her own experiences in New Zealand, and in the United States. As someone who has, at times, occupied each of the roles academic, lawyer and activist simultaneously, she is sensitive to the contradictions and the competing demands of those positions, as well as to the benefits and potentialities in looking to contest the boundaries inherent in the categorisation of those roles as separate and distinct. She is also keen to promote an approach to pedagogy that takes women's experiences and activists' concerns seriously, with the potential for transforming legal education.

Establishing accountability for gendered violence

A key strategy for feminists working in the area of domestic violence has been to seek to make lines of accountability for gendered violence clear. In the international law arena, the struggle has been for states to be seen as having responsibility for the gendered violence practiced by the state's citizens, or by the state itself.

Hilary Charlesworth and Christine Chinkin describe recent developments in international law in response to violence against women. The developments they describe, including the United Nations Declaration on the Elimination of Violence Against Women, seem to represent enormous gains for women. For example, they note that Article 4(c) of that declaration requires that states punish acts of violence against women perpetrated by the state **or by private persons,** a marked shift from the traditional reluctance of international law to regulate behaviour outside the public sphere. However, the authors caution that the achievements to date have been less than might have been hoped for. In the negotiations and compromise that characterise international relations, the final declaration which was agreed to is not as strong as earlier drafts. Violence against women is not explicitly defined as a violation of human rights. And women's human rights issues continue to be relegated to specialist bodies, with poor resourcing, rather than to be dealt with in the mainstream. The appointment of a Special Rapporteur on violence against women is however, a welcome development since it provides one mechanism by which states can be asked to account for their responsiveness, or lack thereof, to gendered violence.

Accountability is also a theme of Ruth Busch and Neville Robertson's chapter, which concerns the response of the justice system to domestic violence at the local level. They describe the Hamilton Abuse Intervention Pilot Project (HAIPP) which was developed in Hamilton, New Zealand, and which was adapted from the Duluth Abuse Intervention Project in the United States. The project attempts to limit the discretion, and the associated variability in response, of different agents within the criminal justice system by introducing a co-ordinated set of policies and priorities for dealing with domestic violence matters. The co-ordination of response across the criminal justice system is obviously a key concern if enhancing the safety of those at risk of domestic violence is to be taken seriously as an objective, and yet the criminal justice system rarely operates in a co-ordinated and systemic fashion with respect to domestic violence or any other matter.[20] Each agent or agency operates with a marked degree of independence such that police, courts, departments of corrections and of community corrections, not to mention community based organisations such as refuges, each have their own concerns and priorities.

The HAIPP scheme is notable not just for the focus on the co-ordination of policy and practice, but also for the mechanisms used to support and empower women, to hold men responsible for their violence, for monitoring whether practice conforms with policy and for holding the agencies accountable where they depart from established policy. Too often where law reform is pursued, it is as a stand-alone response by government which is not resourced to ensure that it has the prospect of success, nor is its impact monitored.

Challenging idealised constructions of the family

The monitoring of judicial decision-making also provides a form of accountability for key agents of the criminal justice system. Whilst it could be argued that judicial decisions, in some form, are typically part of the public record, the power of Ruth Busch's analysis of judicial decisions lies in bringing together a range of judgments to facilitate the identification of underlying themes, and to begin to understand the attitudes which may explain the patterns which emerge. Her work demonstrates the power of an idealised construction of family life in decisions concerning violence. She found that the overwhelming concern of some judges with maintaining or reconstituting families was such that much else, including extreme violence, was ignored, trivialised or reinterpreted in the service of maintaining the family.

Hilary Astor's chapter also explores this theme as she seeks to explain the enthusiasm for mediation as a mechanism for dealing with family disputes. Mediation has a strong appeal as a mechanism for dispute resolution within the family because it is seen as affordable, caring and consensual, especially when compared with more formal mechanisms of dispute resolution. It is mythologised as being particularly well equipped to restore the idealised family. However, it is not simply these qualities which Hilary Astor has identified as crucial to understanding the promotion of mediation in this context. Rather it is the manner in which the public/private dichotomy is invoked by mediators to characterise the process of mediation. Mediation itself is seen as having the qualities of the private sphere, and thus as being especially well suited to deal with "private" disputes. Challenges to constructions of the private as nurturing and caring, by recognising the potential for families to be destructive and violent, provide a fundamental challenge to the ideological basis of mediation itself and are resisted by mediators.

This chapter also highlights the need to be cautious about the renewed interest in alternative, allegedly informal, methods of dealing with domestic violence, often justified by the apparent failings of the justice system to deal with domestic violence effectively. A first reason for concern is that it is often the case that the alleged alternatives are grafted onto the formal justice system, in such forms as court referred or mandated mediation, or as required steps before a grant of legal aid or the right to proceed within a court. Thus what is often presented as a matter of choice on the part of women who seek protection from domestic violence may not be a choice at all. Of greater concern, perhaps, is the danger that any agreement mediated against a background of violence is unlikely to represent a free and equitable agreement and may be to women's significant detriment.

"Offending victims" and the battered woman syndrome

Women on trial for offences committed in response to, or under the effect of, domestic violence, have the potential to disturb conventional practice in the criminal law, and threaten to disrupt the victim/offender dichotomy so prevalent in criminal practice. Their behaviour typically has not been readily understood, nor sympathetically interpreted by courts. The recent acceptance of testimony concerning the battered woman syndrome has been promoted as one avenue by which lawyers, judges and jurors might come to better understand the behaviour of battered women who offend against the criminal law. Two chapters in this collection assess the extent to which this potential to disturb and develop orthodox legal doctrine and practice has been achieved through the use of testimony concerning the battered woman syndrome in Canada and Australia.

Elizabeth Sheehy provides an analysis of Canadian cases in which BWS has been introduced since the important decision in *Lavallee*, a decision which has been relied on in the development of BWS in Australian courts.[21] Whilst *Lavallee* was hailed as a significant development in the law of self-defence, recognising as it did that self-defence was fundamentally gendered in that it presumed male experience, cases determined since that time have not uniformly reflected this development. Several cases indicate a progressive interpretation of the law and a sympathetic treatment by the courts. However, Elizabeth Sheehy demonstrates that in a number of decisions since *Lavallee* the insights of Madame Justice Bertha Wilson into the context in which women who have experienced domestic violence might offend, have not been evident. She cites cases in which women were convicted, or pleaded guilty, yet the facts seemed to conform to the construction of self-defence presented in *Lavallee*, and thus seemed open to an acquittal.

Julia Tolmie and myself provide an analysis of the Australian cases which have been decided to this point in time, in which evidence concerning the battered woman syndrome has been offered. We have found that it is impossible to characterise the Australian cases as representing an unequivocal success for women. Whilst the acceptance of the battered woman syndrome in Australia was seen by some commentators as opening up the opportunity for a further development in the law of self-defence, one which would better reflect women's experience, few of the Australian cases have offered any challenge to traditional self-defence doctrine. In many instances the use of BWS seems to have been used to reinforce orthodox approaches to legal practice. Rather than challenging the victim/offender dichotomy as false and removed from the experiences of many women who have been the target of violence,[22] the use of BWS seems to be most effective where it reinforces the construction of the woman on trial as victim, and erases her agency.

The use of evidence concerning the battered woman syndrome presents a significant dilemma for feminist practice and is highly contested.[23] These chapters share with several others in this collection, a call to be cautious in assuming that recent developments in law and practice, even those promoted as serving women's interests, are achieving that promise. The chapters call into question to what extent, if at all, the use of expert evidence concerning BWS has been a successful means of challenging gender bias in the law.

Law reform and the potential for change

The potential for law reform to provide protection to women in instances of battering, should not be presumed. However, neither should law reform be dismissed as the misguided attempt by liberal feminists to engage with a state which is antipathetic to their interests.[24] The outcome of legislative and policy change is neither predictable nor straightforward and is mediated by many factors, not least of which are the attitudes and commitment of the actors within the criminal justice system charged with implementing those changes. Carol Smart has warned that "law is so deaf to core concerns of feminism that feminists should be extremely cautious of how and whether they resort to law".[25] She also has acknowledged however, that many issues are already in the domain of law so that it is not possible to avoid law. Violence against women is one such issue. Whilst individual women may sometimes choose not to engage with law(s), for many others there is no real choice—law provides one of few resources which might be available to individual women. It is also important, as Margaret Thornton argues, to recognise that:

> [i]n the light of the privileged status of law within our society, it cannot be
> neglected or social relations will continue to be reproduced within legal dis-
> course as they always have been, that is from a masculinist point of view.[26]

In one way or another each of the chapters in this collection is concerned with the possibilities of law and/or policy reform, as expressed in specific contexts. The outcomes which they describe cannot be simply summarised or easily characterised. Some of the developments described and analysed are clearly emergent, and developing—further feminist effort may see them evolve in a manner more clearly articulated with women's interests, and more successful in their application. The developments in the arena of international law could perhaps be characterised in this way. The use of BWS in the courts may yet be open to transformation and application in ways more consistent with feminist concerns. In other areas however, women's interests may be best served by actively resisting the momentum for change- for instance, the use of mediation in violent relationships offers substantial risks to women's personal safety, and to their chances of fair and equitable outcomes.

The chapters outlined above reinforce the value of an approach to law which is critical, cautious, and which resists the "siren call"[27]. They also promote the value of an analysis of law and legal practice which is contextual and situated. Law reform creates a space, a process, an opportunity for addressing violence, but by no means guarantees the outcome. As Smart has argued:

> If we reject the idea of law as a simple tool of liberation or oppression, and look at how it constitutes a kind of institutionalized and formalized site of power struggles—one that can provide resources for women, children, and men, albeit differentially—then it is possible to acknowledge that it remains an important strategic element in political confrontations. Yet it seems we cannot know in advance whether a recourse to law will empower women, children, or men, although there is substantial and well-founded fear that legal power works better for (white, middle-class) men than for anyone else.[28]

Whilst law is a powerful discourse, it is not beyond being contested, nor is it uniform in its practice and effects.

Notes

1   Schneider, E, "Violence Against Women and Legal Education: An Essay for Mary Joe Frug" (1992) 26 *New England LJ* 843 at 848.

2   Edwards, S, "Violence Against Women: Feminism and the Law" in Gelsthorpe, L and Morris, A (eds), *Feminist Perspectives in Criminology* (1990) at 156, emphasis in the original.

3   The use of law(s) is deliberate to indicate that law is not singular, consistent in its goals or unified in its effect. What we call law is really a range of laws, procedures and policies. See Smart, C, *Feminism and the Power of Law* (1989) at chapter 1.

4   Thornton , M, "Feminism and the Contradictions of Law Reform" (1991) 19 *International J of the Sociology of Law* 453-474; see also many of the essays in Watson, S (ed), *Playing the State: Australian Feminist Interventions* (1990).

5   Seddon, N, *Domestic Violence in Australia: The Legal Response* (2nd edn, 1993).

6   [1990] 55 C.C.C. (3d) 97 (S.C.C.).

7   See Minow , M, "Words and the Door to the Land of Change: Law, Language and Family Violence" (1990) 43 *Vanderbilt LR* 1665-1699; Thornton, above n4.

8   Harris, A, "Race and Essentialism in Feminist Legal Theory" (1990) 42 *Stanford LR* 581-616.

9   See McFerren, L, "Interpretation of a Frontline State: Australian Women's Refuges and the State" in Watson, above n4.

10 Thornton, above n4 at 456: "I am adopting an unashamedly essentialist position in focusing on the paradigmatic sex/violence harms which are over-whelmingly perpetrated by men against women **because they are women**, regardless of race, ethnicity or class, although these factors may effect the nature and extent of harm."

11 Behrendt, L, "Aboriginal Women and the White Lies of Feminism: Implications for Aboriginal Women in Rights Discourse" (1993) 1 *Aust Feminist LJ* 27.

12 Harris, A, "Race and Essentialism in Feminist Legal Theory" (1990) 42 *Stanford LR* 581-616; MacKinnon, C, "From Practice to Theory or What is a White Woman Anyway?" (1991) 4 *Yale J of Law and Feminism* 13; Allen, J, "The Masculinity of Criminality and Criminology: Interrogating some Impasses" in Findlay, M and Hogg, R (eds), *Understanding Crime and Criminal Justice* Law (1988); Carrington, K, "Feminist Readings of Female Delinquency" (1990) 8 (2) *Law in Context* 5-31.

13 Lorde, A, "The Master's Tools Will Never Dismantle the Master's House" and "Age, Race, Class and Sex: Women Redefining Difference" in Lorde, A, *Sister Outsider* (1984); hooks, b, *Talking Back: Thinking Feminist, Thinking Black* (1989); Thornhill, E, "Focus on Black Women!" (1985) 1 *Canadian J of Women and Law* 153; Rasche, C, "Minority Women and Domestic Violence: The Unique Dilemmas of Battered Women of Color" (1986) 4 *J of Contemporary Criminal Justice* 150; see also Kline, M, "Race, Racism and Feminist Legal Theory" (1989) 12 *Harv Women's LJ* 115.

14 It is arguably the case that the refuge movement has been much quicker to identify and respond to the needs of Aboriginal and Torres Strait Islander women, and to women from a non-English speaking background, than those working in academic and bureaucratic settings. See McFerren, above n9.

15 Schneider, E, "Particularity and Generality: Challenges of Feminist Theory and Practice in Work on Woman Abuse" (1992) 67 *NYULR* 520; Crenshaw, K, "Mapping the Margins: Intersectionality, Identity Politics, and Violence Against Women of Color" (1991) 43 *Stanford LR* 1241; see also Pettman, J, "Gendered Knowledges" in Attwood, B, and Arnold, J (eds), *Power, Knowledge and Aborigines* (1992) at 120 (special issue, (1992) 35 *J of Australian Studies*).

16 Stubbs, J and Egger, S, *The Effectiveness of Protection Orders in Australian Jurisdictions* (1993); Australian Law Reform Commission *Equality Before the Law: Women's Access to the Legal System* Interim Report No 67 (1992).

17 McGregor, H and Hopkins, A, *Working for Change: The Movement Against Domestic Violence* (1991); see also McFerren, above n9.

18 See Fraser, N, "Apologia for Academic Radicals" in *Unruly Practices: Power, Discourse and Gender in Contemporary Social Theory* (1989); see also McFerren, above n9 especially on the complex relationship between femocrats and feminist workers in the refuge movement; and Schneider, E, above n1 on the dissociation between academics and activists, and on bringing those threads together in her own work.

19 Above n17 at 143; see also McFerren's work on the success of feminist engagement with the state around refuge funding in New South Wales as compared with Western Australia, above n9.

20 See Hogg, R, "Perspectives on the Criminal Justice System" in Findlay, M, Egger, S and Sutton, J, *Issues in Criminal Justice Administration* (1983).

21 The significance of *Lavallee* is discussed by Sheehy, and by Stubbs and Tolmie, both in this volume.

22 See Mahoney, M, "Legal Images of Battered Women: Redefining the Issue of Separation" (1991) 90 *Michigan LR* 1; Schneider, E, "Particularity and Generality" above n15.

23 In the Australian context see the work of Patricia Easteal, who takes a very different position than that of the authors represented in this volume; Easteal, P, Hughes, K, and Easter, J, "Battered Women and Duress" (1993) 18 (3) *Alt LJ* 139; Easteal, P, "Battered Woman Syndrome: What is Reasonable?" (1992) 17 *Alt LJ* 220; Easteal, P, "Battered Woman Syndrome Misunderstood?" (1992) 3 *Current Issues in Criminal Justice* 356.

24 See Thornton, above n 4.

25 Smart, above n3 at 2.

26 Thornton, above n4 at 454.

27 Smart, above n3 at 160.

28 Id at 138.

2

Violence Against Women:
A Global Issue

Hilary Charlesworth and Christine Chinkin*

Our thanks to Dianne Otto who provided very helpful research assistance, and to Jo Crawford and Annie McLean of the Office of the Status of Women who kindly provided valuable documentation and information.

Introduction

Violence against women is a global problem. It occurs in diverse forms across all cultures and in all societies and cannot be narrowly defined. Violence affects examples of women's physical and mental health and includes such acts as: abortion of female foetuses; female infanticide; compulsory sterilisation; deprivation of food for girls and women; wife and partner murder; assault; rape, or threats of such attacks, gang rape, date rape, rape in armed conflict and stranger rape; other forms of sexual abuse and harassment, including those occurring in the workplace; forced marriages; dowry deaths; culturally based practices such as sati and genital mutilation; trafficking, exploitation and slavery.[1] Media coverage of events in the former Yugoslavia has given violence against women a higher profile than ever before.[2] This focus of attention on violence during the exceptional situation of armed conflict, however, may serve to obscure the daily, routine violence suffered by women throughout the world.

Common to all these expressions of violence is the fact that the victims suffer because of their gender. Womanhood means a particular and universal vulnerability to violence. Radhika Coomaraswamy has identified four primary reasons for this:[3] first, a woman's sexuality makes her susceptible to sex related crimes which are "fundamentally connected to a society's construction of female sexuality and its role in social hierarchy";[4] second, a woman's relationship to a man or to a group of men makes her vulnerable to types of violence which "are animated by society's concept of a woman as the property and dependent of a male protector"; third, violence against women may be directed towards the social group of which she is a member because, for example "to rape a woman is to humiliate her community"; finally, there is a strong connection between militarisation and violence against women.[5] Gender-based violence is neither random nor circumstantial. Rather it is a structural problem, directly connected to the universal imbalance in power between women and men. As Margaret Schuler observes, the dominance of male power "reduce[s] women to economic and emotional dependency, the property of some male protector".[6]

Three distinct, but closely connected, institutions can be identified as the major sites of violence against women: the family, the community and the state.[7] The problem of domestic, familial, violence has been well documented. Increasing attention is being given to the role social, cultural and religious groups play in sanctioning gender-based violence. The function that the state has in supporting violence against women has attracted less attention.

This chapter focuses on international attempts to make the state accountable for violence against women. It first discusses traditional international legal doctrine and the problems it poses in attributing state responsibility for gendered violence. It then examines international initiatives, primarily within the United Nations system, to respond to violence against women. There have been significant advances in characterising gendered violence as an international issue, but work remains to be done.

The slow response of international law

Given the universality of the problem, the issue of violence against women has come onto the international agenda very slowly. There are a number of theoretical and practical reasons for this.

First, the public/private distinction which has been the focus of much feminist analysis[8] has had particular significance in the development of international law. International law assumes, and reinforces, a number of dichotomies between public and private spheres of action.[9] One is the distinction drawn between international ("public") concerns and those within the domestic ("private") jurisdiction of states.[10] Within the category of international concerns a further public/private distinction is drawn: international law is almost exclusively addressed to the public, or official, activities of states; states are not held responsible for "private" activities of their nationals or those within their jurisdiction. This more basic dichotomy has significant implications for women. Women's lives are generally conducted within the sphere deemed outside the scope of international law, indeed also often outside the ambit of "private" (national) law.[11] Although human rights law is often regarded as a radical development in international law, because of its challenge to that discipline's traditional public/private dichotomy between states and individuals, it has retained the deeper, gendered, public/private distinction. In the major human rights treaties, rights are defined according to male experiences. The primacy traditionally given to civil and political rights by western international lawyers and philosophers is directed towards protection for men within public life, in their relationship with government.[12] Violence against women does not fit within this paradigm. As Sharon Capeling-Alakiya, the Director of the United Nations Development Fund for Women (UNIFEM) has noted: .

> the home is a metaphor of tremendous power. To debate a government's right or responsibility to intervene in a private home is to raise some of the most explosive issues of our day: What is a nation? What is sovereignty? Under what circumstances must outsiders act?[13]

Second, despite increasing evidence of violence against women its true level has remained hidden.[14] It is viewed in many societies as a private matter. Just as women themselves are reluctant to report violence against them because of shame and the socio-economic pressure to remain in relationships, the incidence of violence against women in the home has been widely underplayed by communities that fear acknowledgment will undermine the integrity of the family.[15] In many cases cultural and traditional attitudes and prejudices lead to tolerance of such levels of violence and the economic and social dependence of so many women makes reporting or combating abuse an unavailable option. These factors have combined to deflect international concern about the extent of violence against women.

Third, on a practical level, the initiatives for most international discussions on gender-based violence have not come from official representatives of states, but from women's groups and organisations which have little domestic and international influence. It is difficult for such groups to make their voices heard within the male dominated structures and institutions of the international legal system.[16] On a legal level, neither women's voices nor actions are influential in the formation of international law since its sources rest upon state consent expressed formally through the negotiation of treaties or through consistent state practice.[17] In both contexts women have almost no influence.

Violence against women and state responsibility

The normative structure of international law has hindered the recognition of violence against women as an international issue. As noted above, traditionally international law holds states accountable only for actions that can be attributed directly to them, for example the "official" activities of government agents. Some violence against women fits clearly into this category,[18] although there is evidence that the international community takes "state" violence against women less seriously than parallel violence against men.[19]

The international legal situation is less clear when the state justice system effectively tolerates violence against women by "private" actors. For example, the Women's Rights Project of Human Rights Watch (WRP) study on violence against women in Brazil found evidence of a structure of discriminatory non-prosecution and indeed sometimes overt acceptance of three forms of violence against women: wife-murder, battery and rape.[20] The study focused on how the substantive criminal law in Brazil and the administration of the criminal justice system had combined to provide effective impunity to men who commit such crimes. With respect to wife-murder, the legal defence of "honor" to the murder of an allegedly unfaithful wife was successful in some regions in 80 per cent of cases in which it was invoked, and in other cases operated to significantly reduce criminal sentences.[21] Husband-murder, by contrast, was treated considerably more seriously.[22] Although over 70 per cent of reported cases of violence against women in Brazil take place in the home (compared to ten percent for men), domestic violence has typically been treated either as a matter outside the criminal justice system, or more recently as a minor, peripheral problem. The WRP also reported the common non-prosecution and non-punishment of rape in Brazil, and the difficulties created for rape victims to prove their cases.[23]

These findings demonstrate how arbitrary the distinction between "public" and "private" action is in the context of violence against women. One reason for the wide scale toleration of violence against women in Brazil was the explicitly stated view that it was a "private" matter, not within the proper scope of the criminal justice system.[24] However, if violence against women is understood not just as aberrant personal behaviour, but as part of the structure of the universal subordination of women, it cannot ever be analysed as a purely "private" or national issue. Charlotte Bunch has pointed out that such violence is caused by "the structural relationships of power, domination and privilege between men and women in society. Violence against women is central to maintaining those political relations at home, at work and in all public spheres."[25] These structures are supported by the male hierarchy of the nation state.

Generally, states are not considered responsible for the conduct of persons not acting on their behalf,[26] although they are required to exercise due diligence to prevent their territory being used by private persons to cause harm in other states.[27] The WRP Brazil report pointed to the discriminatory pattern of state responses to crimes of violence based on the gender of the victims, and founded its argument for Brazil's international responsibility on its violation of the international norm of non-discrimination.[28] But the maintenance of a legal and social system in which violence against women is endemic and where such actions are trivialised or discounted should engage state responsibility directly, whether or not women are treated differently from men in this respect. There is some support for such an approach in decisions of the European and the Inter-American Courts of Human Rights which deal with the failure of states to provide adequate legal remedies for the protection of human rights.[29] In *X and Y v the Netherlands,* for example, the Netherlands was held to be in breach of the European Convention through the inadequacy of its criminal law.[30] A gap in the law meant that there was no action available to a 16 year old mentally retarded child who had been sexually abused. The European Court of Human Rights held that respect for family life includes positive obligations upon states and may require the adoption of measures designed to secure respect for private life even in the sphere of individual relations.

Similarly in *Velasquez Rodriguez v Honduras,* the Inter-American Court of Human Rights referred to "the duty of the States Parties to organise the governmental apparatus and, in general, all the structures through which public power is exercised, so that they are capable of juridically ensuring the free and full enjoyment of human rights". It continued:

> *An illegal act which violates human rights and which is initially not*
> *directly imputable to a State (for example, because it is the act of a private*
> *person...) can lead to international responsibility of the State... because of*
> *the lack of due diligence to prevent the violation or to respond to it...This*
> *duty to prevent includes all those means of a legal, political, administrative*
> *and cultural nature that promote the protection of human rights and ensure*
> *that any violations are considered and treated as illegal acts.*[31]

Although neither of these cases were directly about women, the findings of state liability for private actions could be applied, for example, to the failure of a state to apply its criminal law to prosecute private acts of violence against women. They constitute extremely important statements that states may be held internationally responsible for private actions.

United Nations action on violence against women

Gendered violence has been gradually brought onto the international agenda, with the major work taking place in the specialised women's institutions of the United Nations.[32] Crucial to this has been the work of women's non-governmental organisations and individual women in documenting the incidence of violence against women around the world.[33] Early international initiatives focused upon the issue of domestic violence against women and not on its wider societal incidence and its structural roots. The characterisation of women's freedom from violence as a human right has been a relatively recent, and controversial, development.

The United Nations Decade For Women

The United Nations Decade for Women, 1975-85, witnessed a slow development of international concern on violence against women. The World Conference of the International Women's Year in Mexico City in 1975 launched the United Nations Decade for Women. The objectives of the decade were equality, development and peace; violence against women was not initially perceived as relevant to them. The World Plan of Action adopted by the Mexico Conference did not refer explicitly to violence, although it mentioned the issue of family conflict. It simply drew attention to the need for the family to ensure dignity, equality and security of each of its members and to be provided with assistance in the solution of conflict arising among its members.[34]

The 1980 United Nations Mid-Decade for Women Conference in Copenhagen treated violence in a limited manner,[35] with the final report referring to the issue of violence in the home.[36] The conference adopted a resolution entitled "Battered women and violence in the family".[37] It identified contributing factors to violence as geographic and social isolation, financial difficulties, irregular employment, alcohol and drug abuse and low self-esteem. Violence against women was more clearly on the agenda at the 1985 Nairobi Conference and the parallel forum convened by non-governmental organisations which closed the Decade for Women. The issues of abused women, increasing gender specific violence and the need to intensify efforts to introduce national legislative and other programmes to ascertain the causes of violence and to prevent and eliminate it, were included in the conference report as "areas of special concern".[38] The "Forward-looking Strategies for the Advancement of Women" adopted by the conference identified violence against women as a major obstacle to the objectives of the decade and called for the creation of preventative policies and institutionalised means of assistance to women who were victims of violence.[39]

The concern raised at Nairobi about violence against women has been continued and deepened within the specialised United Nations women's institutions and some of these developments are discussed below. Other agencies, such as the United Nations Development Fund for Women (UNIFEM), have focused on particular aspects of the problem.[40] The review and appraisal of the implementation of the "Forward-looking Strategies" by the United Nations Secretary General in 1990 found that violence against women in the family and in society remained a serious problem everywhere in the world and called on governments to take urgent and effective steps to eliminate it.

Other United Nations fora

Other parts of the United Nations system had meanwhile given attention to violence against women, particularly the Committee on Crime Prevention and Control and the regular United Nations Congresses on the Prevention of Crime and the Treatment of Offenders. In 1985 the United Nations General Assembly adopted a resolution on domestic violence[41] which was a major development in acknowledging the international dimensions of the problem, although the analytical basis of the resolution was very limited. It was based on a resolution of the Economic and Social Council on Violence Within the Family and adopted on the recommendation of the Commission on the Status of Women[42] and the activities of the Congresses on the Prevention of Crime. Its preamble identified the main harms of domestic violence as its undermining of the family structure, and its contribution to psychological harms in and delinquency of children, but did not refer to its effect on women. Among other things, the resolution called on members of the United Nations to make their legal systems more sensitive in response to domestic violence. It associated a non-violent environment with education, equality of rights and equality of responsibilities between women and men.

In 1986, the United Nations Branch (now Division) for the Advancement of Women and the Crime Prevention and Criminal Justice Branch of the United Nations Centre for Social Development and Humanitarian Affairs convened an Expert Group Meeting on Violence in the Family with Special Emphasis on its Effects on Women.[43] The Committee's discussion centred on domestic violence alone and its recommendations were limited to concrete and immediate measures to confront such violence. They also considered methods of crisis intervention. Important aspects of the Expert Group's findings were the global nature of the phenomenon of domestic violence and its considerable under-reporting.[44] This work laid the foundation for more comprehensive international legal responses to the problem.

Committee on the Elimination of Discrimination Against Women

The Convention on the Elimination of All Forms of Discrimination Against Women,[45] (the Women's Convention) adopted by the United Nations in 1979 during the United Nations Decade for Women, makes no explicit reference to violence, although it does deal with specific instances of violence (for example, trafficking).[46] The Women's Convention is monitored by the Committee on the Elimination of Discrimination Against Women (CEDAW).[47] CEDAW has been active in persuading the international legal system to analyse violence against women as a human rights issue.

Two United Nations Covenants, the International Covenant on Civil and Political Rights (ICCPR) and the International Covenant on Economic, Social and Cultural Rights (ICESCR),[48] form the cornerstones of the mainstream human rights canon. The developed world in particular has tended to give priority to civil and political rights over economic and social rights, arguing that the latter are goals rather than legal obligations.[49] While women are formally accorded the same human rights protection as men under the ICCPR and the ICESCR,[50] those documents have not been interpreted to take account of gender specific harms.[51] The Women's Convention built upon the norm of non-discrimination on the grounds of gender contained in the earlier Covenants, and indeed within the United Nations Charter itself.[52] Two significant features of this Convention are its drawing together of civil and political, and economic and social rights in a single instrument and its applicability (albeit limited) in the private sphere.[53]

CEDAW has responded to increasing international concern about violence against women, despite the Women's Convention's silence on the matter. In 1989, CEDAW adopted a General Recommendation that states include in their initial and periodic reports information on the incidence of violence against women and the measures adopted by the state to deal with it.[54] This was followed up by a more substantive recommendation at its eleventh session in 1992. General Recommendation 19 states that "the definition of discrimination includes gender-based violence" and that "gender-based violence is a form of discrimination that seriously inhibits women's ability to enjoy rights and freedoms on a basis of equality with men".[55] These rights include those contained within other mainstream human rights instruments: the right not to be subject to torture, or to cruel, inhuman or degrading treatment or punishment;[56] the right to equal protection under humanitarian law in times of armed conflict;[57] the right to liberty and security of the person;[58] the right to equal protection under the law;[59] the right to equality within the family;[60] the right to the highest attainable standard of physical and mental health;[61] and the right to just and favourable working conditions.[62] General Recommendation 19 reflects the developments in the customary international law with respect to state responsibility by stating that the Women's Convention applies to acts committed by public authorities and also to certain private acts. In particular "states may be... responsible for private acts if they fail to act with due diligence to prevent violations of rights or to investigate and punish acts of violence, and for providing compensation".[63]

General Recommendation 19 then applies these principles to specific provisions of the Convention including those relating to trafficking, prostitution and exploitation (Article 6); equality in employment and sexual harassment (Article 11); equal access to health care (Article 12); the special risks faced by rural women caused by traditional attitudes as to the subordinate position of women (Article 15); and equality within the family (Article 16). Specifically, the recommendation emphasises the discriminatory nature and harmful effects for women's health of certain traditional and cultural practices including genital mutilation, compulsory sterilisation and abortion.

CEDAW included in General Recommendation 19 a number of specific recommendations some of which relate directly to the reporting procedures of states and others to the domestic steps states should introduce. At the twelfth session following the acceptance of General Recommendation 19, the Committee followed up by closely questioning those states whose reports were up for review on these recommended matters, seeking for example identification of the nature and extent of attitudes, customs and practices which perpetuate violence against women, statistical and descriptive data of such violence, and details of measures taken and their effectiveness.[64]

By linking violence against women to human rights norms of non-discrimination, CEDAW asserted that the prohibition of gender-based violence is universally applicable. However the potential of General Recommendation 19 is weakened by a number of factors. First, the recommendation is not part of the authoritative text of the Women's Convention. It is a recommendation by the expert committee as to how States Parties should interpret and apply the Convention and not formally binding upon them. Second, reporting by States Parties is the only method of monitoring the implementation of the Women's Convention (unlike, for example, the ICCPR which provides mechanisms for inter-state and individual complaints).[65] The value of the recommendation will thus depend almost completely on the energy of CEDAW in raising it with reporting states and on the willingness of states to respond. Third, many states have made significant reservations to their obligations under the Women's Convention[66] and may be unwilling to accept a recommendation attributing a broad meaning to its provisions. Fourth, the impact of General Recommendation 19 outside the United Nations women's "ghetto" may be limited. CEDAW is one of six United Nations human rights treaty monitoring committees, and the only one with more than a handful of women members.[67] The other treaty monitoring bodies have displayed little sensitivity to concerns of gender and have generally displayed little awareness of the jurisprudence generated by CEDAW. There are some signs however that this may be changing. For example, in its General Comment No 18 on non-discrimination (37th session 1989) the Human Rights Committee asserts non-discrimination to constitute a basic and general principle (paragraph 1) and emphasises the connection between the ICCPR and the Women's Convention by citing the definition of discrimination contained in the latter (paragraph 6). It also asserts that the Committee is to be informed about states' conformity with the principle (paragraph 5) and in particular that the Committee wishes to be informed whether there remain problems of discrimination which may in fact be practised by public authorities, by the community, or by private persons or bodies. Although this comment does not refer to violence, it is an indication that the Human Rights Committee recognises that it should take account of the Women's Convention. Further, in June 1993 the World Conference on Human Rights asserted that "the human rights of women should be integrated into the mainstream of United Nations system-wide activity".[68] It argued for the integration of the goals and objectives of those United Nations bodies which are primarily concerned with women with those of other United Nations agencies. In particular the Conference stressed the "importance of working towards the elimination of violence against women in public and private life".[69] It is to be hoped that the work of the World Conference on Human Rights will set the parameters for human rights developments within the United Nations and most significantly the approach indicated at Vienna will assist in breaking down the long marginalisation of women's rights reflected in substantive law.

The Declaration on the Elimination of Violence Against Women

The United Nations Declaration on the Elimination of Violence Against Women[70] is the most recent international instrument dealing with gender violence. It was an initiative of the Commission on the Status of Women (CSW) which was established in 1946 as the major United Nations forum for women's policy. The CSW is one of the functional commissions of the Economic and Social Council of the United Nations (ECOSOC) and is composed of 45 governmental representatives.[71] In 1987, CSW selected the issue of violence against women within the family and society as a part of the priority theme of peace in the Forward-looking Strategies adopted at the Nairobi Conference.[72] Its inclusion under the theme of peace indicates that successful eradication of gender-based violence would liberate women to participate actively and effectively in the peace process and in international decision-making, and that violence on a personal and international level are inextricably linked.

In 1991, the CSW recommended to ECOSOC that a framework be developed in consultation with CEDAW and the Committee on Crime Prevention and Control for an international instrument that would address violence against women.[73] Canada, which had raised the issue in the CSW, favoured the preparation of an optional protocol on violence to the Women's Convention. Only those States Parties which formally accepted the protocol would be bound by it. The Canadian proposal raised a number of political and legal issues. A binding international document would take a considerable time to negotiate. It could also undermine the work of CEDAW on violence against women by implying that such violence was not prohibited by the terms of the 1979 Convention. Unless the instrument attracted a broad support from States Parties to the Women's Convention, it could reduce the potential of that document.

After considering a variety of approaches, including the preparation of a protocol on violence to the Women's Convention and a separate treaty on violence against women, an "Expert Group" meeting held in November 1991 as a result of the ECOSOC request decided in the end on an "incremental" approach to the issue by endorsing the notion of a General Assembly declaration on violence against women.[74] Although a declaration is not strictly speaking a binding document in international law, it can contribute to the formation of customary international law by crystallising the views of the international community. Also, declarations on human rights issues have been the usual precursor to binding treaties on the same subject. The Expert Group also recommended the elaboration and strengthening of the work of CEDAW to improve States Parties reporting on violence and the appointment of a Special Thematic Rapporteur on violence against women. In the event that these mechanisms proved ineffective, the Expert Group recommended that optional binding protocols to the Women's Convention be considered.

The Expert Group meeting produced the draft of a declaration, which was submitted to the CSW at its 36th session in 1992. The draft was developed, and changed considerably, at an intersessional working group of CSW in September 1992. The Draft Declaration was adopted at the March 1993 CSW meeting and was finally adopted by consensus by the General Assembly on 20 December 1993.[75]

What is the relationship of the Women's Convention, particularly CEDAW's General Recommendation 19, to this development? Some women's rights activists were concerned that the CSW initiative on violence could work to undermine the work of CEDAW by implying that the Women's Convention was inadequate to deal with gender-based violence. The final text of the Declaration does not properly clarify its relationship with the Women's Convention. The latter is referred to only in the preamble where it is recognised that effective implementation of the Women's Convention "would contribute to the elimination of violence against women and... the present Declaration will strengthen and complement that process"[76] and in Article 4(a) which stipulates that states should consider becoming parties to the Convention or withdrawing reservations to it.

The Declaration makes some significant advances in international treatment of violence against women. First, the preamble acknowledges the structural roots of violence against women. It states squarely that violence against women "is a manifestation of historically unequal power relations between men and women" and that it is a social mechanism whereby "women are forced into a subordinate position compared with men".[77] By recognising power imbalances, this analysis of gender violence takes women's rights out of the confines of anti-discrimination discourse. The fundamental problem women face worldwide is not discriminatory treatment compared with men, although this is a manifestation of the larger problem. Women are in an inferior position because they have no real power in either the public or private worlds. Violence against women reinforces this social and economic reality.

The definition of violence against women in Article 1 is also sophisticated: like the CEDAW General Recommendation 19, it refers to violence as "gender-based" thus emphasising the specificity of the problem. In other words, the right is not an adaptation of a right built on male experience. The definition also is explicit in that it covers violence "in public or private life" and Article 2 refers also to violence occurring within the family. Article 4(c) requires states to punish acts of violence against women perpetrated by the state or by private persons. This is a significant development given the traditional reluctance of international law to regulate behaviour outside the public sphere.

The Declaration also gives prominence, and credibility, to women's groups. It contains a number of references to them. For example the preamble welcomes "the role that women's movements have played in drawing increasing attention to the nature, severity and magnitude of the problem of violence against women" and Article 4(o) calls on states to "recognize the important role of the women's movement and non-governmental organisations worldwide in raising awareness and alleviating the problem of violence against women" and 4(p) "to facilitate and enhance" their work and to cooperate with them. Article 5(h) calls on the organs and specialised agencies of the United Nations to do likewise.

Another advance made by the Declaration is its clarification in Article 4 that custom, tradition or religion cannot be used as a justification to avoid eliminating violence against women. The controversial area of female genital mutilation and "other traditional practices harmful to women" (Article 2(a)) are also included. This provision was included over the protest of some Islamic nations, particularly the Sudan. The text agreed on by the 1992 intersessional CSW meeting read "States should condemn violence against women and should not invoke any custom, tradition or religious or other consideration to avoid their obligations."[78] The underlined phrase was somehow dropped in the draft of Article 4 submitted to the 1993 CSW meeting and has not been restored by the General Assembly.

The Declaration has some problematic aspects. First, as previously stated it does not constitute a binding legal obligation. A "soft law" instrument of this sort creates expectations as to future behaviour but does not formally bind states. Second, the text of the Declaration is weaker in some key respects than the one prepared by the Expert Group in 1991. For example, the Expert Group draft regarded the "degrading representation of women in the media" as a form of violence against women. This was strongly supported by Australia, Canada and New Zealand. The Declaration contains no reference to it because of strenuous opposition by the USA and the Netherlands. Article 4(j) is all that remains of this original provision:

> *States ... should*
> *Adopt all appropriate measures, especially in the field of education, to*
> *modify the social and cultural patterns of conduct of men and women and to*
> *eliminate prejudices, customary practices and all other practices based on*
> *the idea of the inferiority or superiority of either of the sexes and on stereo-*
> *typed roles for men and women.*[79]

Third, the Declaration fails to state explicitly that violence against women is a violation of human rights. Human rights are referred to in the Declaration, but the link drawn between human rights and gender-based violence is rather tenuous.[80] The Declaration's preamble refers to the urgent need for the universal application to women of rights such as equality and security and affirms that violence against women affects women's human rights. But in the operative part of the Declaration this link is not referred to at all. Violence against women is defined in Articles 2 and 3 without any reference to human rights. Article 3 refers to human rights but not to violence against women. Indeed Article 3 appears as a rather redundant provision: it does not advance women's rights in any way, but simply repeats a range of rights which are clearly set out in other instruments. Moreover, the rights given prominence in Article 3 are the classic civil and political rights which traditionally have offered women very little.[81] This is at odds with other innovative aspects of the Declaration which transcend the public/private divide. There is no recognition of the interdependence of civil and political rights and social, cultural and economic rights.

The lack of a clearly stated nexus between violence and human rights reflects the strong opposition to describing violence against women as a violation of human rights which was made in particular by the United States and Sweden during the 1992 intersessional CSW meeting. This was on the basis that it would water down the traditional notion of human rights. It was argued that human rights allowed protection from actions in which there was direct state involvement, and that extending the notion to cover "private" behaviour would reduce the status of the whole human rights canon. Such an argument raises of course the central problem for women in traditional human rights law: fundamental human rights are defined in categories that reflect typically male life experiences and offer protection from actions men most fear. By excluding the "private" realm from international human rights protection, human rights law becomes by and large irrelevant for most women; it offers a thoroughly gendered system of justice.

Conclusion

The evolution of new norms of international law is a slow and tortuous process constantly subject to negotiations, political compromise, governmental agendas and trade-offs. Even where a principle is clearly established as imposing an international obligation, there is no effective enforcement machinery. Is raising the issue of violence against women within international fora a quixotic endeavour, a thankless and fruitless task, especially given the low priority that most national governments accord the issue?

While the advances have been small, there have been some significant steps. Whereas traditional international legal doctrine could not encompass the issue of violence against women, it has a firm standing now on the international agenda: CEDAW's General Recommendation 19 and the United Nations

Declaration on the Elimination of Violence against Women provide a basis for further developments. Moreover, the United Nations Commission on Human Rights in 1994 appointed a Special Rapporteur on Violence Against Women, Radhika Coomaraswamy from Sri Lanka. The reports of "thematic" Special Rapporteurs are considered one of the most effective tools in United Nations monitoring of human rights.[82]

While these developments are to be welcomed, the United Nations response to violence against women raises the general problem of compartmentalisation of women's rights in international law. The development of instruments such as the Declaration on the Elimination of Violence against Women reinforces the United Nations tendency to relegate women's human rights to a special, under-resourced, sphere. It allows the "mainstream" human rights bodies to ignore women's concerns and the gendered nature of the "mainstream" to go unrecognised and unchallenged.

Outside the special United Nations women's institutions, however, awareness of violence against women as an international issue is increasing. An example is the work of the United Nations Compensation Committee, established to consider claims from individuals harmed by the Iraqi invasion of Kuwait.[83] Its Governing Council has decided that "serious personal injury" includes *inter alia* physical or mental injury arising from sexual assault and that compensation will be payable for non-pecuniary injuries arising from mental pain and anguish caused by sexual assault or witnessing such assault on his or her spouse, child or parent.[84] This explicit inclusion of sexual abuse as a compensable harm is encouraging, although it is limited to the extraordinary situation of the Iraqi surrender at the end of the Gulf War and the demands of the Security Council upon Iraq. It is not a general statement of international liability for such actions and does not include, for example, sexual abuse committed by returning Kuwaiti men.[85] The Security Council has also established an International War Crimes tribunal with respect to events in former Yugoslavia.[86] Of particular interest to women is whether the tribunal will consider rape and other sexual abuses independently of other alleged atrocities.[87] However there is a danger that the exceptional situation of providing international punitive mechanisms with respect to events in the Gulf and former Yugoslavia will detract from the less newsworthy, but equally significant, steps that have been taking place to make states accountable for all forms of violence against women. If they are seen as part of an overall condemnation of such acts they are to be welcomed; if instead they are seen as a form of retribution against particular men in extreme situations they will be less effective in combating violence against women.

Statements of international concern cannot eradicate the attitudes that entrench the subordination of women. Both CEDAW and CSW have made a number of positive recommendations as to steps states should take to overcome all forms of gender-based violence by public or private acts. They include legal reform, educational programmes and medical and other support services. Specific recommendations include the requirement of legislating against such behaviour; protective and support services; rehabilitation and counselling services for survivors of gender-based violence; accessible services for women in rural and other isolated areas; gender-sensitive training of law enforcement, judicial and other public officials; compilation of statistics and research on the incidence and causes of violence, its effects and the effectiveness of measures against it; measures to ensure the media promote respect for women; education and public information programmes to eliminate prejudicial attitudes and practices; effective domestic complaints procedures and remedies; monitoring employment conditions for domestic workers; and criminal penalties for domestic violence.

These recommendations are directed towards the state. They give women all over the world a basis for monitoring the progress in protecting women against violence. In particular states should give women the space to express their own needs, incorporate these views in policy formulation and provide the necessary resources to achieve the desired ends.

Until all forms of gender-based violence are regarded as serious violations of international legal standards, the primary goals of the international community will not be achieved. Violence against women undermines international peace and security,[88] just and equitable development,[89] and fulfilment of human rights goals. It is imperative for the international community to develop such norms and to make states accountable for sustaining a legal environment in which violence against women is acceptable behaviour, for example by failure to take action against individual wrongdoers. Such developments require a radical rethinking of the sources and processes of international law, as well as attitudinal changes within states and communities.

Notes

1   For accounts of violence against women worldwide see Schuler, M (ed), *Freedom from Violence: Women's Strategies From Around the World* (1992); Russell, D, and Van de Ven, N (eds), *The Proceedings of the International Tribunal on Crimes Against Women* (1976) at chapter 10; United Nations, *Women, Challenges to the Year 2000* (1991) at 65-78; Connors, J, *Violence Against Women in the Family* (1989); Barry, K, "Female Sexual Slavery: Understanding the International Dimensions of Women's Oppression" (1981) 3 *Human Rights Quarterly* 44; United Nations, *The World's Women 1970-1990: Trends and Statistics* (1991); Ashworth, G, *Of Violence and Violation: Women and Human Rights* (1986); Tomasevski, K, *Women and Human Rights* (1993) at chapter 8.

2   See for example, Amnesty International, *Bosnia-Herzegovina, Rape and Sexual Abuse by Armed Forces* (January 1993); Women Living under Muslim Laws, *Compilation of Informations on Crimes of War against Women in ex-Yugoslavia* (3 December 1992, updated 11 January 1993, available International Solidarity Network, PO Box 23-34790 Grabels, Montpellier, France); Bennett, C, "Ordinary Madness" *The Guardian* (20 January 1993); Mazowiecki, T, Special Rapporteur of the Commission on Human Rights, *Report Pursuant to Commission Resolution 1992/S-1/1* (14 August 1992) E/CN.4/1993/50 (10 February 1993); European Community Investigative Mission into the Treatment of Muslim Women in the Former Yugoslavia, *Warburton Report*, E/CN 4/1993/92.

3   Coomaraswamy, R, "Of Kali Born: Women, Violence and the Law in Sri Lanka", in Schuler, above n1 at 49-50.

4   Further, women in extreme positions of powerlessness, such as refugees, migrant workers and girl children, are especially vulnerable to violence. See Jang, D, Lee, D and Morello-Frosch, R, "Domestic Violence in Immigrant and Refugee Communities: Responding to the Needs of Immigrant Women" (1991) 13 *Response* No. 4 at 2; Executive Committee of the High Commissioner's Programme, *Note on Certain Aspects of Sexual Violence against Refugee Women* United Nations Document. EC/1993/SCP/CRP 2 (29 April 1993).

5   See also Chinkin, C, "Women and Peace: Militarism and Oppression", in Mahoney, K and Mahoney, P (eds), *Human Rights in the 21 st Century* (1993).

6   Schuler, M, "Violence Against Women: An International Perspective" in Schuler, above n1 at 11.

7   Id at 12.

8   See for example, Rosaldo, M, "Women, Culture, and Society: a Theoretical Overview" in Rosaldo, M and Lamphere, L (eds), *Women, Culture and Society* (1974) at 17; Elshtain, J, *Public Man, Private Woman* (1981); Garmanikow, E et al (eds), *The Public and The Private* (1983); Pateman, C, "Feminist Critiques of the Public/Private Dichotomy" in Benn, S and Gaus, G (eds), *Public and Private in Social Life* (1983) at 281.

9   For a more detailed discussion see Charlesworth, H, Chinkin, C and Wright, S, "Feminist Approaches to International Law" (1991) 85 *Am J Int 'l L* 613 at 625-8.

10 United Nations Charter, Article 2 (7).

11 As Professor O'Donovan has pointed out, however, the "private" sphere associated with women is in fact often tightly controlled by legal regulation of taxation, health, education and welfare; O'Donovan, K, *Sexual Divisions in Law* (1986) at 7-8.

12 Charlesworth, H and Chinkin, C, "The Gender of Jus Cogens" (1993) 15 *Human Rights Quarterly* 63; Ashworth, above n1.

13   UNIFEM, "Calling for Change: International Strategies to End Violence Against Women", conference held at The Hague, The Netherlands (6-9 June 1993).

14   ... these figures on domestic violence most probably represent only the tip of the iceberg ". *Women, Challenges to the Year 2000,* above n1 at 70.

15   Connors, above n1 at 17.

16   Charlesworth, Chinkin and Wright, above n9 at 621-5.

17   The sources of international law are set out in the Statute of the International Court of Justice, 1945, Article 38 (1).

18   See for example, Amnesty International, *Women in the Front Line* (1991); Women's Rights Project and Asia Watch, *Double Jeopardy: Police Abuse of Women in Pakistan* (1992); Women's Rights Project and Americas Watch, *Untold Terror: Violence against Women in Peru's Armed Conflict* (1993).

19   Women's Rights Project, *Token Gestures* (1993).

20   Americas Watch, *Criminal Injustice: Violence against Women in Brazil* (1991).

21   Id at 4. Brazil is not alone in its acceptance of the defence of honour. A comparative study on the criminal legislation of a number of Mediterranean and Arab states found it to be widely accepted; Rhoodie, E M, *Discrimination Against Women: A Global Survey of the Economic, Educational, Social and Political Status of Women* (1989) at 29, cited in *Women, Challenges to the Year 2000* above n1 at 70.

22   Id at 35.

23   Id at 54-55.

24   Id at 2-7.

25   Bunch, C, "Women's Rights as Human Rights: Towards a Revision of Human Rights" (1990) 12 *Human Rights Quarterly* 486 at 491.

26   International Law Commission, Draft Articles on State Responsibility, rep. (1980) 2 *Year Bk Int'l Law Comm*, Pt II , Article 11 (1).

27   Cook, R, "Accountability in International Law for Violations of Women's Rights by Non-state Actors" in Dallmeyer, D, (ed), *Reconceiving Reality: Women and International Law* (1993) 93 at 97.

28   See Thomas, D, and Beasley, M, "Domestic Violence as a Human Rights Issue" (1993) 15 *Human Rights Quarterly* 36 for a helpful discussion of the conceptual problems in preparing the report.

29   *X and Y v The Netherlands* (1985) 91 European Court of Human Rights (ser A); *Airey v Ireland* (1979) 32 European Court of Human Rights (ser A); *Velasquez Rodriguez v Honduras* (1989) 28 *Int'l Legal Materials* 294.

30   *X and Y v The Netherlands*, ibid.

31   *Velasquez Rodriguez v Honduras*, above n29.

32 Regional and other international institutions have also considered the issue of violence against women. For example, the Inter-American Commission of Women of the Organisation of American States has drafted a regional convention on violence against women. See Culliton, K, "Finding a Mechanism to Enforce Women's Right to State Protection from Domestic Violence in the Americas" (1993) 34 *Harv Int'l L J* 507. Meetings of the Commonwealth Ministers Responsible for Women's Affairs in 1985, 1987 and 1990 have issued communiques on the subject. The Committee of Ministers of the Council of Europe has adopted Recommendation No R (1985) 4 on "Violence in the Family", Recommendation No R (1990) 2 on "Social Measures Concerning Violence against Women" and at the Third Ministerial Conference on equality between men and women in October 1993 a "political declaration on violence against women in a democratic Europe" was adopted. This was the first step towards the possible adoption of a Protocol to the European Convention on Human Rights on the fundamental right of women and men to equality and a plan of action to combat violence. The First Conference of European Ministers on "Physical and Sexual Violence against Women" was held in 1991. In the same year, the Conference on Security and Co-operation in Europe agreed to seek to eliminate all forms of violence against women.

33 See for example Russell and Van de Ven, above n1.

34 *Report of the World Conference of the International Women's Year, Mexico City, 19 June-2 July 1975*, United Nations Publication, Sales No E 76 IV 1.

35 Schuler, above n6 at 4.

36 *Report of the United Nations Mid-Decade for Women Conference, Copenhagen, 14-30 July 1980*, United Nations Publication, Sales No E 80 IV 3.

37 Resolution 5.

38 *Report of the World Conference to Review and Appraise the Achievements of the United Nations Decade for Women: Equality, Development and Peace, Nairobi 15-26 July 1985* United Nations Publication, Sales No E 85 IV 10.

39 Paragraph 258.

40 See Carillo, R, *Battered Dreams: Violence against Women as an Obstacle to Development* (1992).

41 General Assembly Resolution 40/36.

42 ECOSOC Resolution 1984/14, 24 May 1984.

43 ECOSOC Resolution 1986/10.

44 The United Nations report, *Violence against Women in the Family* (1989) by J Connors was one of the outcomes of the meeting.

45 Adopted by the General Assembly, 18 December 1979, General Assembly Resolution 34/180 (XXXIV), rep. (1980) 19 *Int'l Legal Materials* 33.

46 Convention on the Elimination of All Forms of Discrimination Against Women, Article 6.

47 Convention on the Elimination of All Forms of Discrimination Against Women, Article 17 establishes CEDAW. Reporting obligations of State Parties are specified in Article 18. For a description of CEDAW and its marginalisation within the human rights movement see Byrnes, A, "The 'Other' Human Rights Treaty Body: The Work of the Committee on the Elimination of Discrimination Against Women", (1989) 1 *Yale J Int'l L* 1.

48 International Covenant on Civil and Political Rights, (ICCPR) 16 December 1966, rep (1967) 6 *Int'l Legal Materials* 368, in force 23 March 1976; International Covenant on Economic, Social and Cultural Rights, (ICESCR) 16 December 1976, rep (1967) 6 *Int'l Legal Materials*, in force 3 January 1976.

49 This primacy is illustrated by the language of the respective Covenants and their enforcement procedures. The language of the ICESCR is aspirational and programmatic rather than imposing identifiable and absolute obligations upon states and the only enforcement mechanisms are periodical reports to the relevant treaty monitoring body. There is no provision for the hearing of individual or inter-state complaints as there is in the ICCPR and its First Optional Protocol.

50 ICCPR, Article 2; ICESCR, Article 2.

51 For example, the right to life under Article 6 of the ICCPR has not been interpreted to include the forms of life-threatening violence discussed above. See Charlesworth and Chinkin, above n12; Bunch, above n25.

52 Charter of the United Nations, Article 1 (3).

53 See for example, Convention on the Elimination of All Forms of Discrimination Against Women, Articles 2(e), 2 (f) and 5.

54 Committee on the Elimination of Discrimination Against Women, General Recommendation 12. General Recommendation 14, 1990, deals with an aspect of violence against women, female circumcision. It recommends that parties to the Convention take appropriate and effective measures to eradicate the practice.

55 General Assembly Official Records, 47th Session, Supp No 38 (A/47/38), 1992. The text is reprinted in Fraser, A and Kazantsis M, *CEDAW No 11, the Committee on the Elimination of Discrimination Against Women and the Convention on the Elimination of All Forms of Discrimination Against Women and Violence Against Women*, (1992).

56 ICCPR, Article 7; United Nations Convention Against Torture and Other Cruel, Inhuman or Degrading Treatment or Punishment, adopted by General Assembly Resolution 39/46, 10 December 1984, rep (1984) 23 *Int'l Legal Materials* 1027.

57   Convention for the Amelioration of the Condition of the Wounded and Sick in Armed Forces in the Field, 75 UNTS 31; Convention for the Amelioration of the Condition of the Wounded, Sick and Shipwrecked Members of Armed Forces at Sea, 75 UNTS 85; Convention Relative to the Treatment of Prisoners of War, 75 UNTS 135; Convention Relative to the Protection of Civilian Persons in Time of War, 75 UNTS 287, all at Geneva, 12 August 1949; Protocol Additional to the Geneva Conventions of 12 August 1949, and Relating to the Protection of Victims of International Armed Conflicts (Protocol I), Protocol Additional to the Geneva Conventions of 12 August 1949, and Relating to the Protection of Victims of International Armed Conflicts (Protocol II), 10 June 1977 rep (1977) 16 *Int'l Legal Materials* 1391.

58   ICCPR, Article 9.

59   ICCPR, Article 14.

60   ICCPR, Article 23 (this provision specifies the family itself as the unit of protection).

61   ICESCR, Article 12.

62   ICESCR, Article 7.

63   See above n55.

64   Chinkin, C and Werksman, K, *CEDAW No. 12, Report of the Twelfth Session of the Committee on the Elimination of All Forms of Discrimination Against Women* (1993).

65   The Human Rights Committee has jurisdiction over both types of complaint; ICCPR, Article 41 (inter-State complaints); First Optional Protocol, 999 UNTS 302 (individual complaints).

66   Clark, B, "The Vienna Conventions Regime and the Convention on Discrimination Against Women" (1991) 85 *Am J Int'l L* 281; Cook, R, "Reservations to the Convention on the Elimination of All Forms of Discrimination Against Women" (1990) 30 *Va J Int'l L* 643.

67   On the work of the United Nations human rights treaty monitoring bodies see Alston, P (ed), *The United Nations and Human Rights* (1992).

68   World Conference on Human Rights, Vienna Declaration and Programme of Action (June 1993) at paragraph 37.

69   Id at paragraph 38.

70   United Nations General Assembly Resolution, see appendix 1.

71   On the history and work of the Commission see Reanda, L, "The Commission on the Status of Women" in Alston, above n67.

72   ECOSOC Resolution 1987/24, 1987/121, reaffirmed by decision 1988/27, 1990/213, 1991/18.

73   ECOSOC Resolution 1991/18, 30 May 1991.

74   *Expert Group Meeting on Violence Against Women, Vienna, 11-15 November 1991, Report,* unpublished United Nations Document EGM/VAW/1991/1.

75 General Assembly Resolution 48/103.

76 Above n70 at paragraph 4.

77 Id at paragraph 6.

78 Reprinted in *Women 2000* 4 (1992) 2.

79 Above n70, Article 4 (j).

80 Indeed, the French text of this provision is considerably stronger than the English.

81 See Charlesworth and Chinkin, above n12.

82 Newman, F and Weissbrodt, D, *International Human Rights* (1990) at 145-60.

83 In accordance with SC Resolution 687, 3 April 1991.

84 Decision taken by the Governing Council of the United Nations Compensation Commission, during its second session; S/AC.26/1991/3, 23 October 1991.

85 For a description of such abuse see Middle East Watch, *A Victory Turned Sour, Human Rights in Kuwait Since Liberation* (September 1991). See also Women's Rights Project and Middle East Watch, *Punishing the Victim: Rape and Mistreatment of Asian Maids in Kuwait* (August 1992).

86 In SC Resolution 808, 22 February 1993 the Security Council requested the Secretary-General to prepare a report on the establishment of such a Tribunal. The Secretary-General's report was adopted and the Tribunal established by SC Resolution 827, 25 May 1993.

87 See Chinkin, C, "Rape And Sexual Abuse Of Women In International Law" (1994) *Eur J Int'l L* (forthcoming).

88 "Nairobi Forward-Looking Strategies for the Advancement of Women", above n39 at 15-26, paragraph 13.

89 United Nations Office at Vienna, Centre for Social Development and Humanitarian Affairs, *1989 World Survey on the Role of Women in Development* (1989).

3

"Ain't No Mountain High Enough (To Keep Me From Getting To You)":

An Analysis Of The Hamilton Abuse Intervention Pilot Project

Ruth Busch and Neville Robertson*

We would like to thank Ellen Pence for sharing with us her experiences of the development and operation of the Duluth Abuse Intervention Project, a programme she founded in Duluth, Minnesota approximately 12 years ago. The Hamilton Abuse Intervention Pilot Project is modelled on the philosophy and practices of the Duluth project. In August 1993, Ellen Pence was a Visiting Scholar at the University of Waikato and this paper in part reflects the numerous, lengthy discussions with her about the aims and elements of an intervention approach to domestic violence.

Dedicated to Angelina Julia Poli (aged 21), Taina Huriana Poli (aged 4 years 9 months) and Maria-Luisa Poli (aged 20 months) stabbed to death in Hamilton as we worked on this paper.

The Hamilton Abuse Intervention Pilot Project (HAIPP)[1], launched in July 1991, represents an attempt to reform the New Zealand justice system's response to domestic violence, particularly the violence of men directed against their women partners.

The primary aim of HAIPP is to prioritise safety for victims above all other concerns. Intervention protocols have been developed between HAIPP, the police, the courts, Community Corrections and women's refuges in an attempt to ensure that the safety priority is reflected in the policies and procedures implemented by decision makers at all levels of the justice system. A key feature of intervention protocols is to minimise the discretion available to these decision makers. By establishing explicit procedures which are to be followed in all but the most exceptional instances, intervention protocols aim to maximise the protection afforded by the justice system to victims of spousal violence. They also establish a benchmark by which the justice system's response to spousal violence can be evaluated in any given situation.

A second aim of the HAIPP programme is to enhance the autonomy of victims. This aim implicitly recognises that domestic violence is one of a range of tactics by which abusers seek to maintain power and control over their partners (see appendix 2). Other tactics of power and control utilised by abusers include emotional and verbal abuse; intimidation; isolation; treating the victim as subservient while the abuser reserves the right to make all major decisions in the relationship; minimising and trivialising the violence; blaming the victim for such violence. The use of these two latter tactics is not limited to individual abusers. Such tactics are sometimes used by members of the justice system and serve to deny women's experience of the realities of the violence they face.

Power and control tactics operating on a systemic level legitimise abusers' perspectives of violence and the further victimisation of those who look to the justice system for protection. It is a process that has been identified by certain researchers as "the cultural facilitation of violence".[2] In the area of sexual abuse it has been identified as "the double rape".[3] HAIPP, on the other hand, aims to enhance victim autonomy through the provision of victim advocacy and support services.

A third aim of HAIPP is to hold abusers accountable for their use of violence without abridging their civil rights. Too often abusers escape penalty or face only minor penalties for their use of violence.[4] The message frequently relayed by the justice system has until recently seemed to be that violence within a domestic relationship is different and less important than stranger violence.[5] Moreover, in instances of serious violence, there has sometimes been a message given that "violence works".[6] An intervention approach aims to ensure that there is a negative consequence for violent behaviour and that there will be incremental penalties for additional acts of violence.

A fourth aim of HAIPP is the rehabilitation of abusers, at least to the extent that this is not incompatible with its previous aims. The development of programmes aimed at helping abusers adopt lifestyles which are free of power and control behaviours is a major component of an intervention approach. The input of victims into the development of these men's programmes and the evaluation of their effectiveness are essential ingredients of HAIPP's intervention protocols.

All too frequently victims have been exposed to risks of further violence as a result of their efforts to obtain protection from the justice system.[7] In part, intervention protocols are an attempt to hold decision makers in the justice system accountable for the messages that they give to victims and perpetrators alike about spousal violence. A basic premise of HAIPP's approach is that the justice system colludes in spousal violence if it does not give clear and unambiguous messages that such violence is inappropriate.

In this paper, we outline the philosophy of intervention, describe the intervention protocols which have been developed in Hamilton, analyse the operation of these protocols and assess some of the impacts the intervention approach has had on the administration of justice. In order to demonstrate the wide-reaching changes brought about by the adoption of an intervention approach in Hamilton, we look first at some of the problems identified within the justice system which HAIPP was established to rectify.

The justice system's response to family violence

It is now widely appreciated that the criminal justice system in most Western nations has poorly served those who have been victimised by members of their own families.

> *The criminal justice system is one of the primary institutions to which battered women and their families turn for help and protection. By virtue of its power to enforce existing laws, it is also the institution critical to public condemnation of violence, wherever it may occur. However, the criminal justice system shares the biases of society at large, biases which hold that family matters are private. Such a bias has led to the selective non-enforcement of laws when violence occurs between family members...This stance of non-intervention indirectly condones violence and ignores the frequent escalation which all too often ends in homicide.*[8]

New Zealand studies have identified similar problems. For example, New Zealand police have historically tended to avoid arresting domestic assaulters,[9] in effect screening them out of the criminal justice process. When men have been prosecuted for assaulting their partners, they often appear to have received lighter sentences than men who have committed comparable assaults against strangers.[10]

These problems have not been confined to the criminal justice system but have extended also to the Family Court which, on the breakdown of spousal relationships, has jurisdiction to grant protection orders under the *Domestic Protection Act* 1982 (NZ) and to deal with custody, access, maintenance, and property disputes. Significant problems have been identified for women obtaining protection orders from the Family Court[11] as well as in having breaches of those orders dealt with in the District Court.[12] There is considerable concern about the processes of the Family Court in determining custody and access issues in relationships where there has been a history of spousal violence.[13]

In previous work the authors have identified a disparity between women's experiences of domestic violence and the justice system's response to such violence.[14] We have suggested that this disparity creates a gap between women's experiences of the realities of the violence they are subjected to and the minimisation and trivialisation of that violence by certain police and judges. We have posited that blaming the victim is an implicit feature of this disparity and that at its extreme, the gap is created when the violence suffered by victims is rendered totally invisible by certain decision makers.[15]

A lack of inter-agency co-ordination

Part of the "gap" that we have identified is attributable to a lack of inter-agency co-ordination, both between different branches of the justice system and between government departments and community groups. The problem is starkly illustrated in terms of the lack of co-ordination between the Family Court which grants protection orders and the District Court where breaches of such orders are tried.[16] The result is that a District Court judge often fails to understand the historical context between the parties within which a breach of a non-molestation order has occurred. All too often, therefore, the judge will not understand the intimidatory effect on the victim of what are characterised as "technical" breaches, breaches which do not involve physically violent behaviour. As victim impact reports are typically not called for by District Court judges who hear such breach prosecutions, the consequences of the breach from a victim's perspective are rarely before the court.[17]

The consequences of the lack of inter-agency co-ordination also arise when a spouse against whom protection orders have been granted is receiving psychiatric counselling and confidentiality is privileged above protection concerns. The danger of this situation is illustrated by a case in which a woman was killed by her ex-partner as she emerged from a Family Court ordered counselling session. When it occurred, her death was described by the local police as unpredictable and unavoidable. However, our investigations suggested otherwise.[18]

At least four different agencies were involved with the parties; with minor exceptions, no information was shared between them. Thus the psychiatric unit which was dealing with the abuser treated him entirely as a suicide risk (he was referred there after an attempt to take his own life) and did not make contact with his wife to ascertain what violence or threats of violence he had directed against her. At the inquest, the psychiatrist testified that he had made a practice decision not to make contact with a spouse for such information when parties were separated. Moreover, the psychiatric workers at the unit had no knowledge of the protection orders which had been granted to the estranged wife.

The Family Court counsellor, to whom a referral had been made under section 10 of the Family Proceedings Act 1980 (NZ) at the time the wife applied for a separation order, only found out by accident about the protection orders which had been granted subsequent to the counselling referral. She was informed about the existence of the orders when she ran into the Family Court Counselling Co-ordinator in a lift.

The police in three different districts had had a number of contacts with both parties. These related to the husband's threatening telephone calls and his assaultive behaviour. One time he broke into her parents' home in the early morning and tried to take one of the children. The second incident involved his coming to her workplace and grabbing her. The police were called and escorted her to the airport so that she could return to her parents' home. The husband was not charged by the police with either assault and little information was recorded on their files. No information was recorded in a central place, nor was it available to the Family Court, the counselling service or the psychiatric unit.

From the deceased wife's mother we learned that when the couple's eldest son, a four year old, was told of his mother's death, his first response was, "Did Daddy shoot her?" The poignancy of that comment belies both the sense of surprise and the "unavoidability" of the event that various decision makers expressed when the murder/suicide occurred. The deaths could have been a surprise to people who saw only part of the pattern, viewing single acts in isolation rather than as a whole. We share the belief of the wife's mother that her daughter could be alive today if there had been adequate inter-agency cooperation.

Numerous other examples of the danger to victims due to the lack of an inter-agency approach could be given. In each instance the result was that individual members of different government and health agencies accepted the abuser's minimisation of his violence, interpreted a specific violent incident as a unique, isolated act rather than as part of a pattern of abusive behaviour, and underestimated the cumulative effect of the abuse on the victim. In one case in which a man was convicted 13 times in a four year period of breaching protection orders, he was able to maintain the respect and sympathy of nearly all the police officers in his area.[19] The one police officer who described him as having mounted "a total campaign of intimidation" against his former wife stated, "he was able to convince each new police officer that he was okay".[20]

The elements of intervention projects

Intervention projects aim to "close the gap". At the heart of an intervention approach is a shared philosophy about the nature of violence and the priorities which should guide the community's response to such violence. The elements of intervention entail the development of such a shared philosophy, the adoption of policies and practices to implement the agreed philosophy, networking between agencies to ensure a consistent systemic approach to violence, the monitoring of compliance with intervention protocols, the establishment of programmes for victims and abusers, and the systematic evaluation of the outcomes produced by the intervention model.[21]

The philosophy of intervention privileges addressing the violence above the relationship between abuser and victim. The key concerns of the intervention approach involve a focus on the extent of the abuser's violence and the pattern and impact of his violence. With such a focus, violence cannot be dismissed as a symptom of "relationship problems". Rather, "relationship problems" are recognised as symptoms of the violence. It is a "given" of an intervention approach that one cannot have a good relationship with a partner who enforces his will through the use of violence.

Inherent in the philosophy of intervention is the recognition that an act of physical violence is part of a continuum of power and control, rather than an isolated, uncontrollable eruption. Also implicit in the philosophy of intervention is the view that the use of violence creates imbalances of power. These premises indicate that mediation cannot be viewed as an appropriate process for resolving disputes during marital separation for relationships which have been characterised by violence.[22] Mediation implies equal bargaining positions of the parties. Violence vitiates such equality.

Moreover, a judicial requirement for "fresh and immediate evidence"[23] of physical violence prior to the granting of an *ex parte* non-molestation order belies the perspective that physical violence is only one form of an abuser's pattern of control. The intervention philosophy underscores that one need not hit someone constantly to control them and that a narrow judicial focus on physical violence renders other forms of control invisible.

The second element of intervention is the development of an agreed set of policies and practices, often codified as intervention protocols, which provide concrete and specific ways in which agency personnel must put the safety of victims first. For instance, protocols may require the safety of victims to be the prime consideration in determining whether abusers should be granted bail. Similarly, as a result of the recognition that violence has on-going and disempowering consequences for victims, intervention protocols may mandate that police lay assault charges which arise within a domestic context rather than putting the onus on victims to initiate complaints.

As has been discussed, the emphasis of an intervention approach is on the implementation of intervention protocols so that the justice system becomes more responsive and oriented towards victims. Emphasis on consistent implementation may be contrasted with a focus on the attitudes held by police officers, prosecutors, judges and probation officers about domestic violence. These attitudes are often blamed for the justice system's inadequate response to the victimisation of women.[24]

From a victim's perspective, however, it does not much matter what attitudes police officers, for instance, hold as long as they do their job in accordance with the relevant intervention protocols. The concentration on implementation entails an implicit acknowledgment that attitudinal changes are more difficult to effect than behavioural changes and that the changing of behaviours may in fact be instrumental in the changing of attitudes.[25]

Networking between government and community agencies is a third element of intervention. A common problem facing efforts to curtail domestic violence is that abusers generally can find a decision maker within the justice system who will sanction their analysis of their abusive behaviour. A tendency has been identified for police and courts to trivialise domestic violence and to blame victims.[26] These problems may also arise in respect of probation officers who often do not have access to all the details of an assault or to the historical framework within which an assault has occurred. They may find it easy to accept an abuser's rationalisations (for example, "She never listens to me") and minimisations (for example, "I only pushed her", or "I didn't mean it, I just lost it") and recommend relationship counselling which fails to address the violence.[27] As well, Family Court counsellors typically do not have access to detailed information about violence in the relationship of parties they are working with and are unlikely to obtain it from victims if they hold only joint counselling sessions.[28]

Networking and the sharing of information between different agencies allow for abusers to be held fully accountable for their actions. Often such networking and information sharing may, however, be seen as conflicting with the very philosophies and processes currently adopted by the justice system for dealing with domestic violence, including notions of confidentiality and privacy. This is especially true in the Family Court arena.[29] One contentious element of an intervention approach, therefore, is that confidentiality and privacy will not be privileged over concerns about victims' safety.

A second reason for networking and information sharing arises because members of various agencies all too often do not understand where their "bit" fits in terms of an overview of the system's approach to domestic violence in general or to specific cases involving an individual abuser and victim.[30] It is essential if victims' safety is to be enhanced that decision makers within the justice system gain a better sense of the collective impact of their work, on both a case-by-case and systemic level.

Monitoring, the fourth element of intervention, ensures the intervention protocols are consistently implemented and that abusers receive appropriate, pre-determined consequences for their violence from the justice system. Victim advocates can track the performance of individual practitioners in the criminal justice system and monitor whether such practitioners are holding abusers accountable for their violence by following cases through the processes of arrest, prosecution, sentencing and the enforcement of sentences. The best policies will not enhance the safety and autonomy of victims unless they are implemented.

The fifth element of intervention entails providing services for women who have been battered. These services may include providing safe housing (for example, women's refuges), court advocacy, and support and education groups. They may also involve supplying assistance in obtaining income support benefits, finding employment or obtaining training or education. Any service which will enhance the ability of women to live independently of their abusers falls under this heading. In an offender-oriented justice system, attention is placed on programmes for men who abuse. While the effectiveness of such abuser programmes is still a matter of debate,[31] only rarely is the focus on providing properly resourced programmes for women aimed at reducing the chances that they will remain in or re-enter abusive relationships.

The sixth element of intervention involves rehabilitation of abusive men coupled with an invocation of penalties if men fail to attend court-mandated programmes or are uncooperative. Consistent with the philosophy of intervention, the meaning, power and criminality of violence is central to men's rehabilitation programmes. The programmes help men to understand the origins of the belief systems which give legitimacy to male domination and abuse, and the ultimately self-defeating nature of attempts to enforce their will over partners if what they seek are relationships based on mutual support and trust.

The final element of intervention is evaluation. Regular process and outcome evaluations, especially evaluation from a victim perspective, are needed to identify unanticipated problems in the implementation of intervention protocols so that policies and procedures can be refined. Inherent in this evaluation process is a definition of "success" which concentrates on whether the aims of intervention are achieved rather than on a focus limited to abuser recidivism or minimisation of financial costs.

The Hamilton intervention model

In Hamilton, the elements of intervention have been implemented through the coordinated efforts of the Maori and non-Maori women's refuges, the police, the criminal courts, the Family Court and Community Corrections. Each of these organisations is represented at monthly HAIPP inter-agency meetings which identify and review problems and plan solutions in respect of the implementation of intervention protocols. A project office has been established in the city centre (easily accessible to transport) which employs paid staff to co-ordinate the intervention efforts of the participating agencies, provide advocacy services for women and manage a large pool of volunteers who run the men's and women's educational programmes. Over the two years that HAIPP has been in existence, specific intervention protocols and less formal practices and policies have been implemented which now determine how government agencies and community groups deal with domestic violence in Hamilton.

Police

The police have a pivotal role to play in ensuring that there is a consistent community response to battering. The protocols which have been developed between HAIPP and the police pinpoint several key aspects of policing in terms of domestic violence cases. They are delineated fully in order to demonstrate the significant changes which have occurred in terms of police practice since the advent of HAIPP. The intervention protocols currently entail:

> i.   Mandatory arrest of abusers whenever there is a prima facie case made out that an assault has occurred. An arrest should occur without the police seeking a complaint from the victim: neither should she be required to give evidence in court unless there is no case to answer without her evidence. These aspects of HAIPP's intervention protocols have officially been police policy since 1987.32

> ii.   Notification of attendances at "domestics" by the police to the HAIPP Crisis Line in order to ensure that victims receive immediate follow up support from women's advocates. This should happen whether or not an arrest has been made.

> iii.   Men who commit assaults against their partners are to be charged under section 194 (b) ("male assaults female") of the Crimes Act 1961 (NZ) unless a more serious charge is warranted. All breaches of non-molestation orders will also be charged. This intervention protocol prohibits police from issuing warnings in lieu of charging and rules out assailants being charged with common assault under the Summary Offences Act 1981 (NZ) . It also prohibits police from offering diversion to offenders who admit that they have committed assaults or breached non-molestation orders.33

> iv.   Offenders (whether charged with assault or breach of a non-molestation order) will not receive police bail but will be kept in the cells until the next court sitting after their arrest. If such an arrest occurs on a weekday night, an offender will be brought into the District Court the following morning. If such an arrest occurs on Friday night or over the weekend, the offender will be held in the cells until the Monday morning sitting of the court. This policy provides for victim safety and helps restore victim autonomy by reducing the risk of intimidation.

In addition, HAIPP staff have been involved in police training to improve officers' understandings of the dynamics of abuse.

While aspects of project protocols are consistent with national police policy, the existence of HAIPP has had additional implications for Hamilton police in that they have been asked to place their performance under a greater degree of external scrutiny than is the case elsewhere in the country. In Hamilton, for instance, a victim advocate reviews the log of telephone calls to the police to determine whether the police arrest policy and other police protocols regarding the charging of assaults, have been implemented in every instance.

Women's refuges

The work of women's refuges is fundamental to intervention projects. In conjunction with the HAIPP office, the local women's refuges (Te Whakaruruhau and Hamilton Refuge and Support Services) operate a joint Crisis line which handles after-hours calls from the police as well as women initiating calls themselves. The refuges operate a roster of call-out advocates who attend incidents, provide immediate support for women, discuss the victim services which are available, collect information about the assault (which is forwarded to the HAIPP court advocate[34]) and admit women to a refuge if that is necessary. Call-out advocates also participate in HAIPP's monitoring function by asking women to evaluate the services they have received from the police. Problems with policing can subsequently be raised with the relevant officers; letters of commendation are sent when police officers have been particularly helpful and supportive to victims.

The District Court

An intervention project has important implications for the operation of the District Court and the prosecution of abusers. Prosecutors in cases of domestic violence have faced particular difficulties in obtaining convictions.[35] The most common difficulty is that a significant number of victims decline to give evidence, or seek to have the charge(s) against their abusers withdrawn. This is understandable as abusers characteristically use a variety of tactics, including intimidation, to dissuade their victims from co-operating with the prosecution.

As mentioned above, intervention protocols aim to shield victims from such tactics by not requiring them to lay charges and having police collect sufficient evidence so that a defended prosecution will succeed without the victim being required to give evidence at trial. In addition, when a defendant is remanded on bail, judges in Hamilton will now usually impose, as a condition of bail, an order prohibiting the accused from associating with the victim.[36] This condition is imposed unless the victim specifically requests that the defendant be allowed to return home.

It is now practice in Hamilton for prosecutors to decline victims' requests to have charges withdrawn; instead, victims are advised that they should attend the court and tell the presiding judge why they do not want the abuser prosecuted. Support from the HAIPP court advocate (see below) is available to women who may be considering withdrawing from a prosecution.

Intervention policies also relate to sentencing convicted abusers. There is an informal agreement with Community Corrections that probation officers will recommend the HAIPP men's education programme as part of the sentence for all suitable convicted offenders.[37] And although the Hamilton District Court judges have felt it important not to have their sentencing discretion fettered, they have manifested their support for intervention policies in their sentencing approaches: most convicted abusers are ordered to attend the HAIPP men's education programme, either as a condition of a sentence of supervision or as part of a parole programme following a term of imprisonment (which is a likely outcome for repeated and/or more serious assaults).[38]

A key aspect of the intervention model in the District Court is the role of the HAIPP court advocate. She attempts to demystify court processes for women who have been abused and helps to ensure that they have knowledge of , and input into, those processes. While the court advocate does not give formal legal advice, she does provide information to women about protection orders and other legal issues. She provides support for victims required to give evidence in defended hearings, helps them organise child-care and transportation, talks to them about their fears with regard to appearing in court, outlines court procedures and protocol, and discusses the implication of making a stand against the abuse they have received. She keeps victims informed of what is happening to their abusers as a result of court appearances. She also provides information about victims' safety concerns and the impact of the assaults on victims to both the police prosecutor and the Community Corrections Court Servicing Team. The court advocate represents a crucial part of HAIPP's monitoring process as she tracks abusers through the criminal justice system, and documents departures from intervention policies by prosecutors, probation officers and judges.

Community Corrections

Probation officers have an influential role in the criminal justice system. They make recommendations to judges about the sentencing of offenders, they monitor community-based sentences such as supervision and community care, and they supervise offenders released on parole. Probation officers exercise a significant degree of discretion in terms of their sentencing recommendations and the types of programmes which they require men under supervision to attend. In the past, probation officers have been criticised for being offender-oriented,[39] sometimes to the detriment of the victims of domestic assaults.

As previously mentioned, there is an informal agreement with HAIPP that probation officers in the District Court will recommend the HAIPP men's programme for all domestic abusers, either as part of a sentence of supervision or as part of a parole programme in those instances where offenders are sentenced to imprisonment. The agreement includes a provision that exceptions to this practice should only be made where an offender is clearly unsuitable to attend the HAIPP programme. "Unsuitability" arises when language would be a barrier, when a specific psychiatric condition would severely limit the individual's ability to benefit from the programme, or when an offender is not living within the Waikato district.

Probation officers have been criticised for not obtaining victims' perspectives in the preparation of these pre-sentence reports.[40] The problem has been especially acute when reports have been prepared during a short stand-down period and the victim either has not been present in court or alternatively when members of the Court Servicing Team have been too pressed to have time to interview her. Since the advent of the project, probation officers have had access to victim statements collected by refuge call-out advocates soon after the assault has occurred. This information is supplied by HAIPP to assist probation officers in preparing their pre-sentence reports. The victim statement is aimed at focussing probation officers' attention on the specific instance of violence in question and its consequences for the victim. It also contains a summary of any previous violence that has occurred between the parties.

Probation officers also ensure that offenders comply with the conditions of their sentences. Under HAIPP protocols, if men fail to attend HAIPP as directed, enforcement action will be initiated by the probation officer. Absences for genuine cases of illness or other legitimate reasons (for example, men are sometimes excused if they have unavoidable work commitments) are accepted and usually the first absence without good reason will result only in a warning. In all other cases, offenders will be charged either with breaching the conditions of their supervision orders or else will be subject to an application to have their supervision reviewed and another sentence substituted. A term of imprisonment is most likely when offenders are re-sentenced.

The Family Court

In Hamilton, intervention protocols have been developed to cover aspects of the operation of the Family Court. Respondents who have had protection orders (interim or final) made against them are now directed to attend the men's education programme under the provisions of section 37A of the *Domestic Protection Act* 1982 (NZ).[41] The section 37A direction remains in force even if an applicant who has obtained interim protection orders does not proceed with an application for final orders. Protocols have also been developed for enforcing attendance of respondents at the men's programme through the issuing of summonses and the prosecution of non-attenders. While section 37A of the *Domestic Protection Act* 1982 (NZ) provides for such prosecutions, the prosecutions provisions have hitherto rarely been invoked.[42]

Applicants are recommended to attend the women's programme under section 37 of the *Domestic Protection Act* 1982 (NZ). As a corollary to this section 37 recommendation, the Hamilton Family Court Counselling Co-ordinators have instructed court-appointed counsellors to delay the onset of counselling in respect of custody and access issues (except for an initial, individual appointment) for six weeks to allow women the opportunity to attend women's education and support groups run by the project office. Participation in the women's groups is seen as a way in which women can become more empowered and able to take part in court-ordered counselling and mediation on a more equal footing with their abusers. Concerns about the risks to women of participating in counselling or mediation in the context of domestic violence have been discussed above. However, most women who are applicants for custody orders will face both counselling and mediation conferences if their applications are contested. It is hoped that by gaining some distance from the trauma of the recent violence and by sharing their experiences of custody and access arrangements, women in these HAIPP groups will be able to enter into negotiations about long-term childcare options without resorting to the placation and appeasement tactics which so frequently characterise women's behaviour towards their abusers.[43] They will be better positioned to realistically evaluate which arrangements are likely to work for them. It is believed by Family Court personnel that over time this deferral of counselling will result in a decrease in the number of repeat applications for revision of custody and access orders, thereby saving court time and expense.[44]

HAIPP's women's programmes

The HAIPP office offers a range of services and programmes for women. One-to-one crisis support and advocacy is provided by HAIPP staff and volunteers. These services complement similar services offered by the two Hamilton women's refuges. While quite time consuming for the project, the provision of one-to-one support is a necessary aspect of restoring victim autonomy. Such support may involve listening while a woman painfully recounts the most recent incident involving violence, intimidation during a court appearance or access changeover time, or in a myriad of other situations. On the other hand, it may involve accompanying her to the Department of Social Welfare and helping her apply for a domestic purposes benefit or helping her prepare for and then accompanying her to her lawyer's office if she is applying for protection and other orders from the Family Court. It may take up to three or four hours at the Department of Social Welfare offices for a woman to complete the procedures necessary to obtain the domestic purposes benefit and several hours of waiting at the police station before her statement concerning a domestic incident is taken.

While victims often need one-to-one support, group work is an important part of the women's support and advocacy programme. Group activity breaks down the isolation abusers typically impose on their victims. Through meeting women who are in similar situations, participants can more easily come to understand the systematic (and sometimes systemic) nature of the violence to which they have been subjected. The result is that they are less likely to accept abusers' attempts to make them feel responsible for the violence. Over time, members of women's groups are able to understand their own stories against the backdrop of the commonplaceness of domestic violence as well as the justifications often accepted by the justice system for that violence. Participation in such groups allows women to socially contextualise their spouse's behaviour.

Because of the guilt victims are often encouraged to feel by their abusers and the above-mentioned isolating tactics, it is often difficult to engage women in support and education groups. Some battered women have been "punished" for visiting friends or family and for having interests outside the home; they have been told who they are allowed to speak to and what they can say at social events with or without the abuser being present. These women are, understandably, reluctant to participate in groups where violence is the focus of discussion. Partly because of this, HAIPP has found it helpful to provide a choice of formats for women's groups.

The first of these is the HAIPP Orientation Group. All women whose (ex)partners attend a men's education programme are invited to attend one of these one-off groups. Some women find it easier to attend a group which can be seen as helping their partner than one which is clearly designed for them. The orientation group is an opportunity for women to be informed about the content of the men's programme, to see the control logs and videos used in teaching men about power and control, to learn about the language their partners will probably start to use as a result of their participation in the men's education groups, to find out what will happen if their partners fail to attend the programme, to discuss their personal safety issues and to learn what other women's groups are available to them at HAIPP.

The other type of women's group is the Court Orders Group. The purpose of this group is to inform women about the meaning and scope of protection orders and how to get police to enforce them. The group is run by the HAIPP court advocate, who, in collaboration with others, has produced a guide to protection and other Family Court related orders. This guide sets out in simple language the grounds on which protection orders may be granted, the procedures involved in applying for such orders, information about what behaviour constitutes breaches of those orders and what steps to take to get police to act on those breaches. It also sets out information relating to custody and access issues.

HAIPP's men's education groups

The men's education programme also operates out of the HAIPP office. The programme accepts referrals from Community Corrections and the Family Court. Some men are "self-referred" in that they are not court-mandated to attend the programme. "Self-referral", however, is often a misnomer in that certain men are referred to HAIPP by other social services and some are "partner referrals". The latter attend HAIPP in response to ultimata from spouses that unless they do something to end their abuse, the relationships will be over. Some men apparently "self-refer" prior to court appearances. In HAIPP's first 18 months, five per cent of self-referred men were subsequently ordered by the courts to attend the men's programme.[45]

Approximately 900 men have been referred to the HAIPP programme over the past two years. Of the 193 men on the programme as of 30 June 1993, 70 per cent had been referred by Community Corrections, 6 per cent by the Family Court and 24 per cent were self-referred.[46] Only two women have been referred to HAIPP as a result of their violent behaviour, both from Community Corrections and both in the past two months. Because of their infinitesimal number, there is no group programme established for them; they are dealt with on a one-to-one basis by HAIPP staff.[47]

It is important to note that the HAIPP men's programme is an education programme. It is neither a therapy programme nor an anger management programme. While many men might benefit from therapy or anger management training, such programmes are not a priority for protecting victims and restoring their autonomy. Therapeutic approaches typically address the presumed causes of the violence rather than the effects of such violence.[48] For example, if the presumed cause of an abuser's violence is his lack of communication skills, poor self-esteem or inadequate ways of expressing anger, then providing him with communication skills training, self-esteem enhancement or assertiveness training may be seen as appropriate remedies. Such approaches risk turning out more skilled and confident abusers.

On the other hand, if the violence and the effects of the violence are the focus, then abuser rehabilitation programmes become victim-oriented. Instead of anger being seen as a cause of violence, it is recognised as one of the weapons abusers use to intimidate their partners. Poor self-esteem is recognised as a self-serving justification for using violence which is in fact directed at getting the victim to do something, to stop her from doing something or to punish her for what she has or has not done.

Consistent with the philosophy of intervention, the focus of the men's education programme is on seeing the violence as part of a pattern of tactics utilised by abusers to control their partners. In groups, men are encouraged to re-examine the notions of hierarchy implicit in their belief systems which characteristically condone the use of violence. The curriculum explores the consequences of adopting a "one-up, one- down" model of relationships. For abusers, such consequences may include the loss of their spouse's intimacy, trust, and love. Ultimately, it may result in the loss of the relationship itself and (potentially) in the loss of father-child relationships as well. By exploring the contradictions in their rationalisations and the self-defeating nature of their violence (including arrest and conviction), men are introduced to an alternative model of relationships based on equality and respect.[49]

The men's groups are usually co-facilitated by a woman and a man. In part, this provides an opportunity for the co-facilitators to model an equal relationship between men and women. The women facilitators also play a monitoring role as part of the project's accountability process. They maintain close links with the women's programme so that they bring a victim-oriented perspective on violence and its effects to the men's groups.

Further steps to ensure accountability of the men's programme to victims include women's advocates making regular checks with the partners or ex-partners of men's group participants to gather feedback on the abusers' behaviour outside the group and to offer help to women who need it. Support for women whose partners are undergoing a men's education programme is vital. Both American[50] and local[51] research shows that women are more likely to remain in a relationship if the abuser is undertaking a stopping violence programme. In this context, providing a programme for abusers without support for their (ex) partners may actually increase the danger faced by these women.

HAIPP men's group facilitators sometimes comment that some of the men seem to be less interested in actually changing their behaviour than in convincing their partners that they have changed.[52] Our evaluation data includes instances of women reporting that their abuser has used participation in the programme to further abuse them (for example, by telling her that she has nothing to "moan" about given what other men in his group do to their spouses, or by adopting the terminology of the curriculum to accuse her of using power and control tactics to dominate him).[53] Some women who remain with their abuser as he participates in the men's programme have been characterised as being on a virtual emotional roller coaster as he alternates between behaving himself and relapsing into old patterns.[54] Given the priority on safety and autonomy of victims, support for women can be seen as a necessary part of running programmes for men. This approach has been codified in a standard of practice developed in Pennsylvania which states that:

> No intervention program for batterers should be initiated in a community unless there is a program for battered women that provides safe housing, advocacy and counselling and these services are available to the battered partners of participants in the intervention program.[55]

Indeed we would argue that it is unethical to provide programmes for abusers which do not have built into them processes to ensure accountability to the partners of those abusers. Moreover, a full array of appropriate services for those women must also be provided.

Despite HAIPP's clear priority in terms of victim advocacy services, the men's education programme is frequently seen by the justice system's representatives as the most important part of the project.[56] This view is reflected in many of the enquiries regarding the programme received by HAIPP. Evaluations of HAIPP, moreover, have at times been criticised for not paying sufficient attention to measures of re-offending.[57] The emphasis on offenders is clearly evident in the funding arrangements between HAIPP, the Family Court, and Community Corrections which entail fee-for-service in relation to offenders. The Family Court, for instance, pays a fee for respondents directed to HAIPP under section 37A of the *Domestic Protection Act* 1982 (NZ). It does not fund the women's support and education programme for victim applicants who are referred under section 37.

Whether or not individual men stop their violence is obviously an important measure of HAIPP's success. However, the intervention focus on safety and autonomy of victims means that the most important evaluations of success must be victim-oriented. For instance, as a result of HAIPP's involvement with them, are individual women now living abuse-free lives? This result may occur because former victims have continued to live with abusive partners but the latter have stopped using power and control tactics. Alternatively, former victims may be living independently or may have formed another relationship which is violence-free.

In terms of the systemic problems discussed earlier in this paper, the most salient issues are whether the decision makers in the justice system in Hamilton currently respond to domestic violence in ways which enhance the safety of victims, restore their autonomy and hold abusers accountable for their violence. It is clearly this systemic focus which distinguishes intervention projects from more limited approaches which concentrate on individual abusers and/or victims in isolation. The latter approaches explicitly or implicitly deny the crucial link between the justice system's practices and paradigms about domestic violence and the on-going abuse of victims who turn to police or courts for protection.

The impact of the intervention project

It is not our intention in this section to provide detailed evaluation data on the impact of the project. For that, the reader is referred to the five HAIPP evaluation reports prepared to date. Here, we briefly review some of the major impacts of an intervention approach on women's refuges, police, the courts and Community Corrections.

Women's refuges

For all the agencies, intervention has resulted in an increase in domestic violence related work, at least in the short term. This is most evident for the two Hamilton women's refuges which have reported a four-fold increase in their workload.[58] The increase is due primarily to the refuges' provision of advocacy services to women who do not initiate direct contact with the refuges themselves but who are seen by refuge call-out advocates after police have contacted the crisis line about them. Refuge call-out advocates work long hours under highly stressful and potentially dangerous conditions. The risk to advocates is especially evident when they respond to non-arrest calls. In those situations, the perpetrator may be lurking around the neighbourhood or may even be in the house.

The establishment of HAIPP has resulted in a change of focus for Hamilton refuges from providing services for residents of the refuge houses to community support work. Three-quarters of the work done now by the two refuges involves supporting women who never become refuge residents but who require crisis counselling about the violence they have faced as well as transport to, and assistance in dealing with, the Department of Social Welfare, lawyers, the courts, doctors and police.[59] Moreover, refuge workers perform their call-out advocacy role in addition to all the "traditional" activities of a refuge service, namely running the refuge houses and providing counselling and support services for the women and children who are residents of those houses. Finally, refuge workers carry out various functions within HAIPP's education and support programmes. For instance, both refuges have members who facilitate groups in the men's and women's programmes.

Police

The impact of intervention on police workloads has been difficult to quantify, mainly because police records do not generally distinguish stranger and domestic violence.[60] However, estimates based on a sample of telephone messages suggest that the Hamilton police are now arresting more than twice the number of abusers than prior to the establishment of HAIPP.[61] This seems to reflect a combination of an increase in the number of calls concerning domestic violence and an increase in the proportion of calls resulting in arrest. On the other hand, we have been told by some officers that it is now less common for police to be repeatedly called to the same houses.[62]

While we cannot quantify the level of reduction in repeat calls, this would be consistent with a more effective police response. Here we do have reasonable data.[63] When refuge call-out advocates visit women after a police-attended incident, part of their procedure involves asking the victim how satisfied she was with the police response. The overwhelming majority of victims report

being satisfied with police intervention. Some problems do remain: some officers are considered to be rude, unsympathetic, or victim-blaming. But even
when there are complaints about the attitudes of police officers, it is very rare
for women to be dissatisfied with the outcome of police intervention.

District Court

In relation to the criminal courts, the impact of intervention is more easily
quantified. As we have discussed earlier, prosecuting domestic abusers has
been particularly problematic. This is reflected in Justice Department statistics
for the whole of New Zealand: in 1991, only 64 per cent of the men charged
with "male assaults female" were convicted.[64] During the second year of the
project, on the other hand, 87 per cent of the men charged with "male assaults
female" were convicted in the Hamilton District Court.[65] This is a significant
improvement in holding abusers accountable for their violence and appears to
be the result of a combination of HAIPP related factors. First, the non-association conditions generally imposed on bail[66] presumably help protect women
from being intimidated and increase the chances that they will give evidence in
defended cases. Moreover, the role of the court advocate appears to be crucial;
during the past year, only one woman who has been supported by the court
advocate has declined to give evidence in a defended hearing.[67] This can be
contrasted with the apparent experiences of the Christchurch District Court
where certain judges in that court have commented several times over the past
year that women complainants were refusing to testify at defended assault
hearings, thereby causing substantial problems in terms of the court's calen-
dar.[68]

While statistical analyses can provide a global view, individual cases are
needed to establish exactly how well the intervention approach has been
accepted by the judiciary. The cases monitored by the court advocate show that
there are still times when District Court judges in Hamilton minimise the violence victims have experienced or accept an abuser's rationalisation for his
behaviour.[69] The majority of cases, however, show that clear and unambiguous
messages about the criminality of domestic violence are being given by the
judiciary.[70]

Community Corrections

The increase in the number of abusers arrested in Hamilton has impacted on
Community Corrections: the caseload of domestic abusers on supervision and
parole has increased dramatically.[71] There are efficiency gains however. Because
the direction to attend HAIPP is usually the main focus of the sentence, relatively little face-to-face contact with offenders is required of probation officers.

Thus the officer who supervises most of the HAIPP supervision caseload is able to handle far more offenders than would be possible if they were required to carry out traditional case-work tasks.

Community Corrections officers generally have been consistent in enforcing attendance at the men's programme. In the majority of cases of non-attendance, enforcement action has been taken. Of men referred to HAIPP between July 1991 and December 1992, 11 were not compelled to complete: three went into alcohol treatment programmes, one was deported and seven were allowed by their probation officers to transfer to other parts of New Zealand.[72] Of the 285 men referred by Community Corrections during the first 18 months of the HAIPP programme, 14 per cent have had their sentences reviewed for non-compliance[73] while 10 men (four per cent) have been convicted of further partner assaults.[74]

The Family Court

The first twelve to eighteen months of the HAIPP project also had substantial workload implications for the Hamilton Family Court. The Court staff had to devise procedures for the referrals of women and men to HAIPP under the provisions of sections 37 and 37A of the *Domestic Protection Act* 1982 (NZ) including procedures for summonsing and prosecuting men referred to the men's education programme who fail to attend. While these procedures are now in place, only approximately 50 per cent of the respondents referred to HAIPP under section 37A are actually inducted into the men's programme.[75] The majority of men who fall into the "no show" category cannot be located and therefore have not had HAIPP referral notices or section 37A(4) summonses served upon them. So far, no respondent has been prosecuted for failing to attend HAIPP.[76]

The Family Court has faced an increase in the number of defended applications for final non-molestation orders since HAIPP's establishment.[77] Court staff attribute this increase to the fact that there are now tangible outcomes when protection orders are granted. Non-molestation and non-violence orders are no longer seen as "simply pieces of paper".[78] Specifically, the practice of referring respondents to HAIPP under section 37A after a protection order has been granted, as well as the consistent implementation of police intervention protocols in respect of breaches of non-molestation orders, appears to have resulted in the view that protection orders now have "clout".[79]

Court personnel report that there are also more applications by respondents for discharges of protection orders and/or discharges of section 37A HAIPP referrals.[80] While few of those applications are successful, there have been instances where such orders have been discharged because there is no continuing contact between the parties or where the relationship has ended and there are no children or only adult children.[81] Moreover, if women do not contest their partners' applications, those orders will in fact be discharged. Judges see the fact that the application for discharge is not opposed as evidence that the parties may have reconciled or worked things out and consider that it would be inappropriate not to grant the discharge.[82] However, court staff express concern that some women are too frightened to oppose the discharge applications. As well, the victim may have relocated away from Hamilton and it may be difficult to serve her.[83]

Interestingly, lawyers for men in defended hearings do not appear to be challenging the fact that their clients have been violent; their argument is rather that there is not an on-going need for protection.[84] Court staff underscore the difficulty of proving such an on-going need if the respondent has not been violent during the six months that it takes to get a defended application for discharge of protection orders before the Family Court. They stress that it may well have been the existence of the non-molestation order which deterred further instances of violence.[85]

Judges and court personnel are better informed about the dynamics of domestic violence since the establishment of HAIPP. Some judges have stated that five or six years ago, they did not know what they now know.[86] There is now a focus on the violence in the relationship as well as on other relationship issues and the power and control analysis of such violence is used. This new focus is reflected in recent protection order decisions in which the facts of the violence have been articulated more explicitly.[87] In the past, such facts had often been glossed over or omitted entirely.[88]

With the nationwide and international interest in HAIPP and the establishment of "mini-HAIPPs" throughout New Zealand, the Hamilton Family Court staff has taken on the somewhat time consuming role of sharing its experiences of the HAIPP programme with other Family Court Co-ordinators and overseas specialists.[89] For instance, a paper on HAIPP and the power and control approach to domestic violence was recently co-authored by a Hamilton Family Court judge and the Hamilton Family Court Co-ordinator and presented to a national Family Court judges' conference.[90] The paper emphasised the effectiveness of the inter-agency approach to domestic violence and stressed the positive aspects of having community groups involved in inter-agency meetings.[91]

Conclusion

HAIPP evaluations to date have focused on the results produced by the consistent implementation of intervention protocols. Now that the project is moving into its third year and a reasonable follow up period has elapsed, the evaluation process has begun to focus on the impact of an intervention approach for individual abusers and victims. The data collected so far is encouraging. For example, although some abusers may continue to use violence, 71 per cent of women interviewed for the six month evaluation reported that their partners had shown clearly positive changes (the rest reported either limited changes, no change or ambiguous changes).[92] The majority of women interviewed as part of the 12-month evaluation reported that they felt safer and that their partners (or ex-partners) were less controlling.[93] Comments from interviews conducted as part of the recent evaluations are also positive. One woman commented, "I can stand up to him more." Another woman remarked, "The programme has helped me reclaim what I used to have."[94] In addition, the increased number of women who ring the police when they have been assaulted suggests that there is a perception that women are being taken more seriously by the justice system.

We have anecdotal evidence of men wanting to move out of Hamilton because it has become too "hot" for them. This suggests the power of an integrated approach to domestic violence. Such an approach, however, can only be effective if there continues to be regular and thorough monitoring of the justice system by victim advocates and on-going inter-agency consultation and accountability. There must also be on-going funding of HAIPP and the other intervention projects which are springing up around the country. While it may be difficult to quantify the costs of domestic violence in New Zealand today,[95] it is clear that such costs are substantial not only in financial terms but also in the daily misery experienced by thousands of New Zealand women and children. In Hamilton, HAIPP has clearly been significant in reducing some of that misery for some women. In addition, it has brought hope to some justice system personnel that a constructive approach to this demoralising, chronic problem is being set in place. One member of Hamilton's Family Court staff recently commented: "Those who work within the Hamilton Family Court (judges, court staff, lawyers and counsellors) now have much less of a hopeless feeling, that sense of 'Oh, here we go again' or 'Why bother?'" As she stated, "Even when there is a second referral to HAIPP, we are beginning to see that this has been a perpetrator's behaviour for a lifetime. No wonder he needs a second course. Maybe this time he will get it!"[96]

Notes

1 The Hamilton Abuse Intervention Pilot Project is a three year pilot pro-gramme funded by the Intervention Working Party of the Family Violence Prevention Co-ordinating Committee (FVPCC). At the onset of the pro-gramme in July 1991, the authors were contracted by FVPCC to perform periodic evaluations of the project. To date, five evaluations have been co-authored by us. They describe in detail the workings of the project and the consequences of the development of an inter-agency approach to domestic violence.

2 See, for instance, Pence, E, *The Justice System's Response to Domestic Assault Cases: A Guide for Policy Development* (1986) at 1-8.

3 A discussion of victim blaming within the context of New Zealand rape trials is found in Young, W, *Rape Study: A Discussion of Law and Practice: Volume 1* (1983) at 7-15.

4 Busch, R, Robertson, N and Lapsley, H, *Protection From Family Violence: A Study of Protection Orders Under the Domestic Protection Act* (1992) at 264-5. The authors' discussion of the justice system's approach to domestic violence is drawn largely from this previously published report. The material in the report is derived from the interviews we conducted with and about 21 women whose protection orders had been breached and from our interviews with 73 key informants including six judges, 25 police officers, 15 women's refuge workers, 10 Family Court Counselling Co-ordinators and counsellors, and eight solicitors. Justice Department statistics, police files, and 46 reported and unreported court decisions were also analysed in the report.

5 Ibid.

6 See, for example, *Redward v Redward* (1988) 4 NZFLR 528 (FC) and Esther's case study, both discussed in this volume in the chapter by Busch, R, entitled "Don't Throw Bouquets at Me...(Judges) Will Say We're in Love".

7 See for example, Busch, Robertson, and Lapsley, above n4 at 237-8 for a discussion about safety concerns in Family Court proceedings. From key informants, we learned of an instance where an applicant for protection orders and her refuge worker had hidden in the women's toilet because of the intimidating behaviour of the respondent and his friends in the only waiting area available in that Family Court. Our case studies reveal repeated instances where victims have been verbally and physically threatened in court waiting rooms, emerging from court hearings, and during court-ordered counselling sessions.

8 Family Violence Project, *Domestic Violence is a Crime* (no date) at 1.

9 Church, J and Church, D, *Listen to Me Please: The Legal Needs of Domestic Violence Victims* (1981) at 47; see also Ford, G, *Research Project on Domestic Disputes: Final Report* (1986) at 11.

10 Busch, Robertson and Lapsley, above n4 at 264-5.

11 Moore, J M, "Is a Non-Molestation Order Enough? Women's Experiences of the Family Court", unpublished M. A. Thesis, Victoria University of Wellington, November 1989; see also Busch, Robertson, and Lapsley, above n4 at 207-36.

12 Busch, Robertson, and Lapsley, above n4 at 264-9 and at 277-80. It should be noted that there are three types of protection orders which can be obtained under the *Domestic Protection Act* 1982 (NZ): non-violence orders which can be obtained by an applicant (who either separates from or continues to cohabit with her abuser) if the Court is satisfied that the latter has used violence against or caused bodily harm to the applicant and is likely to do so again (s. 6); a non-molestation order which can be granted if the court is satisfied that an applicant is "in need of protection" but only when the applicant is about to be or has separated from the respondent (s.15); and an occupation order (whose effect is to give the applicant exclusive possession of the household residence) which may be granted if the court is satisfied that the applicant is in need of protection or that such an order would be in the best interests of a child of the family (s 19). Under section 17, non-molestation orders lapse automatically on the applicant's resumption of cohabitation with the respondent; there is no statutory definition of when such "resumption" occurs.

A breach of a non-violence order occurs if the respondent used violence against the applicant or threatens to do so. There is no criminal penalty for a breach of a non-violence order but on a finding that the order has been breached, the respondent may be held in police custody for a period of 24 hours.

A non-violence order is seen as allowing a "cooling off" period by removing the respondent from the scene for a short time. The authors' research indicates that non-violence orders are rarely enforced by police.

Pursuant to section 16, a non-molestation order is breached by the respondent entering or remaining on any land or building the applicant occupies without the latter's consent, molesting the applicant by watching or besetting the applicant's dwelling house, place of business, employment or residence or by following or waylaying her in any public place. Breaches of non-molestation orders are dealt with in the District Court and the penalty for a breach of a non-molestation order is a fine of $500 and/or imprisonment for three months.

It should be noted that in the New Zealand context District Courts are analogous to Local Courts or Magistrates Courts in Australian jurisdictions. The Family Court is a specialist court on the same level of the court hierarchy as the District Court. Problems in terms of protection orders arise, in part, because such orders are granted in the Family Court and yet sentencing for breaches of non-molestation orders are heard in the District Court. One issue involves the fact that the affidavits and other material used to gain the non-molestation order in the Family Court are not available to the District Court judge for sentencing purposes. This lack of contextualising of the conduct which constitutes breaches is one of the factors involved in District Court judges' trivialisation of domestic violence.

13 Id at 239-47.

14 Id at 192-201.

15 Ibid. See, for example, *R v Panoa-Masina*, unreported Court of Appeal, 7 October 1991 (CA 309/91). See further discussion of this case in Busch, R, this volume.

16 See above n12. For a more detailed discussion of this lack of co-ordination in terms of the Family and District Courts' approaches to domestic violence, see Busch, Robertson, and Lapsley, above n4 at 277-80.

17 See Busch, R , this volume.

18 For the full case study, see Busch, Robertson, and Lapsley, above n4 at 149-54.

19 Id at 72-3.

20 Id at 73.

21 Brygger, M P and Edleson, J , "The Domestic Abuse Project: A Multi-systems Intervention in Woman Battering" (1987) 2(3) *J of Interpersonal Violence* 326.

22 A recent New Zealand report entitled *The Review of the Family Court: A Report for the Principal Family Court Judge* (1993) supports this position. It states that "where domestic violence is evident, joint counselling and/or mediation is not appropriate". See also Astor, H, this volume.

23 In our previous work we have recommended that "There should be no requirement for 'fresh' or 'immediate' violence to have occurred as a pre-requisite for issuing *ex parte* non-molestation orders. Past violence coupled with present threats is as compelling a reason for issuing protection orders as is present physical violence." Busch, Robertson, and Lapsley, above n4 at 212. For a discussion of Family Court practices in terms of granting *ex parte* non-molestation orders, see id at 208-12.

24 For a discussion about police attitudes, see Kurz, D, "Battering and the Criminal Justice System: A Feminist View" in Buzawa, E S and Buzawa, C G (eds), *Domestic Violence: The Changing Criminal Justice Response* (1992) at 31. For a discussion about police prosecutors' attitudes, see Cahn, N R, "Innovative Approaches to the Prosecution of Domestic Violence Crimes: An Overview", in Buzawa, E S and Buzawa, C G (eds), *Domestic Violence: The Changing Criminal Justice Response* (1992) at 162-3.

25 Deaux, K and Wrightsman, L S, *Social Psychology* (5th edn, 1988).

26 Busch, Robertson, and Lapsley, above n4 at 165-8 and at 190-208. See also, Busch, R, this volume.

27 These are examples of the rationalisations the second author has heard over eight years working as a probation officer and a similar period facilitating groups of domestic assaulters. For examples of how even experienced workers who have access to only the abusers' stories can easily collude with their violence, see also Pence, E and Paymar, M, *Power and Control: Tactics of Men who Batter* (1986) at 30.

28 Relevant here is the applicability of the Stockholm syndrome to some battered women. The syndrome accounts for the paradoxical psychological reaction of hostages to their captors: when threatened with death by a captor who is also sometimes kind, hostages develop a fondness for their captor and an antipathy to the authorities working for their release. They may become quite protective of their captor. For a description of this phenomena, see Graham, D L R, Rawlings, E and Rimini, N, "Survivors of Terror: Battered Women, Hostages and the Stockholm Syndrome " in Yllo, K and Bograd, M, (eds), *Feminist Perspectives on Wife Abuse* (1988) at 217-33.

29 See discussion concerning issues of confidentiality and privilege in Lapsley, H, Robertson, N and Busch, R, "Family Court Counselling: Part I "(1993) 3 *Family Law Bulletin* 152 and Lapsley, H, Robertson, N and Busch R, "Family Court Counselling: Part II"(1993) 1 *Family Law Journal* 9.

30 See discussion concerning issues involved in the lack of inter-agency co-ordination, above n16.

31 For reviews of abuser programmes, see Tolman, R M and Bennett, L W, "A Review of Quantitative Research on Men who Batter" (1990) *Journal of Interpersonal Violence* 87; Eisikovits, Z C and Edelson, J L, "Intervening with Men who Batter: A Critical Review of the Literature" (1989) *Social Services Review* 384; and McLaren, K, "Programmes to Reduce Domestic Violence: Draft of a Literature Review " unpublished draft of a paper prepared by the Penal Policy Division of the Department of Justice: Wellington, 1992.

32 Police Commissioner, *Commissioner Circular 1987/11* (1987). The mandatory arrest policy has recently been re-stated in *Commissioner Circular 1992/07* (1992).

33 In some police districts outside Hamilton, it is standard practice for domestic abusers to be given diversion for breaches of non-molestation orders and all but the most serious assaults. Such a diversion programme may include a referral to counselling, not only for the abuser but also for the victim; Busch, Robertson, and Lapsley, above n4 at 171. The *Commissioner's Policy Circular 1992/07* (1992), states that diversion may be suitable in domestic violence cases "where suitable local programmes are in place". It states that "there is good evidence that when properly managed, diversion can be a very effective form of treatment".

34 The role of the HAIPP court advocate is discussed more fully below.

35 Police commonly complain that when they do arrest abusers, victims often refuse to give evidence against their partners. This is borne out in the statistics: nationally, less than two-thirds of the prosecutions laid under section 194(b) of the *Crimes Act* 1961 (NZ) ("male assaults female") result in a conviction: 20 per cent are withdrawn and the balance are dismissed. In Hamilton during the period August 1992 to June 1993, 87 per cent of men charged under this section were convicted, in seven per cent of cases charges were withdrawn and six per cent were dismissed. The national statistics were supplied in a letter dated 28 November 1992 from Philip Spier, of the Policy and Research Division, Department of Justice and the Hamilton statistics were produced in Robertson, N and Busch, R, *Hamilton Abuse Intervention Pilot Project Report No. 5: The Two Year Review* (1993).

36 Id at 9-10. Between August 1992 and July 1993, of the 344 men charged with domestic violence related offences, 22 per cent (77) were remanded in custody, 60 per cent (207) were remanded on bail with non-association conditions and 17 per cent (60) were remanded on bail with no non-association conditions.

37 See below for examples of "unsuitability".

38 Robertson and Busch, above n35 at 11.

39 Penal Policy Review Committee, *Report to the Minister of Justice* (1981) at 116-17.

40 Department of Justice, *Submission to the Committee of Inquiry into Violence* (1986) at 177.

41 Section 37A (1) states that "the Court may, on making an order under this Act, **direct** the respondent to participate in counselling of a nature specified by the Court". (emphasis added) The language of section 37A(1) is mandatory, and subsections (4) and (5) lay out provisions for summonsing and prosecuting for non-participation. On the other hand, section 37 states that "On making an order under this Act, the Court may **recommend** either party or both of them to participate in counselling of a nature specified by the Court." (emphasis added)

42 Busch, Robertson and Lapsley, above n4 at 260.

43 A cliche often used by battered women to describe their appeasement tactics is, "He said, 'Jump!' And I said, 'How high?' "

44 See Robertson, N and Busch, R, *Hamilton Abuse Intervention Pilot Project Report no. 2: Six Month Evaluation Report* (1992) at 39-40.

45 Robertson and Busch, above n35 at 27.

46 Id at 25-6.

47 Information given by the HAIPP court advocate in a discussion held 3 October 1993.

48 Adams, D, "Counselling Men Who Batter: A Pro-feminist Analysis of Five Treatment Models" in Yllo and Bograd (eds), above n28 at 176-99.

49 Pence and Paymar, above n27. The curriculum used in the HAIPP men's programme was developed in Duluth, Minnesota and then adapted for New Zealand conditions, for example, separate men's groups for Maori and non-Maori abusers, separate Maori and non-Maori women's groups, and production of local video vignettes of abusive behaviour.

50 Gondolf, E W, "The Effect of Batterer Counselling on Shelter Outcome" (1988) 3 *Journal of Interpersonal Violence* 275.

51 Furness, J A, "From a Woman's Perspective: A Multiple Case Study Evaluation of an Education Programme for Abusers", unpublished M.Soc.Sci. Thesis, University of Waikato, (1993) at 203.

52 Robertson and Busch, above n35 at 29-30.

53 Robertson, N, Busch, R, Glover, M and Furness, J, *Hamilton Abuse Intervention Project: The First Year* (1992) at 44.

54 Id at 213-14.

55 Foster, B and Bicehouse, T, "Principles of Practice" in Hart, B J (ed), *Accountability: Program Standards for Batterer Intervention Services* (1992) at 5.

56 For example, a discussion paper prepared for FVPCC by a senior police officer regarding the evaluation of HAIPP suggested nine measures which could be considered as indicators of the success of the project. The first was "reduced levels of recidivism and therefore a reduced incidence of violence". The next five indicators related exclusively to abusers. Only the last three related to

victims and each of these related to reduced need for medical services (for example, hospitalisation and specialist services such as psychologists). No mention was made of increased victim autonomy as an indicator of success. Only the first indicator related (indirectly) to victim safety. (Smith, D C, unpublished discussion paper prepared for the 3 December 1992 meeting of the Intervention Working Party of FVPCC.)

57 This was evident from a discussion paper prepared by Bruce Asher of the Department of Justice and tabled at the 24 March 1993 meeting of the Intervention Working Party of FVPCC.

58 Robertson and Busch, above n35 at 6.

59 Ibid.

60 For instance, it is not possible to provide an analysis of all the prosecutions in respect of domestic abusers because Justice Department statistics do not distinguish domestic assaults from other assaults. However, the analysis of section 194(b) prosecutions provides a reasonable measure. While not all domestic assaulters are charged with "male assaults female" (for example, "common assault", "assault with intent to injure" and "threatening to kill" charges may be laid), police informants have told us that nearly all prosecutions for "male assaults female" are related to domestic assaults.

61 One impact that HAIPP has had is that record keeping is now much improved compared to prior to the project's establishment. For example, we can determine with considerable accuracy the number of abusers arrested in Hamilton each month. Establishing comparable figures for the months prior to the project's launch is more difficult. An approximation can be obtained by searching the records of telephone messages received at the Watch House. This requires making a judgment on limited information as to which calls were domestic-related. This method fails to include some arrests—for example, where a complaint was made in person rather than over the telephone or where an offender was arrested more than a day after the telephone call was made. Police advise that few arrests are made in those latter circumstances. Working from a sample of telephone messages for January to June 1991, we calculated an estimate of 16 domestic violence related arrests per month. During the same period in 1993, an average of 42 arrests per month were recorded by HAIPP.

62 From conversations with Hamilton police sergeants in February 1992.

63 Robertson and Busch, above n35 at 5-6.

64 See above n35.

65 Robertson and Busch, above n35 at 10. For a comparison of outcomes of prosecutions for "male assault female" charges for HAIPP and national samples, see Table 3, id at 12.

66 Id at 9-10, especially table 1. See also above n35.

67 Id at 10.

68 Reported in NZ Herald, 14 January 1993, at 3; Waikato Times, 11 March, 1993, at 8. For example, Erber J commented that, "The failure of victims of domestic violence to testify against alleged offenders could lead to a lowering

of concern about domestic violence assaults." It is perhaps ironic that a graphic illustration of how dangerous it can be for women to testify against their abusers occurred last year in the Christchurch District Court when a woman was attacked by her ex-boyfriend while waiting to give evidence against him. He cut her face severely with a razor. *The Christchurch Press*, 10 August, 1993, at 1.

69 For a discussion of several of these cases, see Section 5 of the *Criminal Justice Act: Recent Criminal Court Cases* in Busch, this volume.

70 Ibid

71 J. Davies, personal communication (October 1993). Collated Community Correction statistics cannot be used to track the HAIPP-related consequences for caseloads because those statistics do not distinguish domestic assaulters from other offenders.

72 Robertson and Busch, above n35 at 15, 28.

73 Id at 28.

74 Id at 27.

75 Id at 16.

76 Ibid.

77 Id at 17.

78 Ibid.

79 Ibid.

80 Id at 16-18. See for a general discussion of present Family Court practices in terms of discharges of protection orders and discharges of section 37A directions.

81 Id at 17.

82 Ibid.

83 Ibid.

84 Ibid.

85 Id at 17-18.

86 Id at 20.

87 Ibid.

88 Busch, Robertson and Lapsley, above n4 at 193.

89 Robertson and Busch, above n35 at 19.

90 Twaddle, A J and Wasey, J F, "Hamilton Abuse Intervention Pilot Project (HAIPP)", unpublished paper delivered to the Family Court Judges' Conference, Wellington (April 1993).

91 Ibid.

92 Robertson and Busch, above n44 at 19.

93 Robertson, Busch, Glover and Furness, above n53 at 43.

94 Comments recorded in 1992 by evaluation interviewers and held on HAIPP database.

95 For a discussion of the financial costs of domestic violence in New South Wales, see Cox, E, "Costs of Domestic Violence" in New South Wales Domestic Violence Committee (ed), *Local Domestic Violence Committees Conference: Papers and Proceedings* (1992).

96 Robertson and Busch, above n35 at 20.

4

Aboriginal Women and Domestic Violence in New South Wales

Pam Greer

Introduction

Violence against women and children in Aboriginal and Torres Strait Islander families and communities is widespread and extreme. Until recent times this violence has been given little if any acknowledgment. Now that it has begun to be acknowledged, both by Aboriginal and Torres Strait Islander communities, and by the wider community, it is vital to ensure that this recognition translates into effective service provision. Research, policy development and service delivery concerning domestic violence in Australia to date has paid too little attention to the needs and concerns of Aboriginal women and their children. There is an urgent need to remedy this. But in doing so, it is also important to ensure that policies and services are appropriate for the communities they are intended for.

This chapter will focus on responses to domestic violence, as experienced by Aboriginal and Torres Strait Islander women, in New South Wales. It will also identify priorities for the future.

Research: the findings and the gaps

What we know about domestic violence in Aboriginal communities is derived primarily from research undertaken in the Northern Territory and Queensland. Aboriginal researchers Marcia Langton,[1] and Judy Atkinson[2] are among those who have been instrumental in bringing this violence to public attention. Their research has been extremely valuable. However, there is relatively little research available from other states and territories. The limited research which has been undertaken indicates a very high level of domestic violence in some Aboriginal or Torres Strait Islander communities.

Research concerning homicide in Australia provides shocking evidence of the extent of violence within Aboriginal communities, and demonstrates that Aboriginal women are at substantially higher risk of fatal domestic violence than are other women in Australia. Heather Strang found that in 1990-91 six-teen per cent of all female victims of homicide in Australia were Aboriginal.[3] Whilst the rate of homicide victimisation for all Australian women in 1990-91 was 1.7 per 100,000, the rate for Aboriginal women was 10 times that figure.[4] In that year 21 per cent of all homicide victims were killed by their spouse. However, 51 per cent of Aboriginal homicide victims were killed by their spouse.[5] Strang also found that the over-representation of Aboriginal people among homicide victims, relative to their proportion within the general com-munity, varied between states and territories: Aboriginal victims of homicide were two and a half times over-represented in the Northern Territory,[6] more than six times over-represented in Queensland and approximately ten times over-represented in Western Australia.[7]

Strang's findings are consistent with those of previous research undertaken in the Northern Territory. In 1987 Aboriginal females were the victims of 79 per cent of all chargeable homicides in the Northern Territory, yet made up only 11.5 per cent of the population.[8]

Indirect evidence of the level of domestic violence among Aboriginal com-munities is also available from the Royal Commission into Aboriginal Deaths in Custody. The Royal Commission found that 53 per cent of Aboriginal men who died in prison cells over the past ten years were there because of acts of vio-lence: 9 per cent for homicide, 12 per cent for assault and 32 per cent for crimes of sexual assault.[9] The Royal Commission report provides little detail concerning who this violence was directed against, except to say that in nine cases the offences for which men were imprisoned related to violence against women and in two cases it related to violence against girls.[10] The Royal Commission report acknowledges that violence against women and children by young men in Aboriginal communities is a significant problem.[11]

While too many Aboriginal men have died in custody, too many Aboriginal women have died in their communities. In two states more Aboriginal women have died from violence in their communities than all of the total national Aboriginal deaths in custody. In one town in the Northern Territory five women died because of violent assault over the last five years, whilst the total custody deaths for Northern Territory were less than five. In one Queensland communi-ty more women have died as a result of violence than all the deaths in custody in that state.[12]

The level of sexual violence suffered by Aboriginal and Torres Strait Islander women is also estimated to be extremely high. Judy Atkinson cites research which found that rape and assault were the most under-reported offences in the Queensland Aboriginal Community, and that in one Queensland town, there was concern that there was no Aboriginal girl over ten who had not been raped.[13] It has been reported that a study carried out of 120 households in the Adelaide Aboriginal Community found that 90 per cent of the women and 84 per cent of the girls reported having been raped at some time in their lives.[14]

Other research undertaken in Queensland has also demonstrated high levels of violence generally in Aboriginal and Torres Strait Islander communities. Paul Wilson analysed homicide and serious assault statistics for Queensland over a three year period from 1978 to 1981. The homicide rate was 39.6 per 100,000 in Aboriginal communities, compared to 3.28 per 100,000 in the general community. The serious assault rate was 226.5 per 100,000 in the Aboriginal community, compared with 43.85 per 100,000 in the general community.[15] More recently it has been estimated that domestic violence affects 90 per cent of Aboriginal and Torres Strait Islander families living in Queensland Trust areas.[16]

It has taken a great deal of courage for Aboriginal women to begin to talk about the violence they and their children have been experiencing, and it has caused some controversy within Aboriginal communities. Judy Atkinson has reported that she was challenged by a senior male member of an Aboriginal organisation not to talk about the violence women experienced because "if we continue to talk about these problems we will cause more men to suicide as they worry about what they are doing".[17] More recently Aboriginal anthropologist Dr Eve Fesl has been reported as saying that "[a] lot of trouble has been caused by white feminists going into Aboriginal communities and pushing their anti-male line".[18] Yet the figures cited above present a horrifying picture of the extent and nature of the violence endured by Aboriginal women and children. Feminism is not to blame for the destruction of our communities.[19] We need to acknowledge the pain and the fear of women. They should not be ignored.

However, the figures reported above do need to be interpreted with caution since we can't assume that all Aboriginal communities have the same problems and needs. Care needs to be taken in applying knowledge derived from some Aboriginal or Torres Strait Island communities to Aboriginal communities generally. Aboriginal people in this country, both individually and in groups, can be vastly different. As Marcia Langton reminds us:

> Aboriginal cultures are extremely diverse and pluralistic. There is no one kind of Aboriginal person or community. There are regions which can be characterised, however, with reference to history, politics, culture and demography.[20]

New South Wales indigenous peoples have had a longer history of European colonisation than elsewhere in Australia, and have survived differently from Aboriginal and Torres Strait Islander peoples in other states and territories. The research findings from Queensland or the Northern Territory may not be applicable to communities in New South Wales. It is crucial that specific research is undertaken in this state, and that appropriate forms of consultation are developed in order that Aboriginal women's voices can be heard, and their needs identified and acted upon.

A decade of consultations

The needs of Aboriginal women in the context of domestic violence were first considered by the government in New South Wales in 1981. Pat O'Shane was commissioned by the New South Wales Task Force on Domestic Violence to prepare a report concerning Aboriginal women.[21] She undertook consultations in some urban and rural centres of New South Wales and found that "it is clear that wherever Aboriginal women lived, domestic violence is an aspect of their lives which looms large".[22] During the consultations for the report comments such as "it's fairly widespread" to "very widespread" were made, whilst others said "it's part of being black, isn't it?" and "It's so commonplace—there is nothing remarkable about it."

While most people consulted at this time saw alcohol as the cause of domestic violence, they also said that it was more than just alcohol. However, only two women said that it was because men saw women as their property.

The Task Force made a range of recommendations concerning Aboriginal women, including the need for land rights as a precondition for addressing social problems experienced by Aboriginal people, the establishment of more Aboriginal women's refuges, the provision of transport to get women to distant refuges, the extension of services of the Aboriginal Medical Service, and the expansion of advice and information by the Aboriginal legal services to Aboriginal women who had been victims of domestic violence.

Despite the acknowledgment of Aboriginal women's experiences of domestic violence in the 1981 Task Force report, it was not until 1986 that an Aboriginal Domestic Violence Committee was established in New South Wales to advise the government's Domestic Violence Committee. A temporary position of Aboriginal Project Officer within the New South Wales Women's Co-ordination Unit was established, initially for three months and then for a further six months. I held that position for the first three months and Bonita Byrne then took over from me. A permanent position was then created, which unfortunately on several occasions has not been filled for long stretches of time bringing into question the government's level of commitment to meeting the needs of Aboriginal women.

My role, in three short months, was to take the legislation concerning domestic violence out to Aboriginal communities throughout the state and to inform them about the law. It was totally unrealistic to cover the whole state, and at my request, the target area was narrowed to focus primarily on the Orana and Far West regions. During this time workshops, forums and community meetings were held in places such as Bourke, Walgett, Wilcannia, Broken

Hill, Coonamble, Nowra, Newcastle and inner city Sydney. The response by Aboriginal and Torres Strait Islander women was enthusiastic and they encouraged further workshops to provide information and to increase awareness about domestic violence.

At all times during that period the single most amazing fact was that Aboriginal women did not know that a crime was being committed. Denial was evident at one level. A lot of communities were closed to "outsiders", with domestic violence and sexual abuse being seen as "white fella's problems". It was claimed that the extended family in Aboriginal communities was a mechanism for prevention and protection. Throughout the project this perception began to change. There began to be a recognition that domestic violence was a widespread problem within Aboriginal communities and the feeling began to develop that "we can do something about this". Individual women began to speak out which was a courageous thing for them to do since communities were practised in saying "you are splitting our community and calling attention to us and therefore giving further ammunition to an already racist situation".

The next important initiative which emerged in terms of responding to the needs of the Aboriginal women was undertaken under the auspices of the Department of Health in 1988 and with the support of the Women's Legal Resources Centre. The project initially focused on the town of Wilcannia which was, and is, a particularly under-resourced community. It aimed to undertake consultations with the local community and to provide specific women's services, and was known as the Women's Business Workshop.[23] In planning the project those of us who were involved were very aware of, and indeed critical of, the fact that most services to the town were visiting services. There are no chemists, or doctors, or dentists in Wilcannia, and neither the Department of Social Security nor the Department of Community Services has a permanent office in the town. Services which came to the town often dealt with individual cases but left nothing behind them in terms of resourcing or empowering the women in the town.

The project involved a camp on the river bank with workers from the Department of Health, the Family Planning Association, sexual assault services, domestic violence workers, and the Women's Legal Resources Centre, interacting with local service providers and Aboriginal women. The learning was a two way thing—we learnt from them about the land, and the environment, and bush tucker. We let the women tell us what they wanted to hear about from us. We didn't set the agenda until the last day. It was a great success. The Aboriginal women made it clear that they felt that they had control at all times, aware that we were taking our direction from them. And it was good for them to meet a woman lawyer, to see a lawyer who wasn't a man in a suit but a woman with something to offer them. Now they specifically ask if Marion (the lawyer) is coming to visit them.

This project was repeated in 1989, and 1991, and provided the basis for the Women Out West Project undertaken in 1992 by the Women's Legal Resources Centre and funded by the New South Wales Law Foundation.

The Women Out West Project was developed to provide training for community workers and community legal education concerning sexual assault, domestic violence and family law in remote western regions of New South Wales. The project drew on the experiences of the earlier Women's Business Workshops, but also undertook a great deal of planning and co-ordination with the participating communities. Whilst the programme covered a range of health and legal issues relevant to the women, the consultations undertaken in planning the project confirmed that domestic violence was the issue of most concern to the women participating.[24]

Women Out West focused particularly on Aboriginal communities in New South Wales and visited Gilgandra, Dubbo, Narromine, Wellington, Peak Hill, Bourke, Enngonia, Brewarrina, Walgett, Lightning Ridge, Collarenebri, Broken Hill, Menindee and Wilcannia. In all 656 individuals participated in workshops carried out by the project during 1992.[25] The project found widespread concern at the level of domestic violence and sexual assault against women and children, and the belief that the violence was increasing. It also found that police and legal services were not providing adequate support to women and children who were the victims of this violence. The services available in this region were extremely limited and the women and children had little access to the available services.

This has been a good model for consultation and service provision; however, we need to be careful not to assume that all communities have the same needs, nor to assume that a single model will be appropriate for all Aboriginal communities. We also need on-going funding so that such projects can continue.

Further consultations with Aboriginal women about domestic violence were undertaken in 1990 during the development of the New South Wales Domestic Violence Strategic Plan, and an Aboriginal Working Party was convened for the duration of the development stage of that plan. Two Aboriginal women project officers undertook consultations in 12 towns—the towns chosen were those which gave state-wide representation geographically, and/or those in which strategies or ideas about the issue of domestic violence already existed.[26] In all, 151 Aboriginal people attended these meetings. Discussion papers were also distributed and women from towns other than those directly consulted were encouraged to attend meetings, or to send written responses.

Once again these consultations found concern about the amount of domestic violence in Aboriginal communities. There was an urgent need for community education, particularly about legal and individual rights, and information about resources available to women and to communities. The consultations found that some women were unaware of their legal rights, whilst others did not use the legal system because they had little faith in laws and government policies. Many women were critical of the Aboriginal Legal Service, since its policy of not representing one Aboriginal person against another often left Aboriginal women without effective, or culturally appropriate legal advice or representation, and in some cases with no legal representation at all. Criticisms of police failure to do their job in domestic violence cases were voiced in each of the communities visited. Women also raised concerns about the Aboriginal Police Liaison Officers, all of whom were male, and many of whom seemed to be unclear what role, if any, they had with respect to domestic violence. The consultations demonstrated that there was also an urgent need for Aboriginal services, and Aboriginal workers in mainstream services.[27]

During 1990, the first New South Wales Aboriginal Women's Conference was held in Dubbo which saw 400 Black women come together for three days to look at a range of problems and issues, including violence against women and children. The conference was funded by the Women's Co-ordination Unit and the Aboriginal and Torres Strait Islander Commission.[28]

Yet more consultations were undertaken during 1991 in conjunction with the release of the New South Wales Domestic Violence Strategic Plan, which had identified that special strategies needed to be developed for Aboriginal women. More recommendations were produced.

Despite the successive rounds of consultation which clearly identified and reiterated the problems and the needs, relatively little has been achieved in addressing those problems or meeting those needs. Violence continues to escalate. Where programmes have been introduced they have tended to be one-off, of limited duration and with inadequate funding. Being one-off or operating in isolation, projects have not made links with other services which could perhaps build on the particular project. Knowledge of the project remains with the participants and is not passed on. Often too, targeted positions for Aboriginal workers have been left vacant, or have not been supported so that turnover of staff has been high. It is also the case that these consultations have not replaced the need for careful and appropriate forms of research to be undertaken in New South Wales to gather appropriate data, data which can be used effectively to lobby for appropriate services, and to extract funding for on-going services.

Mainstream services and Aboriginal women

Equality Before the Law: Women's Access to the Legal System is the most recent of many reports to have demonstrated failures by mainstream services to meet the needs of Aboriginal and Torres Strait Islander women. The report documents unhelpful attitudes by police and police aides, a lack of cultural sensitivity by lawyers, judges, magistrates and other legal staff, cultural barriers which prevent Aboriginal women from discussing certain matters with men, isolation and lack of services as limiting women's access to legal protection.[29] The Human Rights Commission report *Racist Violence* goes further in analysing the historical basis for the antipathy between Aboriginal and Islander peoples and police,[30] and documents the continued use of threats and actual sexual or other violence by the police against Aboriginal and Torres Strait Islander women.[31] It also has been the case that Aboriginal women who have a criminal record are even less likely to get assistance from the police—it seems that having previously been prosecuted for a criminal offence, they are deemed to have foregone the right to police protection—they are judged as undeserving victims.

Numerous reports have also documented failings to meet the needs of Aboriginal and Torres Strait Islander women in the areas of welfare, health and housing, each of which are crucial in the context of domestic violence. Inadequate or inappropriate services, a lack of staff with relevant training, little or no commitment to employing Aboriginal staff, and outright racism have been found to limit Aboriginal women's access to a range of crucial services.[32]

The failure by these services to meet the needs of Aboriginal and Torres Strait Islander women and their children is associated with a certain level of suspicion or cynicism concerning mainstream services. This should not be used however, as an excuse for those services to continue to ignore the needs of Aboriginal and Torres Strait Islander women. Nor should it be presumed that Aboriginal women do not wish to use these services. In the context of legal services Carol Thomas has argued:

> *As a result of being denied information, women remain unsupported and unaware of their legal rights and the court process, and are reluctant to become involved. There are women, however, who are aware of the legislation but do not use it because they have no faith in government policies and laws, and because they believe (in common with all Aboriginal communities) that the solutions are to be found, and should therefore be developed, within each community.*
>
> *It would be wrong, therefore, to assume that legislation and access to the legal process is the answer for all Aboriginal women and communities. It is also wrong to assume that women are not using the law because they do not want to.*
>
> *All Aboriginal women need to know their legal rights and the processes involved in using the law. They need to have this option and to be confident that if they choose this path, they will receive all the help and assistance to which they are entitled.*[33]

While there have been significant problems documented with mainstream agencies in their failings to meet the needs of Aboriginal and Torres Strait Islander women and children, there are a number of mainstream agencies or services which have offered meaningful and sensitive support to Aboriginal women.

The women's refuges have been significant in recognising the needs of Aboriginal and Torres Strait Islander women, and in adapting their services to meet those needs. There are three refuges in New South Wales run for and by Aboriginal women,[34] and there are now 72 Aboriginal women employed in women's refuges throughout New South Wales. Working in a refuge is often doubly difficult for Aboriginal women who may experience pressure from their community who may perceive them as turning against men.[35] However, the Aboriginal women's refuge workers are getting stronger and are supporting each other from within. They are demanding that Aboriginal women's needs and interests be acknowledged, and that appropriate forms of training be provided for themselves, and for other key service providers.

One service which seems to be working very well and which is beginning to attract many Aboriginal women clients is the Redfern Women's Domestic Violence Court Support Scheme. This scheme is co-ordinated by Redfern Legal Service and staffed co-operatively by a number of community legal services including the Domestic Violence Advocacy Service and an Aboriginal women's resource centre. It has a holistic approach which acknowledges that women who have experienced domestic violence have a range of needs which go beyond legal issues. Aboriginal women are very happy with the service, and women are even beginning to come to it from other regions.

A number of government departments are also now beginning to pay greater attention to the need to provide more appropriate training for their staff concerning Aboriginal issues more generally, and the needs of Aboriginal women who have experienced domestic violence specifically. The Department of Courts Administration recently began a series of Aboriginal cultural awareness workshops in which court staff visited Aboriginal communities and received education from Aboriginal people about Aboriginal culture and lore, and about domestic violence. The Department of Health has a pilot programme called the Koori Community Care for Women which is based in Lismore. The project is funded by the National Women's Health Program. The project aims to reduce violence towards women and children through Outreach Education and Community Development. It also includes advocacy with local services. Two Aboriginal educators are employed to work in conjunction with Aboriginal workers in existing services in the area. The pilot project began really well but is now under a great deal of pressure to produce data justifying its continued existence.

The Ministry for the Status and Advancement of Women (previously the Women's Co-ordination Unit) has once again appointed an Aboriginal Policy Officer after that position had been vacant for some time. The domestic violence unit of the Ministry is currently producing a video and brochures concerning domestic violence within Aboriginal families and communities.

In a joint initiative of the Women's Health and Sexual Assault Education

Unit, the Department of Community Services and the Women's Co-ordination Unit, a core training package was produced concerning domestic violence. This package is now being updated and used in training Aboriginal workers and community members in responding to Aboriginal women and children who experience domestic violence.

The New South Wales Police Service has begun to recognise violence against Aboriginal women and children as an issue. In recent years they have invited Aboriginal women to participate in their training of police concerning domestic violence. In 1993 the Police Service provided funding to the Taree Aboriginal Community to address domestic violence within that community. A part-time Aboriginal worker was employed to support women and to assist women who go to the police and to the court seeking protection from domestic violence. The worker also provides important feedback to the police and the courts about the effectiveness of their responses to the needs of Aboriginal women in the context of domestic violence. This service has a lot of potential but unfortunately the funding is only sufficient to pay one worker for 18 hours per week, which is entirely inadequate.

The Aboriginal Police Liaison Officer (APLO) Scheme operated by the New South Wales Police Service has not been effective in dealing with domestic violence. It seems that many APLOs remain unclear as to their role in domestic violence, or actively avoid dealing with such violence. There continues to be concern among Aboriginal women that almost all of the APLOs are men, and that they are typically unwilling to assist women who experience domestic violence. [36]

Initiatives from the Aboriginal community

This year has seen the Aboriginal and Torres Strait Islander Commission (ATSIC) begin to fund community awareness programmes concerning domestic violence. This is an important initiative but more care needs to be taken in recruiting appropriate and adequately trained people to implement this programme. ATSIC continues to have too few women in decision making and policy positions, and the funding allocated to provide services to Aboriginal and Islander women is insufficient and denies the seriousness of the situation. There is an urgent need to act to protect women and children and ATSIC must become more responsive to women's concerns.

Aboriginal women from around Australia have begun to speak out about the violence and are challenging Aboriginal and non-Aboriginal organisations to take the issue seriously. They are also setting up their own mechanisms for dealing with the problem.

In 1993, with the support of the Women's Legal Resources Centre, and with funding from the Year of the World's Indigenous People, the Aboriginal

Women's Legal Issues Group held a conference which was attended by Aboriginal women from throughout New South Wales. The issue of violence against Aboriginal women and children was high on the agenda. In particular Aboriginal women were concerned with factors which limited their access to the law. These included:

> The lack of appropriate information given to Aboriginal women about their rights, particularly in rural and isolated areas, has meant that they are generally unaware of their options and continue to remain unsupported.
>
> The lack of available services in rural and isolated areas means that Aboriginal women have nowhere to go for protection, advice or counselling.
>
> There appears to be inconsistent responses from Government agencies in relation to Aboriginal victims of domestic violence.
>
> Racism and sexism within the legal system lead to incorrect assumptions about Aboriginal women's positions within Aboriginal society. In addition, this has led to incorrect assumptions about the role of violence within Aboriginal society.
>
> Concern regarding the over-representation of Aboriginal people as defendants has meant that Aboriginal female victims have been placed in the position of not wanting to be the "reason" for Aboriginal men being imprisoned. This has also meant that Aboriginal women victims have been overlooked both within research and the development of strategies which address the issues of Aboriginal people and the law.
>
> In many instances, Aboriginal women are unable to obtain legal advice and representation. Women have spoken about the difficulties they face in accessing the Aboriginal legal services as victims of violence. Aboriginal legal services mainly represent people who have been charged with a criminal offence and as such, are defendant focused. Ethically, no legal service can represent the victim if they are acting for the defendant in the case. [37]

The major recommendation arising from the conference was that an Aboriginal women's legal service should be established which would: provide advice, referral and representation to Aboriginal women; educate women about their rights and about victims of crime compensation; provide resources and education to the community on domestic violence, sexual assault and child sexual assault; and act as an advocate for Aboriginal women in law reform and the legal process. [38]

The idea for an Aboriginal women's legal service had originated with the Wilcannia women who had participated in the Women Out West Project. Similar recommendations have recently been made in Queensland at the First Conference on Violence Against Indigenous Women, sponsored by the Department of Health, and at the conference on Challenging the Legal System's Response to Domestic Violence, sponsored by the Department of Family Services and Aboriginal and Islander Affairs. They have also been endorsed by the Australian Law Reform Commission in the report *Equality Before the Law: Women's Access to the Legal System.*[39]

Concerns about the failure of the various Aboriginal legal services to represent women's interests are now widespread. Whilst there are a number of Aboriginal legal services operating in New South Wales, and their practice differs somewhat from one to another, in general it is Aboriginal women who are not well served. The various Aboriginal legal services typically focus on protecting Aboriginal men from the effects of racism and discrimination by police and the criminal justice system. In protecting Aboriginal men from the court system, they fail to provide support for Aboriginal women. The consequences of having a policy of not representing one Aboriginal person against another is, typically, that women miss out. Either they are referred on to a non-Aboriginal lawyer, or receive no assistance at all. In some areas the legal services have a budget from which they will pay another lawyer to represent an Aboriginal woman where both parties to the matter are Aboriginal. Too often it is the women who miss out on culturally appropriate and effective legal representation.

The Aboriginal Women's Legal Issues Group has recently received funding from the Law Foundation of New South Wales to set up a project investigating Aboriginal women's needs for legal services and advocacy.

In addition to lobbying for access to legal protection from domestic violence, Aboriginal communities have also begun to establish their own services to support women and children who have experienced violence within the family. One such service is Mygunya Aboriginal Corporation, a crisis outreach service which operates in the north-west of New South Wales. The service is run by Aboriginal women for Aboriginal women who suffer domestic violence in isolated or poorly resourced areas of rural Australia. The services offered include information and advice, assistance with transport to the nearest women's refuge, assistance in accessing mainstream services, counselling, self help and community education. It also aims to develop links with the police and other agencies.[40] However, there are some doubts whether Mygunya can continue. The small group of women providing the services are getting burnt out and it is not clear whether there is a commitment to on-going funding by the government.

Future priorities in New South Wales

The need to provide protection to Aboriginal women and children who experience violence remains urgent in this state. Despite more than a decade of consultations, the violence remains commonplace and is escalating. I have yet to visit an Aboriginal community in this state in which the violence is not rife—often being repeated in successive generations. It is not unusual for Aboriginal women in workshops that I have conducted to discuss their own experiences of violence, and most chillingly, to tell of the number of women they have known who have died due to domestic violence.

We know that the violence is widespread and extreme. However, we are often hindered in lobbying government by the absence of systematic research concerning domestic violence affecting Aboriginal women and children in New South Wales. Such research remains vital for several reasons. First, it is basic to any attempt to lobby for better services for Aboriginal women. Secondly, it is important to help identify which services Aboriginal women use: we need to know if Aboriginal women are using services, whether they are Aboriginal specific or mainstream services. Information about Aboriginal women's use of services will help us ensure that services are appropriate and sensitive to meet their needs. Where Aboriginal women do not use particular services we need to think seriously about what that tells us about their access to those services, the quality of the services provided and how to improve those services. All too often Aboriginal women are not given sufficient and accurate information about the services available or their entitlements to those services. Thirdly, we need this data to hold government, and especially the legal system, accountable where it fails to respond to the needs of Aboriginal women and children.

We also need to provide adequate and meaningful support for community initiatives in dealing with violence. Not all communities will have the same needs, nor the same preferences for mechanisms and services to deal with violence. We need to take the communities seriously and listen to what they have to say.

Policy development and service delivery must be co-ordinated, and consistent across government, and between government and non-government agencies. Services must be adequately resourced, and on-going, if they are to be effective. We have seen too many part-time, short-term, "pilot projects" which leave Aboriginal women and children with little real protection. Services must be culturally appropriate and there needs to be a much greater commitment to employing Aboriginal people in those services. There is a widespread need for training, both to provide skills for Aboriginal workers and to assist non-Aboriginal workers to develop a greater understanding of Aboriginal culture. Much can be achieved through "training trainers" so that the message is spread further and more people become involved in, and committed to, on-going training.

There is a pressing need for an Aboriginal women's legal service to be responsible for appropriate representation, advocacy and referral. This service must also provide much needed community education concerning domestic violence and women's right to legal protection.

Aboriginal women in New South Wales have been talking long and loud about these issues. It is time that our voices were heard and taken seriously.

Notes

1 Langton, M, "Feminism: What Do Aboriginal Women Gain?" (1989) 2 *Broadside* 3; "Aborigines and Policing: Aboriginal Solutions from Northern Territory Communities" (1992) 2 *Aust Aboriginal Studies* 14.

2 Atkinson, J, "Violence Against Aboriginal Women: Reconstitution of Community Law—the Way Forward" (1990) 2 (46) *Aboriginal Law Bulletin* 6; "Violence in Aboriginal Australia: Colonisation and gender" Parts 1 & 2 *The Aboriginal and Islander Health Worker* (June and September 1990).

3 Strang, H, *Homicides in Australia 1990-91* (1992) at 25.

4 Id at 25.

5 Id at 37.

6 See also Bolger, A, *Aboriginal Women and Violence* (1991).

7 Unfortunately these figures are not presented separately for men and women, nor is this data supplied for New South Wales. Id at 25-6.

8 National Committee on Violence, *Violence: Directions for Australia* (1990) at 37.

9 Royal Commission into Aboriginal Deaths in Custody, *Research paper no. 11* (1989) at 12.

10 Royal Commission into Aboriginal Deaths in Custody, *National Report* Volume 2 (1991) at 101.

11 Id at 98.

12 Atkinson, J, and Morton-Robinson, A, "Violence Is Contagious: Gender Relations in Aboriginal Communities in Queensland" (1991).

13 Barber, G J, Punt, J and Albers, J, "Alcohol and Power on Palm Island" (1990) *Australian J of Social Issues* 23 (2) 87 as cited by Atkinson, J, *Aboriginal Law Bulletin,* above n2 at 6.

14 Sam, M, *Through Black Eyes* (2nd edn, 1992) at 4.

15 *Black Death: White Hands* (1982) at 4-5.

16 Domestic Violence Task Force, *Beyond These Walls* (1988) at 256.

17 Atkinson, above n2 at 7.

18 Bone, P, "Crying Out For Justice" *The Age* (11 February 1994) at 18.

19 See also Langton, above n1, on this point.

20 *Well I Heard It On the Radio and I Saw It On the Television* (1993) at 11.

21 O'Shane, P, "Report on Aboriginal Women and Domestic Violence" in *Report of the New South Wales Task Force on Domestic Violence* Volume 2, Appendix 2, at 99.

22 Ibid.

23 Women's Legal Resources Centre, *Women Out West* (1994).

24 Ibid.

25 Id at 15.

26 Thomas, C, *Report on Consultations with Aboriginal Communities* (1991).

27 Ibid.

28 Greer P, and Thomas, C, *Report of the NSW Aboriginal Women's Conference 1990* (1991).

29 Australian Law Reform Commission, *Equality Before the Law: Women's Access to the Legal System* Interim Report No. 67 (1994) at 31-32.

30 Human Rights and Equal Opportunity Commission, *Racist Violence* (1991) at Chapter 3.

31 Id at 88; see also Atkinson in each of three papers cited above n2.

32 Thomas, above n26 at 5.

33 Id at 3-4.

34 Id at 5.

35 Ibid.

36 *Women Out West* (1994) above n23 at 13.

37 Aboriginal Women's Legal Issues Conference Report, at 2 (no date, or publisher provided).

38 Id at 3.

39 Above n28 at 57.

40 Smith, S and Williams, S, "Remaking the Connections: an Aboriginal Response to Domestic Violence in Australian Aboriginal Communities" 1992 (16) 6 *Aboriginal and Islander Health Worker* 6.

5

Lawyering and Domestic Violence:

A Feminist Integration of Experiences,

Theories and Practices

Nan Seuffert

Introduction

In recent years there has been a resurgence of interest in exploring theories of lawyering. Feminists have shared this interest, which has resulted in useful and insightful additions to the literature on lawyering from critical, feminist, the so-called "minority" and other perspectives. As a feminist active in the movement to end domestic violence who has practiced law and is currently a legal academic, my interest in theories of feminist lawyering flows from my commitment to integrating feminist theories and practices with the diverse experiences of women.

Feminists have long recognised the importance of integrating the experiences of women in feminist theories.[1] Phyllis Goldfarb has suggested that the integration of feminist theories, practices and the experiences of women in the area of lawyering might be facilitated by a "theory-practice spiral",[2] a conception of feminist theorising that is grounded in the experiences of women.

> *Feminist theorising begins with the concrete experiences of particular women,... These experiences are then questioned, probed, examined, explored, and analysed, a process that produces tentative theoretical conceptions. Once formulated, these theories are continually held up to the light of new experiences for evaluation, refinement, modification, and development. In short, feminist thinkers view concrete situations as containing strong theoretical potentialities. Theory then circles back to guide future behavioural choices which, in turn, test and reshape theory. (citations omitted.)[3]*

This chapter considers **how** we can integrate theories and practices of lawyering with the experiences of women, recognising both the commonalities and the diversity of those experiences and the situated character of the resulting theories. It focuses on a particular context: lawyering for survivors of domestic abuse in civil actions. First, it considers the epistemology and methods of a research project designed to explore and analyse the experiences of survivors of domestic violence with their legal representation in a manner that facilitates the generation of feminist theories of lawyering. Second, this chapter considers some of the experiences of survivors of domestic violence: survivors' perceptions of lawyers' lack of understanding of the dynamics of domestic violence. The chapter proposes a pedagogy[4] for educating lawyers about the dynamics of domestic violence which was developed by survivors and incorporates the experiences of survivors. The chapter next illustrates how educating lawyers about the dynamics of domestic violence might influence legal representation. Both a focus on teaching lawyers about domestic violence, and this method of teaching, are manners of facilitating the integration of the diverse experiences of women, feminist practices of lawyering and the development of feminist theories of lawyering.

Epistemology

Much of traditional research theory and design have been subject to feminist critique and re-development.[5] This section considers feminist developments in epistemology that have been essential to the development of the research design for this project.[6]

An epistemology is a theory of knowledge. It answers such questions as who can be a knower; what is knowledge; and what can be known?[7] Feminist epistemologies approach these questions from the perspective that women can be knowers and that the experiences of women can produce knowledge. Feminists have critiqued traditional or scientific empiricism and the related epistemology to reveal that it has generally been based on the assumption that the experiences of men, clothed in the myth of objectivity, are essential to the production of knowledge. The experiences of women have been excluded from knowledge production:

> a process will be considered to be "scholarship" to the extent that it appears to conform to norms of objectivity, rationality, and so on; and it will be considered to be "not scholarship" to the extent that it overtly attempts to take account of women's social experiences, as expressed through a deconstruction of falsely universalised knowledge and theory.[8]

Goldfarb's theory-practice spiral, mentioned above, illustrates one manner in which feminists have constructed feminist theories based on the assumption that the experiences of women can produce knowledge.

The centrality of the experiences of women to feminist epistemologies and to Goldfarb's conception of theorising suggests an inquiry into what experience means. The experiences of women are diverse, and they are also, at least to some extent, socially constructed. Experiences are not, however, totally determined by social construction:[9]

Subjects are constituted discursively, but there are conflicts among discursive systems, contradictions within any one of them, multiple meanings possible for the concepts they deploy. And subjects have agency.

The social construction of the subject means that any inquiry into the experiences of women will not provide access to a "true" or "authentic" nature of all women which can provide a foundation of knowledge upon which to base one universal feminist theory. Experience remains a useful category for theorising:[10]

Experience is not a word we can do without...[i]t serves as a way of talking about what happened, of establishing difference and similarity, of claiming knowledge that is "unassailable." ...Experience is at once always already an interpretation and is in need of interpretation. What counts as experience is neither self-evident nor straightforward; it is always contested, always therefore political.

Some feminist epistemologies recognise the diversity of experiences among women[11], as well as the constructed nature of experience. In their discussion of epistemology, Liz Stanley and Sue Wise suggest that recognition of the diversity of experiences among women and the constructed aspect of experiences results in recognition of "contextually grounded truths". The perspectives of different groups, located within specific contexts, have epistemological validity and produce contextually grounded knowledge that is true for that context.[12] This attention to contextually grounded truths suggests a focus on practice that is local, contextualised and immediate.[13]

Similarly, Katharine Bartlett identifies "positionality" as an epistemological stance that "acknowledges the existence of empirical truths, values and knowledge, and also their contingency".[14] Positionality recognises that experience can reveal new understandings of current perceptions from women's positions of exclusion. It also recognises that both experiences and the resulting knowledges are situated and partial, and that the relationships of the "knower" provide the location for meaning, identity and political commitment.[15] Experience is therefore retained as a useful category and basis for knowledge, but is coupled with the insight that the knowledge thus obtained is limited by context, and never assumed as a monolithic category.

Bartlett also suggests that increasing knowledge requires extending one's limited perspective by attempting to expand sources of identity and understand other perspectives.[16] This effort can assist in identifying both differences and commonalities with other perspectives. Positionality thus provides a manner of recognising experience as a basis for grounding assertions of truths and of increasing one's knowledge beyond one's limited experiences while continually deconstructing the category of experience.

Donna Haraway recognises the political construction as well as the partiality of experiences in her brilliant argument for the production of embodied knowledges that are **situated**, and that take responsibility for inherent limitations. Her argument is that "objectivity", or rational knowledge claims, should be recognised as those claims that take responsibility for the partiality of the knowledge produced, rather than those that make what can only be false claims of universality[17] : "I am arguing for politics and epistemologies of location, positioning, and situating, where partiality and not universality is the condition of being heard to make rational knowledge claims."[18] The knowledge producers thereby become accountable for the knowledge produced. Experience remains a useful category upon which to begin to formulate theories which are partial, fluid and context-based.

The experiences of women recognised by feminist epistemologies include the experiences of both the researcher and the research participants.[19] The researcher's knowledge is as contextually specific as the knowledge of the research participants; it is grounded in the researcher's political, historical, emotional and intellectual context.[20] Haraway's approach requires that the researcher not only identify, but take responsibility for the partiality of the knowledge produced. It is therefore appropriate to place the researcher(s) in the research, as well as to discuss the manner in which the research was designed to facilitate recognition of the standpoints of the research participants based on race, class, culture, sexual orientation and placement in other socially constructed categories.

Feminist approaches to epistemology have also resulted in rethinking the power hierarchy inherent in the traditional researcher/research participants relationship. Traditionally, the researcher has been cast as the knower, or subject of the research and the research participant as the object of inquiry, without any recognition that the research participant can possess knowledge. Feminist epistemologies require the recognition of the research participants, who are often women, as subjects who possess knowledge.[21] One of the goals of feminist research is to:[22]

> [M]inimise the tendency in all research to transform those researched into objects of scrutiny and manipulation. In the ideal case we want to create conditions in which the object of research enters into the process as an active subject.

In New Zealand, Maori critiques of traditional research designs, often used by Pakeha researchers studying Maori, have noted this same tendency of these designs to transform Maori people into objects of study.[23] Addressing this issue requires an epistemology that recognises Maori people not as objects of study, but as knowing subjects. Structuring research teams to include people of each ethnicity or culture involved in the research at every level and in all of the processes is one manner in which these issues are partially addressed.[24] It also requires recognition that research for Maori people will originate with Maori people, and be based on their experiences.[25] In *Attitudes to Family Violence*,[26] studies of several cultural groups in New Zealand were designed and implemented by people of the same culture. This structure recognised both that members of all cultural groups have knowledge and that truths are culturally specific.

Feminist and Maori critiques of the traditional researcher/research participant power hierarchy have spurred attempts to break down the power disparities in the relationship:

> the goal of emancipatory research is to encourage self-reflection and deeper understanding on the part of the researched at least as much as it is to generate empirically grounded theoretical knowledge. To do this, research designs must have more than minimal reciprocity.[27]

Although attempts to address power disparities in the interview context are both laudable and necessary, it is unlikely that power disparities can be completely overcome. An on-going awareness of the possible effects of power disparities is therefore necessary.

Stanley and Wise, Bartlett and Haraway all argue for feminist epistemologies that recognise both the diversity and the situated character of the experiences of women and a resulting multiplicity of fluid and partial theories developed out of those experiences. Goldfarb's theory-practice spiral also recognises the diversity of women's experiences and the contingent nature of feminist theories, always subject to revision in light of new, or new constructions of, experience. In the development of feminist theories of lawyering for survivors of domestic violence, this revision might come from the experiences of the survivors , the experiences of feminist lawyers, or the shared experiences of both in the process of lawyering. The next section considers research methods designed to recognise the diversity and the situated character of women's experiences.

Research methods

Feminist approaches to epistemology influenced the development of the specific methods used in this project. This section presents the research methods used in the project. Consistent with the epistemological stance of positionality, and with the recognition of situated knowledges, this chapter recognises the perspectives of both the researcher and the research participants.

A. Recognising perspectives

1. The researcher's perspective

(a) As a middle-class white American woman

As an American who had been in New Zealand for less than one year at the time of the commencement of this research project, I was aware of my "Americentrism", and my status as a non-Maori women, as well as my middle-class background. Although the English language is spoken both in the United States and in New Zealand, I soon learned that any similarity this commonality seems to indicate between the cultures is largely superficial. Feminism, and the connections between the women's movement and the anti-racism movement also take different forms in the two countries.[28] In designing the research project I attempted to "improve my perspective by stretching my imagination to identify and understand the perspectives of others"[29], while recognising that my own perspective is, ultimately, limited.[30] Therefore I designed and organised the research project with the National Collective of Independent Women's Refuges (NCIWR)[31] , and considered myself accountable to the women in this organisation. The NCIWR women provided an activist-based input into the project.

I also made a conscious effort to distribute some of the power and the resources connected with the research project. Maori women law students chose the Maori research assistant for the project. The research participants were chosen by refuge collective workers. Refuge workers who participated in the Maori and non-Maori pilot interviews provided feedback about the interview methods.

(b) As an activist in the movement to end domestic violence

I began learning about domestic violence as a volunteer in refuges for survivors of domestic abuse in 1986 and have worked as a volunteer in refuges fairly consistently since then. My work has included co-ordinating refuge training programmes, acting as a legal advocate and doing crisis call-out visits to survivors of domestic violence.

This work has made me acutely aware of activists' concerns with academic research in the area of domestic violence. Many refuge workers are sceptical about the role that academic research plays in the on-going oppression of women.[32] Activists have challenged the use of funds and energy for research when funds for responding to life and death crises are unavailable or severely limited.[33] They place priority on research that arises in response to problems identified by workers in the movement and survivors of domestic violence and that involves workers and survivors directly:[34]

To the extent that research was to be undertaken, concern was expressed about the level of activists' participation in the process, whether their insights would be built upon or ignored, and whether their own source of knowledge founded on a growing base of direct experience would be used, ignored, subverted and/or lose its legitimacy in the face of academic knowledge. There was concern about who was to do the research, what their orientations might be, and how the privacy, integrity and safety of abused women would be respected. Would the research be useful to women and to the agenda of change, or would it be an abstract enterprise destined for the lecture halls and the library shelves of academia?

These concerns are not to be taken lightly by any academic researcher. It is important that feminist researchers use the resources available to them in **furtherance** of the aims of the women's movement, and do not perpetuate the oppression of women.

Activists' concerns illustrate some of the issues considered by feminist epistemologies. The feminist epistemologies discussed above promote the use of the experiences of women as a basis for rational knowledge claims. Consistent with this approach, the experiences of activist women might provide a focus for the research and resulting knowledges, rather than being ignored. For example, in this research the experiences of activists and survivors are gathered to form the basis of feminist theories of lawyering in the context of civil actions concerning domestic violence.

(c) As a lawyer and legal academic

While practicing law in Boston in 1989 I co-founded a programme at the firm where I practiced to represent indigent survivors of domestic violence in obtaining restraining orders under the *Massachusetts Abuse Prevention Act 1978.* Eighteen lawyers participated. My role in the programme, in addition to taking cases myself, included co-ordinating initial and on-going training for these lawyers and co-ordinating training and supervision in the programme as interested new associates arrived at the firm.[35]

(d) Tensions in roles

Throughout the past eight years, my various activist and professional roles have been sometimes gracefully integrated and sometimes precariously balanced. As a trained member of the legal profession and a legal academic, I fit into the category of professionals, sometimes to be mistrusted at the grassroots level.[36] As an activist, I participated in many discussions about the roles and training of lawyers, which were accompanied by the cynicism that seems to prevail about lawyers in society generally. There were many examples of women who felt unfairly treated by the legal system and questioned the role of lawyers in either convincing them that they were being treated fairly, or coercing them into accepting arrangements with which they were unhappy. Not surprisingly, women questioned this behaviour from lawyers paid to act as their advocates.

Questions also arose for me, acting as a lawyer for survivors of domestic violence.[37] My activist self was highly critical of some of the practices that I observed other lawyers engage in and the effects that they had on the women represented, while my professional self recognised heavy caseloads and monetary and time constraints on lawyers, as well as training inadequacies. The tension between my professional role and my role as an activist provided the creative spark[38] for this research project.

2. Recognising the perspectives of the research participants

(a) Maori women

The unique perspectives of Maori women were recognised to some extent by providing for separate interviews for Maori women, to be conducted by a Maori woman. Due to the scarcity of information available and studies conducted using this type of research model, methods for the Maori interviews were necessarily determined to some extent by the discretion of the interviewer. This made the choice of interviewer extremely important. Ideally, the Maori interviewer would have been a co-researcher knowledgeable in law and active in the area of domestic violence funded to fully participate in the project.[39] As funding was unavailable for that purpose, I decided to hire a Maori woman law student research assistant to conduct the Maori interviews. At the suggestion of a Maori colleague, the process of choosing a research assistant was turned over to the Maori women law students to conduct in a manner that they thought was appropriate. I will briefly describe my part in the process, as an illustration of one way in which privileged white feminists might re-distribute some of our power, in attempts to take responsibility for the partiality of our perspectives.

I requested that an announcement be made at the Maori law students forum asking any women interested in a job as a research assistant to attend a meeting. The students who attended included Riparata, a mature woman who was a member of a refuge collective and Kura, a mature woman who had a social science degree and several years experience working as a cross-cultural communicator for the Department of Social Welfare. At the meeting, after I introduced the project, the students had a general discussion of the skills that they thought would be necessary for a Maori interviewer on this type of project. The students then went away to make their choice of research assistant, using a Maori process to arrive at the decision.

Robyn, a woman well-versed in Maori culture and communication was chosen. Neither Riparata nor Kura, one of whom I might have chosen had I made the decision, took the job. They explained that this job was a good opportunity for a younger woman to gain important experience and insight: while they could find other summer employment, it was unlikely that Robyn would find another job. Both women indicated that they would maintain contact with Robyn and would be available for consultation should she feel uncertain about the processes that she choose to use for the interviews. In fact, Riparata accompanied Robyn on the initial pilot interview, which was conducted at the refuge where Riparata was a member. Later, when Robyn was unable to travel on an interview trip due to unexpected family commitments, Riparata was able to accompany me on short notice and to conduct the Maori interviews. All of these arrangements were made by the Maori women as they thought appropriate.

Robyn drew on Maori protocol in conducting the Maori interviews. I indicated that she should use whatever methods she felt comfortable with and made explicit that I would not impose any criteria or methods on her. The Maori women students' process for choosing a research assistant resulted in a better choice than I would have made. I also learned an immense amount from these women. The information obtained from the Maori women in the interviews, after being transcribed and proofread, was given to a Maori woman colleague for interpretation, and so that a Maori person could control what happened to the information. The information about the interview process and the findings of the Maori interviews will be the subject of a separate report by Maori women. The separate presentation of the Maori interviews in a report by Maori women is consistent with the theoretical and methodological issues discussed above.

(b) Non-Maori women

As the interviewer of the non-Maori women, I was aware of my own status as a middle-class white American women, as discussed above. In an attempt to limit my influence on the project, research participants were approached through the refuges from which they had received support and refuge workers were requested to be available during and after the interviews for support. The research participants were also given the option of bringing other women to the interviews for support.

(c) Further recognition of standpoints

In recognition that many of the experiences that are the subject of this research differ for women of different classes and sexual orientations, as well as for women in other socially constructed categories, we offered individual interviews to all of the women, either as substitutes for the group interviews or in addition to the group interviews.

It may have been appropriate to further divide both the Maori and non-Maori group interviews to allow women of similar classes, for example, to share their experiences of their legal representation and the system. However, due to the small size of the study and limited resources, this was not possible.

B. Working with the National Collective of Independent Women's Refuges

The first step in ascertaining interest in NCIWR was initiating discussion about the possibility of a research project into the roles of lawyers at the collective where I am a member. I then facilitated two workshops at the NCIWR Annual General Meeting in 1991, attended by paid and unpaid refuge workers from around the country. As the interest level among both Maori and non-Maori women was high, an informal discussion of the proposed research project with a national coordinator of the NCIWR took place. The project was formally proposed to a member of the Core Group of NCIWR,[40] who placed the proposal before the Core Group. The Core Group agreed to support the project.

The project was initiated by the use of a questionnaire which introduced the project and allowed individual refuges to indicate an interest in participating in the research by coordinating interviews of survivors with the researchers. Grassroots support for the project was evident in an excellent response to the questionnaire, combined with the interest and support indicated at the Annual General Meeting, by the Core Group, and communicated in various other informal discussions with survivors of domestic violence and refuge workers.

The locations chosen for the research were those where there had been an expression of interest in participating in the project. The refuge workers who organised the interviews selected the research participants. The criterion for selection was simply that the women had hired lawyers to obtain non-molestation, non-violence and/or other orders under the *Domestic Protection Act* 1982 (NZ). The women could be current residents in a refuge, and currently going through the legal process, or they could be refuge collective members who had been through these legal processes at some point in the past. As some of the collective members were never residents in a refuge, it was hoped that the interviews would include women who had selected lawyers in a variety of manners, including choosing from the telephone directory, and by recommendation from friends as well as by recommendation of refuge workers. In addition, interviewing both women currently involved in the process and previous participants would facilitate an exchange of information between the research participants, as well as provide the researchers with both recent impressions and thoughtful reflections on legal representation.

C. Designing interviews for abused women

The interviews were designed to be consistent with the feminist epistemologies discussed above. As noted above, the methodology and results of the Maori interviews will be reported separately by Maori researchers. This section therefore focuses on the interviews with non-Maori women.

The interviews were generally conducted in groups of three. Each group attended two two-hour sessions. The interview style adopted recognised feminist critiques of traditional interviewing.[41] Information about my status as a refuge collective member and a lecturer at a university was given at the beginning of each set of interviews, and questions asked by participants were answered.[42] Providing the information about involvement in a refuge collective indicated my familiarity with stories of survivors of domestic abuse, in an effort to encourage the women not to edit their own stories for fear of shocking me.

1. The pilot interview

In an effort to recognise the limitations of my perspective in the design of the interviews, a pilot interview was conducted, after which the participants were asked for feedback on the interview process and methods. Three women with varying experiences and backgrounds participated in the pilot interview. Two of the women were refuge workers, one of these a paid refuge worker. One of these women was also a university student and one a lesbian.

The feedback from the pilot interview was generally very positive. It also alerted me to such issues as child care and smoking breaks.

2. The first interview session

In the first session open-ended questions about legal representation were asked. The format included standardised questions with general prompts.[43] The questions began with each woman's story of her abuse and then took the women chronologically through their legal representation. Standardised questions were used in an attempt to keep the stories and discussion focused on the legal representation, due to the limited time available and the quantity of information sought.[44] However, the goals included allowing the women to relate their experiences of their legal representation, and for this reason the interviews were not strictly controlled. The questions were truly open-ended.[45] The first part of the first interview session consisted of questions designed to elicit the emotional reactions of the women to their legal representation.[46] The first interview session concluded with some general questions about the effects of going through the legal procedure. The women were also asked what would be important to them if they were choosing a lawyer at the present time. This question was intended to allow women to have direct feedback to lawyers and to ensure that their opinions of what was important about their legal representation were recognised.

3. The second interview session

The second "interview" session was the most exploratory aspect of the project.[47] It was designed specifically to recognise the participants as active subjects, with important contributions to make to the research project, and important expertise to share. It was also designed partially in response to the question often asked by activists, and specifically asked by refuge workers about this project: how will the women who participate in the project benefit? An obvious answer was to give the women access to information that could be relevant to the legal processes that they were currently involved in and which are the subject of the research. The session was therefore designed to be an informal exchange of information in which the women interviewed could ask questions and receive information on these legal procedures.[48] Flow charts of the legal procedures were presented and discussed. These included information about how to obtain non-violence, non-molestation, custody and occupation orders, the procedures to be followed upon breaches of non-violence and non-molestation orders, and the penalties that abusers could receive for breaches. The flow charts were intended to clarify the processes for the women and to stimulate questions and discussion about the processes and their lawyers' roles. Exchange of information occurred at several levels in these sessions, among the research participants as well as between the researchers and the research participants. Further, the women were able to point out ways in which the processes varied at the local level, as well as providing information about their lawyers.

At the end of the second interview session a brainstorming session about legal representation was held, which usually included discussion of the women's perceptions of the roles of lawyers in society, their understanding of the legal system and their understanding of their relationships with their abusers. Group interviews are recognised as excellent for creatively generating ideas.[49] Further, this aspect of the discussion was intended to recognise the expertise that the participants possessed with respect to legal representation as a result of their experiences. The resource of the participants' combined knowledge about the ways in which lawyers deal with survivors of domestic violence is crucial to the development of lawyering.

D. Experiences

One consistent theme easily identified from the interviews was a sense by many of the women, both refuge workers and non-refuge workers, that their lawyers did not understand the dynamics of domestic violence. This was seen by some women to directly affect the quality of legal representation that they received, as well impacting directly on their physical safety.

For example, Robin approached several lawyers to obtain protection from her violent partner and was told that she could not get protection. Robin described the abuse in the following terms:

> Mine was mainly emotional, verbal and sexual abuse actually and he didn't start any abuse until after we got married and the day we got married I remember feeling this terrible sense of dread and being trapped… If he didn't get his own way or I wouldn't agree with him he would start arguing with

me and it was constant. It was little things like never supporting me, never affirming me, putting me down and later on he would start screaming... he ended up smashing the place up and had me backed up in the corner with an arm chair thrown at my feet and it was that kind of level and I was with him for about twelve years... I tried several times to get away... This was before I had children and then about the last four years of the relationship it was something like screaming at me for about three or four hours a day and smashing the place up. I was so shaken emotionally that I couldn't cope and my whole life was focused on looking after him and nurturing him so he wouldn't abuse me and the kids, yell and scream, and it was constant, the sexual abuse was constant at me physically. In the day time ...Always touching me, and then at night time he was demanding sex all the time whether I wanted to or not. Even in my sleep he would have his arms around me so there was just like no escape. No escape ever...

Robin described her first visits to two different lawyers:

I went to him and I tried to explain to him I was just so terrified I was shaking, I was anorexic, I could hardly speak, I was really really distressed, I was so frightened, frightened of my own shadow, terrified of going to his office. I had nobody. No one would believe me, people used to think that I was sick, that I was making it up or I was just being nasty to him because my ex-husband was very sweet to people. In front of other people he was really sweet and very nice to them. I didn't feel that this man understood the danger that I felt myself to be in. I was terrified I was going to be killed and so I went away to a girlfriend's place and she said you need a woman, and I duly went and got a female lawyer that she recommended and I felt this woman was very much like "I'm a woman lawyer, I'm very important" and she sat behind this huge desk and I was sitting there and I was just...I didn't feel comfortable. Again nobody was listening to me about how scared I was.

Robin further described the reactions of these two lawyers:

I didn't feel I was being taken seriously because I couldn't show any bruises and it would have been obvious I was drawn, I was very very thin and I was shaking and it was obvious there was something dreadfully wrong and no one took me seriously...As people they were lovely people, they listened, but I couldn't make them understand the danger I was in. Even though he had been violent early in the marriage against my person, and the rest of the marriage it was smashing the place up, and because I hadn't been actually physically touched for about 5 or 6 years they felt I was in no physical danger, whereas I felt he was so sick that he would stalk me and they wouldn't listen to this and they said I had no grounds to get any kind of legal protection, and he did stalk me later.

Betty also felt that her lawyer lacked understanding of the dynamics of domestic violence. She described her abuse in this way:

> The abuse went on for the duration…of the twelve year relationship. It was physical, it was emotional, it was verbal, it was sexual… So every type of abuse was involved. My children were abused in all those ways as well except for my son who wasn't sexually abused…

Betty describes what happened at the final hearing on the non-molestation order:

> [before] the non-molestation hearing, my lawyer said to me that I would probably come out without it, without any protection orders because [during] the interim period between the…interim order being put on him, and the [final] hearing…he actually hadn't done anything terrible… the only thing he'd done was to find out our phone number somehow, which was confidential, and wait until Louise's birthday and ring her on the morning of her birthday and abuse her. But he hadn't done anything physical to warrant having [the non-molestation order] made permanent…

Betty noted that her lawyer did not make any argument to the judge that the non-molestation order should be made permanent, with the result that she was left without any protection orders. Now a refuge worker, Betty concluded:

> I think [lawyers] need to have a really good understanding of abuse, to have a really good analysis of what that is. I also think that they should have some sort of training of skills in listening, not necessarily counselling, but being able to kind of use some feedback or some sort of creative listening skills, so that you know that what you are saying is being understood and you know that they hear what you are saying.

Finally, Ann, who survived eight years of constant physical, emotional and sexual abuse, described her situation in relation to her lawyer subsequent to receiving protection orders:

> I think that he just, he had absolutely no idea of the situation that I'd been in, and, yeah, just really cold and expecting me to come up with all this information, like this, this, this and this. I felt like I was going go be murdered, any day and every day. That just went in one ear and out the other ear, with the lawyer…I can just remember sitting there and saying, I feel like I am going to get murdered tonight, I really do, and that wasn't crazy… that was a real thing, I mean I had guns held to my head, there was no problem getting a non-molestation order for me, but these people would sit at the other side of the desk and [ignore me].

Ann, who has also been a refuge worker, concluded:

> I think that lawyers, dealing with this stuff should have a really good

analysis, they should have a really good understanding of what abuse is about. I think that would greatly improve [the way that they represent women]. It's got to. And I can't see why it's not ... a specialist area.

These are some passages from the interviews that most directly address lawyers' understandings of the dynamics of domestic violence. Numerous other passages indirectly reveal women's concerns about their lawyers' understanding and knowledge of their situation. Some of these concerns arose around contact that women were required to have with their abusers as a result of their use of the legal system to obtain protection orders: for example in joint counselling sessions, mediation and negotiation sessions and in the arrangement of access to children.

Several limitations of these interviews must be acknowledged here. First, and most importantly, the interviews drawn on here do not include interviews of Maori women. As discussed above, interviews of Maori women were conducted in a parallel Maori/non-Maori interview process and the transcripts of the Maori interviews were given to a Maori woman to interpret. While the concerns expressed by non-Maori women are not totally irrelevant to the representation of Maori women, Maori women may place priority on other issues. Lawyers who represent Maori women who are survivors of domestic violence must take responsibility for learning about the concerns that Maori women have with their legal representation.

Secondly, due to the difficulty in locating a sample of survivors of domestic violence, all of the interviews were conducted through refuges, and are therefore limited. It may be that women with knowledge of refuges are relatively well-educated about the availability of social services. This may mean that these women had information available that enabled them to choose lawyers who had a reputation for excellence in representing survivors of domestic violence.

Third, the number of women who expressed concerns about lawyers' understanding of the dynamics of domestic violence and the scope and depth of those concerns make this a major theme emerging from the interviews. Its identification as a theme involved a process of analysis of qualitative research data which was informed by my perspective as the researcher. This finding does not mean that no lawyers understand the dynamics of domestic violence,[50] or even that this conclusion can be made about a representative sample of lawyers working in this area. Nor does it suggest that such an understanding is all that is required of a good lawyer in this area. Anne's comment that the representation of survivors of domestic violence should be recognised as a specialist area of lawyering is not a radical suggestion. Lawyers who specialise in construction contract litigation, for example, would be expected to learn something about construction, trade practices and other related matters, as well as to keep informed of current developments in the area. Suggesting that lawyers who work in family law, and particularly in representing survivors of domestic violence, educate themselves about the dynamics of domestic violence is consistent with the on-going self-education that is the responsibility of all lawyers.

Theories and practices: A pedagogy for teaching about domestic violence

Recognising the experiences of survivors of domestic violence in practices of lawyering, consistent with the development of a theory-practice spiral, suggests creating a direct link between those experiences and our lawyering practices. This section proposes establishing that link through a specific pedagogy and method for teaching lawyers and law students.

A. Groups for education and action

Drawing on the experiences of survivors of domestic violence, and the pedagogy of Paulo Freire, women in the movement to end domestic violence in the United States have developed a method for teaching about domestic violence.[51] The manner in which this pedagogy has been developed recognises commonalities as well as differences in women's experiences. It is also explicitly contingent and situated: it is constantly open for revision in light of changing experiences or changing interpretations of experiences. All teaching materials are drawn from the personal experiences of survivors of domestic violence. Freire suggests five phases to be followed to establish the content and method for the "Education Groups": conducting a survey, choosing a theme and posing a problem, analysing the problem, developing a code, and providing for discussion on possible action.[52]

The first phase of developing Education Groups for survivors of domestic violence has involved informal surveys of hundreds of survivors. The women were asked to identify issues that they would like to know more about. Surveys provided the basis for choosing the themes and posing problems and such surveys continue to be conducted annually.

One of the themes that emerged from the original survey was a high incidence of the repetition of specific abusive behaviours. When asked what they would like to learn, women repeatedly replied with questions such as, why doesn't he let me see my friends? Why does he treat my friends so badly? Why do men think they can treat women like servants? Why does he keep accusing me of being a lesbian? Is emotional abuse battering? Why doesn't he want me to make money? These questions suggested that abuse consists not only of physical abuse and threats, but also of abusive acts that reinforce physical violence.

The theme of repetitive abusive behaviours was analysed at three levels: the **personal** (relating basic physical and emotional needs to the problem);

the **institutional** (relating the policies of community institutions to the problem); and the **cultural** (relating the values and beliefs of a group of people to the problem).

The next step in developing the content for the Education Groups involved developing a code to represent the abusive tactics. The code is a teaching tool used to focus group discussion. The method used to develop the codes recognised the partiality of the experiences drawn upon and the contingent character of the production of knowledge in at least two manners.[53] First, culturally appropriate codes were developed: the Native American women in the United States have developed their own codes for teaching about domestic violence.[54] Second, the method of developing codes, based as it is in on-going surveys, is always open to evolution and change—any code developed and any theme upon which a code is based is constantly re-examined in the light of the experiences of survivors of domestic violence. Once a code is developed, discussion of possible actions in response to the problem follows.

The power and control wheel (see appendix 2) was developed as a code, or teaching tool to focus group discussion; it is not the only code developed, and it can be used in many different ways. It was developed to represent the theme of the high incidence of specific non-violent abusive behaviours used by abusers, as well as to represent the role played by physical abuse in gaining and maintaining power and control. It represents physical abuse and the other tactics as intentional acts used to gain power and control over another person, rather than as an anger management problem or a problem with loss of control by the abuser. The hub, or centre of the wheel represents the intention of all of the abusive tactics—to establish power and control. Each spoke of the wheel represents a particular tactic used by abusers. The rim of the wheel, which gives it strength and holds it together, is physical and sexual abuse.

The design of the wheel is important to an understanding of abuse in all of its forms; physical abuse is only one part of a whole system of abusive behaviour that an abuser uses against his partner. Physical violence is never an isolated behaviour; it is used to back up and reinforce other tactics. For example, when a women requests a protection order and she hasn't been beaten recently, it does not necessarily mean that she is not abused; it simply means that other tactics of her abuser are currently working to maintain his power and control.

B. Using the Power and Control Wheel to teach about abuse

This section briefly outlines some specific teaching methods used with the wheel to teach about abuse, and relates the methods to developments in feminist pedagogies generally.

1. Storytelling

The power and control wheel, as a code, is used with stories of the experiences of abused women to teach about abuse. Storytelling has been identified as a feminist teaching method. Storytelling in law can work to disrupt the legal categories created by the dominant groups in society by presenting moving stories of experiences that do not fit.[55] The stories of outsiders work in two ways: they create bonds between those who share the experiences that the stories represent, and they challenge the dominant characterisation of the experiences of these groups. They may also serve to open up space within the dominant groups and the legal categories for the recognition of these experiences.

Three types of stories are used with the power and control wheel to teach about abuse: videos illustrating specific tactics of abuse, as re-enacted by survivors of domestic violence, are shown; women tell their stories on video of how each tactic represented in the wheel was used by their abuser; and group members tell their own stories of power and control in their lives. Stories of group members come from both the facilitator, who is often a survivor and/or a refuge worker, and from the participants in the group.

Stories of survivors of domestic violence are the stories of outsiders. The dominant construction of survivors is that they deserve what they get. Physical abuse of women in the home continues to be condoned by society and, to a large extent, the legal system.[56] The stories of survivors can challenge the tendency of society to condone abuse. The stories of group members can encourage other group members to identify and recognise abuse in their own lives, and may also confront societal stereotypes of survivors such as the notion that abuse doesn't happen to intelligent, well-paid women, and isn't used and perpetuated by intelligent, well-paid men.

2. Sharing life experiences

Sharing life experiences in the classroom, with the possibility of creating the "collaborative, questioning spirit of the consciousness-raising method", has been identified as another feminist teaching method:

> Feminist teachers endeavour to create a cooperative classroom climate that
> welcomes students and other persons to share their life experiences as the
> basis for further inquiry and speculation. In so doing, the feminist classroom
> recreates, in part, the collaborative, questioning spirit of the consciousness-
> raising method.[57]

Consciousness-raising is based on group members sharing life experiences with each other. The commonalities of the experiences and patterns that emerge are explored,[58] to reveal "the social dimension of individual experience and the individual dimension of social experience",[59] and to facilitate structural critique,[60] which have both been identified as goals of feminist teaching and methods.

Education Groups incorporate aspects of consciousness-raising. Stimulated by the stories told in the videos, experiences of group members are shared and analysed at the personal, institutional and cultural levels. This type of analysis facilitates connections between individual experiences and the social dimensions of those experiences. For example, a specific group education session for women might begin with the screening of a video vignette titled "No judge would give you custody of the kids." This vignette depicts a scene in which a woman, having obtained a protection order, is subjected to emotional abuse. The scene ends with the abuser implying that the women is at fault.[61]

After showing the video, the facilitator might pose the following questions: What happened in the scene? Why did it happen? What tactics were used? Tactics could be identified by using the power and control wheel, but are not limited to those represented there. How did she respond? Why did she respond that way? What was the intent of the behaviour? These questions might be asked with respect to each of the three levels of analysis identified above: the personal, the institutional and the cultural. At the personal level, group members might discuss experiences similar to the ones portrayed in the video. At the institutional level, group members might discuss the role of community institutions and organisations in giving him more power and reducing her power. At the cultural level the values and beliefs operating might be discussed, focusing on the values and beliefs that were operating on his part, on her part, and in the community where they lived. The discussion might also cover how those values and beliefs define his power and her power. Finally, the group might discuss options for actions. These might include personal options to reduce the power of the tactics used in group members' lives, what women in the community can do to make changes in the institutions and what actions might be taken to influence the way that personal and community values are shaped. This is only one manner in which the vignette and the power and control wheel can be used; the teaching method is meant to be open to possibilities for discussion posed by facilitators and group members.

The Education Groups have the potential to enlighten the law students and lawyers not only to comprehend "how their clients cognitively and emotionally perceive the world",[62] but to recognise some commonalities of their (the law students and lawyers and the clients) standpoints in the world with respect to the effects of abuse. Linking this understanding to the institutional and cultural facilitators of violence has the further potential to inform the law students' and lawyers' lawyering, by providing insight and stimulating action for change at the societal level.

Education Groups using the power and control wheel are appropriate methods for teaching lawyers about domestic violence. The experiences of survivors of domestic violence point to the need for this training. It draws directly on the experiences of survivors. It is constantly subject to re-formation, thereby providing a direct link between these experiences and legal representation, consistent with the creation of feminist theories of lawyering. It requires lawyers to confront issues of power and control in their own lives, facilitating their recognition of such issues in the lives of their clients.

Practices: Influences on legal representation

This section investigates the impact that an understanding of the dynamics of domestic violence might have had on the legal representation of Robin and Betty. This discussion is not meant to second guess strategic decisions actually made by the lawyers in those situations. Rather, the situations are used simply as examples of the types of situations actually facing lawyers in representing survivors of domestic abuse in court, and as such, as vehicles for the discussion of the possible impact on legal representation of an understanding of domestic violence as an issue of power and control.

Betty did not receive a final non-molestation order, apparently because her abuser did not abuse her during the period for which the interim order was in effect. The *Domestic Protection Act* 1982 (NZ) provides that non-molestation orders may be applied for on an *ex parte* basis, without the other side having a chance to defend. *Ex parte* orders may be granted where the Court is satisfied that the delay caused by giving the defendant notice prior to issuing the protection order might entail risk to the personal safety of the woman or might entail serious injury or undue hardship.[63] An *ex parte* order is issued to ensure that the woman has protection immediately. A date is then set for a final hearing, at which time the woman must prove that an order is necessary for her protection in order to justify a permanent order.[64] The law does not require the applicant to show that the abuser perpetrated further abuse during the period covered by the interim order, it simply requires proof that the applicant is in need of protection at the final hearing.

The fact that Betty was not abused during the period covered by the interim order is likely to mean that the interim order was effective in protecting Betty from violence. It did not mean that Betty was no longer in danger: power and control are rarely relinquished without strong intervention and clear messages. In this case, the message provided by the interim order, combined with the fact that Betty was in hiding in a women's refuge during the interim period, was enough to protect Betty.

Betty's lawyer made no argument to the judge in support of finalising her order, apparently because the judge had a policy of not granting final orders where there was no abuse during the period covered by the interim order. An understanding of the dynamics of domestic violence might have changed the way in which Betty's lawyer represented her. It would have clarified that Betty remained in danger despite the fact that her abuser had not used physical violence during the period of the interim order. The lawyer might also have been aware of the need for change in dealing with domestic violence at the institutional level. She might have argued to the judge that the lack of abuse during the period covered by the interim order was simply an indication that the order was working effectively, not that the protection was not necessary. The importance of educating the judge about the on-going danger to her client, in the interests of both her client and institutional change, could also have alerted the judge to the possibility of on-going danger for other women in similar situations.

Similarly, had the lawyers that Robin approached been aware of the range of tactics used by abusers to gain and maintain power and control, they might have recognised Robin's need for protection as defined by the *Domestic Protection Act* 1982 (NZ). The fact that Robin had not been physically abused recently in her relationship did not mean that she was not "in need of protection". The importance of obtaining protection for Robin, and of educating the judge and making changes at the institutional level, might have been more apparent to a lawyer with an understanding of the dynamics of domestic violence.

Conclusion

The concrete experiences of women are central to feminist theorising. This chapter has explored **how** we might focus on integrating the diverse experiences of women into feminist theories and practices of lawyering. It has focused on a particular context: legal representation for survivors of domestic violence, and discussed epistemologies and methods that elicit women's experiences. Drawing on these experiences while recognising context and limitations, it has proposed a pedagogy for teaching lawyers about domestic violence. Every aspect of the pedagogy also draws on the experiences of survivors, and is consistent with developments in feminist teaching methods generally. Using the pedagogy proposed to educate lawyers about the dynamics of domestic violence could have a positive impact on the practices of lawyering for survivors of domestic violence. This chapter has demonstrated **how** the integration of the concrete and diverse experiences of women into theorising about lawyering can result in theories and practices that reflect and respond to those experiences.

Notes

1 For example Schneider, E M, "The Dialectic of Rights and Politics: Perspectives From the Women's Movement" (1986) 61 *NYU LR* 589; Minow, M, "Feminist Reason: Getting It and Losing It" (1988) 38 *J Leg Educ* 47; Mossman, M J, "Gender Equality and Legal Aid Services: A Research Agenda for Institutional Change" (1993) 15 *Syd LR* 30 at 50.

2 Goldfarb, P, "A Theory Practice Spiral: The Ethics of Feminism and Clinical Education" (1991) 75 *Minn LR* 1599 .

3 Id at 1614.

4 I use "pedagogy" to refer to the process by which knowledge is produced, reproduced and transmitted, which requires attention to epistemology, the politics of the processes and the political context. Gore, J, *The Struggle for Pedagogies* (1993) at 3-6.

5 A number of feminist critiques of "traditional", "scientific" or male-dominated social science research behaviours exist. For example Oakley, A,"Interviewing Women: a Contradiction in Terms" in Roberts, H (ed), *Doing Feminist Research* (1981) at 30-61; Addelson, K P, "The Man of Professional Wisdom" in Fonow, M and Cook, J (eds), *Beyond Methodology: Feminist Scholarship as Lived Research* (1991) at 16-34; Jayaratne, T and Stewart, A, "Quantitative and Qualitative Methods in The Social Sciences: Current Feminist Issues and Practical Strategies" in Fonow and Cook, id at 84-106 (a list of feminist criticisms of traditional quantitative research at 86); Stanley, L and Wise, S, *Breaking Out: Feminist Consciousness and Feminist Research* (1983) at 12-32. For an excellent critique of the use of social science data in a legal context see Fineman, M and Opie, A,"The Uses of Social Science Data in Legal Policymaking: Custody Determinations at Divorce" [1987] *Wisc LR* 107.

6 Space does not permit a full discussion of the development of feminist epistemologies. See eg Hekman, S, *Gender and Knowledge: Elements of a Postmodern Feminism* (1990); Stanley, L and Wise, S, "Method, Methodology and Epistemology in Feminist Research" in Stanley, L (ed), *Feminist Praxis* (1990) at 20-59.

7 Stanley, above n6 at 26; see also Harding, S, "Introduction: Is there a Feminist Methodology?" in Harding, S (ed), *Feminism and Methodology* (1987) at 3.

8 Lahey, K A, "...Until Women Themselves Have Told All That They Have To Tell..." (1985) 23 *Osgoode Hall LJ* 519 at 525.

9 Scott, J, "Experience" in Butler, J and Scott, J (eds), *Feminists Theorize the Political* (1992) 22 at 34.

10 Id at 37.

11 Stanley, above n6 at 27; Harding, above n7 at 187-9.

12 Stanley, above n6 at 28; Farina, C R, "Getting From Here to There" [1991] *Duke LJ* 689 at 707; "Feminist theory typically understands knowledge as contextual—that is, as embedded in situation and experience, rather than derived from principle through abstract logic."

13 Bartlett, K, "Feminist Legal Methods" (1990) 103 *Harv LR* 829 at 878.

14 Id at 880; see also Haraway, D J, *Simians, Cyborgs, and Women* (1991) at 188.

15 Bartlett, above n13 at 880-1; Haraway, above n14 at 190.

16 Bartlett, above n13 at 881-2.

17 Haraway, above n14 at 190.

18 Id at 195.

19 Rather than use the traditional language of researcher/researched, which connotes a subject/object relationship, I use "researcher " to refer to myself and my research assistants and "research participants" to refer to everyone else who participated in the research project. Below n22-7.

20 Stanley, above n6 at 23.

21 Haraway, above n14 at 198 : "Situated knowledges require that the object of knowledge be pictured as an actor and agent, not a screen or a ground or a resource, never finally as slave to the master that closes off the dialectic in his unique agency and authorship of 'objective' knowledge."

22 Acker, J, Barry, K and Esseveld, J, "Objectivity and Truth: Problems in Doing Feminist Research" in Fonow and Cook, above n5 at 136.

23 Te Awekotuku, N, *He Tikanga Whakaaro: Research Ethics in the Maori Community* (1991); Jackson, M, *The Maori and the Criminal Justice System — He Whaipaanga Hou: A New Perspective, Pt 1* (1988) at 42; *Pt. 2* (1988) at 3.

24 Family Violence Co-ordinating Committee, *Attitudes to Family Violence—A Study Across Cultures* (1988) at 9. For an interesting discussion of both class and race bias in qualitative research methods see Cannon, L W, Higgenbotham, E and Leung, M L A, "Race and Class Bias in Qualitative research on Women" in Fonow and Cook, above n5.

25 Te Awekotuku, above n23 at 14.

26 Above n24.

27 Lather, P, *Getting Smart: Feminist Research and Pedagogy With/In the Postmodern* (1991) at 60; Acker, above n22 at 140-1.

28 For a discussion of feminism in Australia and the United States, some of which is also applicable to New Zealand, see Eisenstein, H, *Gender Shock: Practising Feminism on Two Continents* (1991).

29 Bartlett, above n13 at 881-2.

30 Id at 882.

31 "Refuge" is the New Zealand term for feminist safe houses maintained by women for women escaping situations of domestic violence. NCIWR is an organisation of independent refuge collectives founded by activists in the movement to end domestic violence in New Zealand.

32 Dobash, R E and Dobash, R P, *Women, Violence & Social Change* (1992) at 221-35; Lahey, above n8 at 522.

33 Dobash, ibid at 255-7.

34 Id at 256-7.

35 While in Boston, I was also a member of the Governor's Anti-Crime Commission, Battered Women's Working Group, which undertook such tasks as drafting amendments to *Massachusetts Abuse Prevention Act* 1978. I was also a founding member of the Domestic Violence Council, which established the role of coordinating services offered to survivors of domestic violence in the Boston area.

36 Lather, above n27 at pxviii, a discussion of "[f]eminism's grassroots, 'no more experts' credo."

37 My role as co-ordinator in the programme to represent survivors of domestic violence involved keeping open communication with all the organisations that provided services to battered women. I was therefore constantly aware of problems with lawyers, judges and court personnel in different areas of Boston.

38 Haraway, above n14 at 196 : "We do not seek partiality for its own sake, but for the sake of the connections and unexpected openings situated knowledges make possible."

39 For a description of an exploratory study that attempts to respond to race and class bias factors see Cannon, above n24 at 113 :
    we made explicit in every communication about the study that the coprincipal investigators for the study were a Black and a White woman, that the research team was biracial, and that we sought both Black and White subjects. We also sent Black members of the research team to speak to exclusively Black groups, White members to speak to exclusively White groups and a biracial team to speak to every group that had both Black and White women. Only Black interviewers interviewed Black subjects, and White interviewers interviewed White subjects.

40 The Core Group of NCIWR is a group of eight activist women, four Maori and four non-Maori, elected each year at the Annual General Meeting of NCIWR to make policy decisions for the organisation.

41 Oakley, above n5 at 30, 31;Stanley, above n5, at 48-9.

42 Oakley, above n5 at 47.

43 Patton, M, *Qualitative Evaluation and Research Methods* (2nd edn 1990) at 280.

44 Id at 285.

45 Id at 295.

46 Id at 291.

47 Above n22 at 136. Feminist methods are methods of exploration and discovery:
    [e]xploration means...an open and critical process in which all the intellectual tools we have inherited from a male dominated intellectual tradition are brought into question, including ideas about the basic nature of human beings, the nature of social life, the taken-for-granted world view

of traditional science, what concepts and questions might help to illuminate our shared condition, and how we should go about developing such knowledge.

48 Lather, above n27 at 72: "[i]n praxis-oriented inquiry, reciprocally educative process is more important than product as empowering methods contribute to consciousness-raising and transformative social action".

49 Goldman, A, *The Group Depth Interview: Principles and Practice* (1987) at 73.

50 This paper is not intended, nor should it be construed, to suggest that lawyers are not necessary to the process of obtaining protection orders. Nor does it suggest that the problem of understanding the dynamics of domestic violence is unique to lawyers.

51 Minnesota Program Development, *In Our Best Interests: A Process for Personal and Social Change* (no date) at 9. This section draws on the training manual to describe the development of the teaching method. Due to space constraints, Freire's pedagogy has not been discussed in detail here. For a full explication of his theory, see Freire, P, *Education for Critical Consciousness* (1974); Freire, P, *Pedagogy of the Oppressed* (1972). Freire's pedagogy has been critiqued as modernist and defended as post-modernist (see above n4). My discussion partially responds to critiques of his pedagogy as modernist and as regimes of truth by focusing on the contingency of both the pedagogy and the theories to which it might lead, as well as by recognising the limitations of both the pedagogies and the theories of lawyering. For discussions of Freire see McLaren, P and Leonard, P (eds), *Paulo Freire: A Critical Encounter* (1993); above n4.

52 Freire (1973), above n51 at 42-58.

53 See discussion above at n12.

54 Freire (1973), above n51 at 93-7.

55 Abrams, K, "Hearing the Call of Stories" (1991) 79 *Calif LR* 971 at 975-6; above n2 at 1630-1.

56 Busch, R, Robertson, N and Lapsley, H, *Domestic Violence and the Justice System: A Study of Breaches of Protection Orders* (1992).

57 Above n2 at 1670 citing Cain, P, "Teaching Feminist Theory at Texas: Listening to Difference and Exploring Connections" (1988) 38 *J Leg Educ* 165.

58 Bartlett, above n13 at 863-4.

59 Schneider, above n1 at 603.

60 Above n2 at 1627.

61 Pence, E and Paymer, M, *Power and Control: Tactics of Men who Batter ; An Educational Curriculum* (1986) at 124.

62 Above n2 at 1678.

63 *Domestic Protection Act* 1982 (NZ) 14(1).

64 *Domestic Protection Act* 1982 (NZ) 15.

6

"Don't Throw Bouquets at Me... (Judges) Will Say We're In Love":

An Analysis of New Zealand Judges' Attitudes Towards Domestic Violence

Ruth Busch

The domestic violence report: an introduction

Neville Robertson, Hilary Lapsley and I (the University of Waikato Domestic Protection Team) were commissioned by the Victims Task Force in 1990 to conduct research into repeated breaches of domestic protection orders. It was believed by members of the Task Force and ourselves that repetitive breaches of such orders could only be understood within the broader context of victims' lives and their experiences with the justice system. Therefore, the perspective of victims of domestic violence shaped the project's research design. Twenty detailed case studies of battered women who had experienced breaches of their protection orders (including two women who had obtained protection orders and were subsequently killed by their husbands) were made a central part of the resulting report. In addition, over 70 interviews were conducted with key informants connected with the justice system, including Family and District Court judges (9), Family Court Counselling Coordinators and counsellors (10), police officers (25), refuge workers (10) and solicitors (8). Archival materials from police files and log books, 46 published and unreported decisions of the courts and Justice Department statistics added to the data collected by us.

A three hundred page report entitled *Domestic Violence and the Justice System: A Study of Breaches of Protection Orders* was presented to the Victims Task Force in early 1992. Since that time, the report has been surrounded by controversy. The version of the report available to the public, renamed by the Task Force *Protection from Family Violence: A Study of Protection Orders Under the Domestic Protection Act 1982 (Abridged)*, has been significantly "edited". Missing from this version is the analysis of 21 Family Court cases as well as the names of all 46 Family and criminal court judges whose decisions were discussed. The very words used by victims to describe their experiences of Family Court hearings and counselling sessions have in places been deleted. In protest at this censorship of our work, the author and the other researchers have had our names removed from the expurgated version.[1] The full version of the report is available to a restricted audience through the Justice Department, also under the title *Protection from Family Violence*.[2]

This chapter presents an important area of that report's findings: judicial attitudes towards domestic violence. Drawing on the author's interviews with judges in 1991 and an analysis of New Zealand case law concerning domestic violence, this chapter examines judges' attitudes as expressed in the following contexts: in Family Court protection order proceedings; prosecutions and appeals heard in the District and High Courts concerning breaches of non-molestation orders; cases of serious violence under section 5 of the *Criminal Justice Act* 1985 (NZ); and in custody and access applications in the Family Court.

Adopting the intervention model developed by the Duluth (Minnesota) Abuse Intervention Project[3], it is a basic premise of this chapter that physical violence is one of a range of tactics by which abusers seek to maintain power and control over their partners. Other tactics of power and control utilised by abusers include emotional and verbal abuse; intimidation; isolation; treating the victim as subservient while the abuser reserves to himself the right to make all major decisions in the relationship; minimising and trivialising the violence; and blaming the victim for such violence.[4]

The minimisation and trivialisation of violence and the blaming of victims for the violence which they suffer are not tactics limited to individual abusers. Such tactics are sometimes used by members of the justice system and serve to legitimise abusers' perspectives of violence. The result of such power and control tactics operating on a systemic level all too often leads to the further victimisation of those who look to the justice system for protection, and has been referred to as "the cultural facilitation of violence".[5]

It is a further premise of this chapter that abusers must be held accountable for their violence. Penalties for their use of domestic violence[6] must be appropriate and must challenge the view that domestic violence is less significant than stranger violence.[7] Moreover, there has sometimes been a message given that "violence works".[8] It is a third premise of this chapter that unless clear and unambiguous messages are given that domestic violence is wrong, the system purporting to afford protection to victims colludes in such violence.

Judicial attitudes about domestic violence convey powerful messages to victims and abusers alike. If they are to portray the justice system's commitment to stopping domestic violence, it is essential that judges convey unequivocal messages that the existence of violence in a relationship is a "real" and significant problem.

"The gap" between women's experiences and judicial responses to domestic violence

The material presented in this chapter highlights a disparity between victims' experiences of domestic violence and the response of some members of the judiciary to such violence. This "gap" is manifested in a number of ways: in the analysis of spousal violence as a form of family dysfunction in which both parties are responsible; holding family reconciliation as the predominant consideration for the court, irrespective of the victim's wishes; the use of language which minimises, trivialises or effaces the violence which has occurred; blaming the victim for the violence; and/or constructing the violent man as pathetic, inadequate or to be pitied.

Common to many of the cases analysed below is an idealised construction of family life in which the maintenance (or re-constitution) of the family is valued over and above the safety of individual members of the family. It is this construction which helps explain the predilection of some judges to require counselling rather than grant protection orders, and to characterise serious violence as a dispute or disagreement between parties rather than to name it as rape or attempted murder or serious assault. It is also this privileging of family which has rendered violence as irrelevant in some cases for the purposes of custody and access determinations; thus the court is able to determine that an abuser who has raped his wife[9] or even beaten her to death[10] may still be a proper custodial parent.

Such an approach is also evident in some of the cases in which judges took very seriously the violence which had occurred and the need for on-going protection against the likelihood of further violence. In some such cases it is evident that it is the victim's status as "a good mother" who stands blameless before the court which constitutes her as being worthy of the concern of the court, rather than the objective circumstances in which she finds herself.[11]

Family Court protection order cases

From the author's research findings, it is clear that repeated spousal violence is the reason that many applicants for protection orders approach the Family Court.[12] As one of the Family Court judges interviewed noted:

> In most cases we'd see this is not the first time the violence has happened. It may be going on for two or three years but he's getting worse; he's been drinking more often or whatever it might be and maybe he's hitting her more.[13]

A second Family Court judge concurred: "Inevitably there will tend to be a history of violence. It is unusual to get an application where there has been just one incident."[14] Women, therefore, come to the Family Court looking for protection from what they perceive as an important problem. What they often receive is a judicial interpretation which is strikingly at odds with their own experience. The case of *P-W v P-W*[15] provides a good illustration of the ways in which the gap between women's experiences and judicial interpretations are manifest.

The facts of the case, in which Mrs P-W sought a final non-molestation order, were summarised by Inglis J in language which erased the violence itself:

> *The parties are going through a crisis in their marriage and it has got to a stage where neither of them is coping very well. As often happens in such situations the difficulties and their consequences have fed on themselves and spiralled. The wife could not stand the situation in the home any more and she left with the three children. The husband's response to that led her to come to this Court for the urgent protection of an interim non-molestation order which was granted ex parte.*[16]

There are no specific details given of the reasons which "led the wife" to leave her husband nor of that part of "the husband's response" which led the court to conclude that the wife was in need of an *ex parte* non-molestation order. The statutory criteria under the *Domestic Protection Act* 1982 (NZ) for the granting of such an order make it clear that not only did the judge need to be satisfied that Mrs P-W was "in need of protection"[17] but that proceeding on notice "would or might entail risk to the personal safety of the applicant or a child of the applicant's family" or alternatively "that the delay…would or might entail serious injury or undue hardship".[18]

While Inglis J found that "it is unlikely that the husband will moderate his attempts to see and communicate with the wife unless a (final) non-molestation order is made", he refused to make such an order. He argued that such an order would be "overkill" and found instead that what the applicant needed was "a temporary respite from the husband's persistent overtures so that **the real problems in the marriage** can be addressed".[19] Further, the judge expressed his preference that "the problems faced by this husband and this wife" be addressed therapeutically, and in a way which "did not close the door against the reconstitution of the family".[20] The judge also attached considerable weight to the likely effect of a final non-molestation order on the husband. As part of the obiter of the decision, Inglis J concluded that:

> *A final non-molestation order would be seen by the husband in his present condition not only as a destructive blow to his already fragile self esteem but also as closing the door against any possibility of resuming the marriage.*[21]

Instead of granting the final order sought by the wife, Inglis J adjourned the hearing part-heard for three months, extended the interim order until that date, and reserved leave for either party or counsel for the children to bring the matter back for hearing at an earlier date. During the three month adjournment period, the judge stated that he "expects" the husband "in the interests of the whole family" to obtain a full medical assessment of his condition and to undergo such medical or other treatment as may be prescribed. He also directed the parties to have therapeutic counselling, separately or together.[22]

G v G[23] is another clear example of "the gap". In *G v G*, the wife was applying for final non-molestation and occupation orders, her husband having already consented to the issuing of a final non-violence order. While granting the application, in the course of his decision, Inglis J made several telling points. Firstly, he stated:

> Mrs G has told the Court that she wishes to terminate the relationship and in effect that the only way she can obtain peace for herself and her son is for the home to be sold and for her and the boy to establish themselves in a place where Mr G cannot find them. **I do not really take Mrs G seriously in much of what she said about this because I am quite certain that her feelings for Mr G are not entirely dead** although obviously they have been put under a great deal of stress.[24]

One problem with the judge's approach is that while the applicant stated that she was prepared to live "underground" so that her husband could not locate her and her son, the judge interpreted the fact that she might still have "feelings" for her husband as indicating that she was not actually as desperate as her "only" solution might suggest.

It is not unusual for a wife to have some feelings of love for a husband, even a violent one, after 15 or more years of marriage. The real issue is what relevance do these have, among what is probably a myriad of contradictory feelings, in terms of the applicant's need for protection? Needless to say, a "dead feelings" test is not a statutory requisite under the *Domestic Protection Act* 1982 (NZ). Any equation which leads a judge to refuse or defer protection because of the presence of "feelings" in the hope of a reconciliation of the parties indicates a misunderstanding of the complexities inherent in domestic violence situations. In terms of how difficult it is for battered women to air their histories of domestic violence in court proceedings and to articulate (sometimes for the first time) how desperate they are about their situations, what does it mean to them if a judge says he cannot take their desperation seriously,[25] yet can take seriously, as a mitigating factor, a husband's desperation?

A second important element of "the gap" is highlighted through the characterisation by Inglis J of Mr G as "a gentle sort of person (who) finds it hard to detach himself from the home and the family life which I'm afraid some of his actions have helped to weaken if not destroy".[26] The "gentle abuser" view is a repetitive theme in domestic violence cases. To give just one example, in the case of the *R v Panoa-Masina*, the Court of Appeal took into consideration in its sentencing for manslaughter that the appellant "was described by a number of people as being a man of quiet disposition who was kind and gentle and there was no evidence of any previous incidents of violence".[27]

Through this depiction of Mr G, Inglis J emphasises that the respondent is in some way not responsible for the desperate situation his wife finds herself in :

> Mr G I am sure clings to the hope that in some way or another his family unit can be restored and that I think is evidenced by the fact that every now and then he gravitates instinctively towards his home even though his condition when he arrives there regrettably sometimes makes him an unwelcome visitor.[28]

Just as in *P-W v P-W*, there is a view that the husband cannot really help himself, that in some way he is not accountable for his actions.[29] Rather than seeing the abuser as responsible for what he has done, courts often see him as pathetic and childlike, a person who should be the object of pity (and therapy) rather than as someone from whom a victim needs protection.[30] This view may also lead to the conclusion that the abuser's violence is out of character.[31] This characterisation may then lead judges to find that victims are over-reactive or partly to blame for the abuse they suffer.[32] As can be seen in *G v G*, it clearly results in a trivialisation of the victim's feelings of fear and danger.

Titter v Titter[33] is a recent example of the victim-blaming aspects inherent in "the gap". In that case, the wife was seeking a final non-molestation order. Inglis J refused to grant that order and instead discharged the *ex parte* interim non-molestation order and ordered a further interim non-molestation order in its place.[34] The judge found that the applicant had an on-going need for protection, stating that the respondent "had reacted badly" to her decision to separate from him, "pestering her to resume the marriage and at various times threatening to do away with himself, her and the new male friend with whom she is apparently living in a de facto relationship". The judge found, moreover, that "the same kind of threats are continuing".[35]

But in *Titter*, Inglis J obviously felt that the applicant was to blame for the separation and in obiter he appeared to offer excuses for the respondent's threats and "pestering" behaviour. The judge said that the applicant's decision to leave her husband, and live with a man who for 25 years had been a close personal friend of her husband,

> could have been seen as adding to the fact of separation with the intention of ending the marriage the additional elements of betrayal and humiliation of the husband and the destruction of a longstanding friendship.[36]

The judge also expressed the view that it is often the case that the two parties view a separation in different ways:

> **the separating spouse may see the other spouse's approaches as unwarranted and annoying pestering; the abandoned spouse may see those same approaches as a perfectly reason-**

able means of trying to restore the relationship. The danger is that the non-molestation procedure may be misused to prevent perfectly proper and understandable efforts to reconcile, or conciliate, the differences which led to the separation. Those efforts cannot be regarded as "molestation" against which the law can or should provide protection. But those efforts may become "molestation" if they go beyond what is reasonable in all the circumstances.[37]

The judge went on to say that it was too early to determine whether the husband's behaviour "went beyond what was reasonable" and he questioned instead whether the applicant's beliefs were reasonable:

Indeed she might reasonably have expected a strong reaction. The question may well arise whether she could reasonably have interpreted the husband's wild statements as a genuine threat, or whether those statements were more properly to be interpreted as perhaps unwise efforts on the husband's part to demonstrate the depth of his distress and to bring home to the wife some sense of what she had done to him.[38]

The query must of course arise as to how the judge can determine which threats to kill are genuine and which are simply "wild statements". Is it when those threats are acted upon? When do such threats fall into the category of statements "more properly to be interpreted as perhaps unwise efforts on the husband's part"? In terms of current research into lethality assessments in domestic violence situations, threats of homicide and/or suicide have been identified as behaviours which are primary indicators of an increased likelihood of homicide. Two other significant indicators are obsession about the partner ("I can't live without her") and recent separation.[39]

The view Inglis J has of the husband as "abandoned", "betrayed", and "humiliated" leads him to minimise the significance of the death threats, which he euphemistically describes as "threatening to do away with". There is a clear sense that the husband's threats to kill may be "reasonable" in the light of the wife's behaviour and that it is her behaviour which has "caused" his pestering. There is an implicit assumption that she is an unworthy victim. While few people might dispute the probable feelings of the respondent as described by the judge, it is not "feelings" but threats and behaviour which are under scrutiny in an application for a non-molestation order.

Inglis J states, "…in the unlikely event of the husband acting immoderately and unreasonably, there is the possibility that the Court might decide that the wife needed the protection of a 'final' non-molestation order".[40] He expresses no sense that the threats may be "immoderate and unreasonable" nor that they may represent criminal behaviour. Moreover, he also does not give details of the respondent's other earlier conduct which led to the *ex parte* non-molestation order being granted. He privileges the respondent's hurt and angry feelings over the applicant's desire for a final non-molestation order, even though she clearly has met the statutory criteria for such an order. The very issuance of the second interim non-molestation order demonstrates that Inglis J was "satisfied" that she was in need of protection.

Titter can be seen as falling squarely within the parameters of a line of domestic violence cases previously characterised by the author as "the fortress cases".[41] Those cases involve a judicial view that protection orders may be weapons in the hands of applicants who have unilaterally (often "selfishly") decided to separate and who want to fend off conciliation attempts by their deserted spouses. The idea is that non-molestation orders may create a "fortress" against the possibility of the reconstitution of a marriage or, as a minimum, against communication between the parties aimed at conciliation. This perspective is clearly present in the instant case. In his discussion about why he has refused to grant the final non-molestation order, the judge states:

> *The advantage of a further interim order is that it is possible to attach effective conditions to it, designed to provide a constructive approach to the parties' problems. For instance, in the present case,* ***it would have been possible to allow for review, with a view to discharge of the order, or with a view to making a 'final' order, if the parties or either of them declined to attend counselling.*** *That is not necessary at the moment, but I draw the flexibility of the Court's powers to the parties' attention so that they will realise that the interim order made in this case is temporary only and is aimed at achieving a period of calm so that the parties can apply their minds to the consequences of their separation and the orderly reorganisation of their affairs* ***in an atmosphere of fairness and justice.***[42]

After stating that a final non-molestation order might be granted "in the unlikely event of the husband acting immoderately and unreasonably", Inglis J then continues:

> *On the other hand, in the unlikely event of it appearing that the wife was using the interim order as* ***a shield to avoid reasonable discussion of their matrimonial difficulties, that might well be a ground for discharging the interim order on review.***[43]

If a primary reason for denying a final non-molestation order at this point is to compel the wife to attend counselling with her husband, several issues arise. First, pursuant to section 37 of the *Domestic Protection Act* 1982 (NZ), judges may only "recommend" that **applicants** participate in counselling. This is to be contrasted with section 37A of the Act which allows a judge to "direct" **respondents** to anger management counselling or other forms of violence focused counselling. Under section 37, applicants cannot be compelled to attend such counselling whereas if respondents fail to attend section 37A directed counselling, they may be prosecuted. By implicitly making Mrs Titter's non-molestation order conditional on her attending counselling, Inglis J forces her to participate in counselling on the pain of losing the protection provided to her by the non-molestation order, this despite his finding that she is in need of such protection. What he has no authority to do under section 37, he purports to accomplish under section 15 of the Act.[44] And he emphasises his satisfaction at this outcome by commenting:

> It is comforting to find that in these respects the Domestic Protection Act is capable of being used constructively, and to further the Family Court's statutory objectives of reconciliation and conciliation.[45]

In terms of reservations currently being expressed in New Zealand[46] and overseas[47] about the appropriateness of counselling and mediation in relationships characterised by violence and abusive behaviour, one must question how an "atmosphere of fairness and justice" is to be created during counselling and mediation sessions in the face of repeated suicide and homicide threats.

A final example of "the gap" in Family Court protection order cases is *Redward v Redward*[48]. The case indicates a failure by the Court to recognise certain tactics and strategies of domestic abuse for what they are, further aspects of violence against the victim. And it is significant as a clear example of how courts faced with a very threatening abuser may, in fact, appease him in an attempt to deter him from carrying out his threats. Rather than giving a clear and unambiguous message that violence is wrong, the judge's actions indicate to the respondent that violence works.

In *Redward*, Mrs Redward had previously sought protection from the Family Court by obtaining *ex parte* non-violence, non-molestation and occupation orders. In order to grant such orders, the Court had to be "satisfied" that Mrs Redward was in need of protection and moreover that her husband had used violence against her, had caused her bodily harm or had threatened to do so. The Court also had to find that complying with the normal service requirements for such orders would have entailed risk to Mrs Redward of serious injury or alternatively would have jeopardised her personal safety.

The legal issue in this subsequent Family Court proceeding involved Mr Redward applying under section 21(1) of the *Domestic Protection Act* 1982 (NZ) for a condition to be imposed on his wife's occupation order that no one other than his wife or children should be able to have access to the former matrimonial home. Specifically Mr Redward sought an order excluding Baker, the wife's principal support person, from the home. Given that isolation of the victim is a well-described tactic of power and control,[49] the intent of Mr Redward's application is obvious. That his aim was a product of his jealousy (rather than a result of sadism or malice) does not lessen its abusive consequences for his already victimised and now to be isolated former spouse.

It was commonly agreed that Baker visited the wife frequently at home. In terms of Baker's relationship to Mrs Redward, McAloon J found:

> I do not believe that the issue of the sexual relationship is the all important factor. It is quite plain that Mr Baker has an intimate relationship with the wife in the sense that he is her closest confidant, is supporting her financially and is an effective person in the decision-making relating to the children which she undertakes. I further accept that this is a cause of substantial annoyance and frustration and anger to the husband. He spoke of Baker moving into his house, having access to his wife and taking over his children. I must accept the depth of Mr Redward's abhorrence of the situation which has occurred.[50]

Various threats had been made by Baker and Mr Redward against each other. A psychologist testified that Mr Redward's threats to kill Baker "could become a reality".[51]

McAloon J granted the condition sought by Mr Redward in respect of Baker. The latter was prohibited from having access to Mrs Redward and the children at her home. McAloon J based his decision on his assessment of the best interests of the Redward children:

> I would state that I believe that a consideration of the welfare of the children is imperative in determining this case. The situation between Baker and Redward is one of extreme jealousy, of overt threats and of simmering fury as far as Mr Redward is concerned toward Baker. **He has made an overt threat to kill Baker during the course of these proceedings.** I hardly need to say that the consequential effect of this depth of feeling alone is not conducive to the children's welfare **even if the threat should not be executed.** Quite plainly it is a matter which is of major significance in Redward's mind and I believe that it is appropriate in the interests of the children that I give favourable consideration to his application and make an order excluding Baker from the household residence, such order to be effective forthwith and to be until further order of the Court.[52]

It is important to fully understand the placatory nature of the Court's action in the face of Redward's threats to kill. The wife had been awarded exclusive possession of the former matrimonial home. Now, through the imposition of the condition sought by him, the husband is able to control who comes into that home. Whatever else he may have been, Baker was the wife's principal support person and the Court's action prohibited him from even visiting her at her home. The judicial result was arrived at in the face of the respondent's threats to kill Baker made even during the court hearing and was justified under the heading "best interests of the children". It should be noted that there is no indication that Redward was charged with any criminal offence in respect of his threats against Baker. Instead he "won"; he obtained the condition he sought as a direct result of his repeated threats to kill.

As part of his decision, McAloon J discussed the atmosphere in the court-room during the hearing and in a very revealing comment, acknowledged that the condition was imposed despite his own reservations about his jurisdiction to order such a condition:

> Because of the extraordinarily tense situation present in the Court I have
> determined that it would be inappropriate not to give a judgment in this
> matter this evening, although the time is now 5.50pm. I would also mention
> that this case was not scheduled to be heard today but was allocated some
> time this afternoon because of its urgent nature in an effort to defuse a situ-
> ation which is potentially dangerous....I have had cause to request the Chief
> Bailiff to be present as a court-taker in Court, a situation which I have not
> done before in 10 years on the Bench and I have also requested the Deputy
> Registrar of this Court who is in charge of the Family Court section to be
> present in the Court throughout the hearing. Indeed I believe that the
> Deputy Registrar has arranged for members of the police to be within the
> Court precincts. I furnish these details solely to set the scene as to my belief
> that it is urgent that a decision is given today notwithstanding the some-
> what novel legal proposition which is contained in the application. I am
> unable to ascertain in the time available to me, any cases which give an
> illustration of the extent of the (s.21(1)) conditions likely to be imposed by
> the Court.[53]

It would appear that the Court itself has been abused by Redward's threats of violence and has colluded in the abuse.

Rather than the appeasement approach representing an anomaly in protec-tion order cases, *Redward v Redward* highlights a recurring problem discerned from the author's interviews with Family Court judges. This is that certain judges are reluctant to grant *ex parte* protection orders because of their belief that such orders may alienate spousal abusers from court conciliation efforts in respect of future custody and access issues. Instead of assessing whether the applicant meets the statutory criteria set out in section 14(1) of the *Domestic Protection Act* 1982 (NZ), these judges assess the application's merits from the point of view of the respondent's likely response to the granting of such an order. Some judges justify this placatory policy, as in *Redward v Redward*, in terms of the best interests of the children. As one Family Court judge stated:

> If you've got matters such as custody and access which are going to have to
> be resolved further down the track, it doesn't help the resolution of those
> long-term issues by granting ex parte protection orders. That's the reason
> why in a lot of cases my approach is to direct the application for orders on
> notice but drastically abridge the time within which the victim can come
> back to court—such as 2-3 days or even less. If you have issues which must
> be resolved down the track, you're going to lessen the chances of a conciliato-
> ry approach. That's just one of the factors to be taken into account. Other
> factors—such as violence toward the victim—must be the first and overrid-

ing consideration. But I must say that I do place some weight on the fact that the granting of orders ex parte may exacerbate the tension between the couple.[54]

A second Family Court judge interviewed by the author said:

I may be wrong in my approach but I perceive continuing problems if respondents feel that orders are made against them without their knowledge and that those orders are going to affect their ability to have contact with their children. I have seen cases that have developed into horrendous files as far as violence is concerned and also problems involving the children because an ex parte order was made rather than putting the application on notice and abridging the time. So if there are dependent children involved, I'll take that into account and bring the respondent before the court rather than grant the orders ex parte. You can describe my practice as involving a two-tiered test. First I look at what's contained in the application in terms of the protection that is sought and the reasons for it. Then there's the question of whether children are involved.[55]

Here, the statutory criteria for the making of *ex parte* orders become less relevant than judicial concern that respondent abusers may be alienated from court processes. Facts, such as that the parties may have dependent children or may have not previously engaged in court ordered couples counselling, are not factors for consideration found in sections 14(1) or 15 of the *Domestic Protection Act* 1982 (NZ). Yet they are utilised by judges to determine whether *ex parte* non-molestation orders should be issued. The end result is that *ex parte* protection orders for some victims are withheld, not because the applicants fail to meet the statutory criteria but because certain judges prioritise concerns for the respondents' future participation in counselling and mediation over immediate protection for the victim. As a Family Court judge commented in a classic example of "the gap": "Now I know that this may be contrary to how the victims see their situation and they want nothing further to do with the perpetrator. In my view, it isn't as simple as that."[56]

A problem with the approach taken by these judges is that by their own report it is very rare for applicants to pursue their applications for protection orders once those applications are put on notice, even if the time for service is abridged to a few hours or a few days.[57] Ironically, as in *Redward v Redward*, the upshot of this judicial practice appears to be that in certain instances victims who are in need of protection orders are left further exposed to their abuser's power and control tactics by the court's actions. While the abusers may be "kept in the ballpark", it is those seeking protection who are often alienated from the court processes.[58]

Judicial approaches to breaches of non-molestation orders

Judicial attitudes which exemplify "the gap" are also found in criminal cases, in both District Court and High Court judgments. The judicial focus in many of these decisions is again on the relationship rather than on the violence or behaviour constituting the criminal offence with which the accused is charged. Implicit in these decisions is "the two to tango"/family dysfunction analysis apparent in the previously discussed Family Court judgments. Even in "male assaults female" cases under section 194(b) of the *Crimes Act* 1961(NZ), the violence which gives rise to the assault charge is sometimes not defined as "the real problem" between the parties. In many cases, moreover, the victim is explicitly blamed for her behaviour which is seen to have "provoked" the accused's violent response.

In *Lynch v the Police*,[59] after quashing a conviction for breach of a non-molestation order, Ellis J ordered that the appellant be granted a discharge without conviction under section 19 of the *Criminal Justice Act* 1985 (NZ). While Ellis J concurred with the District Court judge that there had been a breach of the order, he neither stated what sentence the District Court judge had imposed nor did he give any facts of the case except to state:

> From my reading of the transcript the hearing was a difficult one. It was a matrimonial dispute where feelings and hurts were of long standing. The facts complained of fall into two parts. Firstly, what happened between the husband and the wife at the bus stop and between there and the house and then what occurred inside the house itself.[60]

From this brief statement, it would appear that in fact the appellant could have been charged with several distinct breaches of the non-molestation order.

The importance of the case lies in the echoing by Ellis J of the family dysfunction paradigm about domestic violence which has been so commonplace in Family Court judgments: :

> As is so often the case in domestic disputes that end up in the Criminal Court on matters such as this, **the resolution of the real problem** is impossible. I bear in mind the fact that the District Court judge was plainly of the view that this matter did not warrant a penalty of any great substance and it is also plain to me that this incident is part of a wider dispute and that **a conviction of the appellant on this charge may well militate against final resolution of the problems that have arisen between the husband and wife and I bear in mind, a conviction may also militate against the welfare of the children.**[61]

The relationship between the complainant and the accused rather than the *actus reus* of the offence becomes the focus of the judge's comments and concerns. In a manner reminiscent of the decision of McAloon J in *Redward*, the "best interests of the children" are found to lie not in providing protection to the complainant by imposing a (nominal) sentence on the appellant for breaching the non-molestation order; instead, such "best interests" appear to lie in privileging the resolution of relationship issues over the enforcement of the protection order. Given that the judge states that "the resolution of the real problem is impossible," an obvious question which arises is whether the quashing of Mr Lynch's conviction will "militate against" further breaches of the non-molestation order granted by the court to Mrs Lynch.

A further example of the "the gap" is *Newlands and the Police*.[62] In this case, Tipping J clearly adopts the abuser's perspective of his assaultive behaviour. *Newlands* concerns the appellant's tenth conviction in less than a two year period for breach of a non-molestation order against the same complainant. The facts involved the accused grabbing the arm of the complainant "with a significant degree of force"[63] as she got up to leave a pub in which both had been drinking at separate but adjoining tables.

In describing the assault, Tipping J stated that the appellant "then addressed certain remarks to her which the learned judge below discreetly described as uncomplimentary".[64] One can only query why in the relating of the facts of the case, the High Court judge has opted for such "discretion"? How can one understand the impact of the incident on the complainant and therefore evaluate the appellate court's approach to the case without knowing the verbal context within which the assault on her occurred? It should be mentioned that Newlands was not charged with assault by the police. As has been quite typical in breach of non-molestation order cases, Newlands was charged only with the status offence (that is, breach of a non-molestation order) but not with the substantive conduct which constituted the breach.[65]

While agreeing that Newlands did in fact "waylay" the complainant and therefore was in breach of the non-molestation order, Tipping J substituted a fine of $200 without court costs for the sentence of three months periodic detention which the District Court judge had imposed. It perhaps needs to be reiterated that this $200 fine represents the penalty for the tenth conviction for breach of a non-molestation order by this appellant against the same woman in a period of less than two years.

The sentencing approach of Tipping J is quite significant. First, the judge found that "there is more than a suggestion"[66] that the complainant knew that Newlands had left one pub and gone to the one which she eventually went to also. "She chose to follow him into the Royal Hotel and to sit at a table very close to his. I'm told that there was no other table available but in the circumstances her actions can only be seen as provocative."[67] The judge continued:

> Having reviewed all the evidence I am by no means satisfied that her subsequent actions were not designed to be provocative also. **If she was trying to get a reaction from Newlands that would lead him into yet further trouble on the non-molestation order front she has**

succeeded because unfortunately he was unable to restrain himself. He certainly delivered, on the view which the learned Judge formed, a message to her in distinctly uncomplimentary terms. However, it **is my view that on the evidence Mrs Walker was substantially the author of her own misfortune on this occasion.** There is no doubt however that Mr Newlands did commit an assault on her and to that extent he was at fault....For the future Mrs Walker would be wise to refrain from any action which could be seen as provocative or ambivalent as to the need for a non-molestation order. Mr Newlands would be wise to avoid doing anything which could possibly be construed as a breach of the order while it remains in force.[68]

This case illustrates a common aspect of "the gap" in that it expresses the view that offenders who assault may not be accountable for their actions because they ("unfortunately") are unable to restrain themselves. This approach sees certain victims as provocative and at least as blameworthy as their abusers when they try to live their lives free of "molestation". Why does Tipping J warn the complainant that she may not be seen to be in need of protection (and therefore may no longer be eligible for a non-molestation order) if she chooses to frequent a pub where the appellant is also drinking? The fact that the complainant is waylaid and forcefully assaulted by the appellant when she attempts to leave the pub at the end of the evening indicates that she has a current need for a non-molestation order. But in terms of "the gap", does Tipping J perceive Newlands or the complainant as the victim in this pub incident? In the judge's analysis, who has molested whom?

An irony of this decision is that it was made only five months after Tipping J rejected an appeal by Newlands against his conviction in respect of five charges of breach of non-molestation order.[69] Tipping J then pointed out, "These breaches represented the 5th, 6th, 7th, 8th, and 9th offences of Newlands of a breach of a non-molestation order in respect of the same woman."[70] The trial court judge had sentenced Newlands concurrently to two months imprisonment on each charge (four of which involved persistent phone calls with the fifth involving the accused entering the complainant's property). In rejecting the appeal, Tipping J made a clear statement about the seriousness of repetitive breaches:

One can accept the submission that was made by the appellant to some extent that the earlier breaches may have been trivial in themselves but **cumulatively and when added to this further five, the time had come in my judgment to indicate to him firmly and clearly that this sort of conduct simply cannot be tolerated.** It is not a single isolated lapse. It is a consistent course in my view....a consistent course of breach of non-molestation order. **The whole purpose of these orders would be undermined if the Court did not in the appro-**

priate case, this being one, deal firmly with people who are in breach.[71]

While the statement from Tipping J is clear and laudatory, in the second appeal just five months later he himself failed to deal firmly with Newlands. In so doing, he gave the appellant a clear message that the complainant was at least partly, if not totally responsible, for his apparently uncontrollable violent behaviour.

It will not be surprising that one learns from his police file that Newlands was charged almost immediately after the outcome of this second appeal with breaches 11, 12, 13, 14, 15, and 16.[72] Rather than prosecute him for these breaches, however, the police decided to warn him, on the condition that Newlands promised not to harass the complainant again. Moreover, even when he did commit further breaches—and began to threaten the police themselves—the police did not prosecute.[73]

As part of a discussion about criminal court judges' responses to "technical" breaches,[74] District Court judges interviewed by the author provided insights into the way in which judges generally deal with breach of non-molestation order cases. They stated that judges see such breaches as insignificant, partly because they are viewed in isolation. Often the sentencing judge fails to understand the historical context between the parties within which the breach has occurred. The result is that judges often do not understand the intimidatory effect on the victim of such breaches. As one District Court judge stated:

> Judges who work daily in the criminal court regard a breach of a non-molestation order case as of very minor significance—in terms of the criminal law—and they wouldn't be very interested in the case at all. I mean they are dealing every day with serious violence—people perhaps being killed in motor accidents, all that sort of thing. When you get a diet of that, day in, day out, sending flowers or sending a letter through the letterbox really pales into insignificance. And so you can sort of understand, from their point of view, "Oh, breach of non-molestation order through leaving flowers on the back step. What's this in my court for? Oh, I'm not interested in this."[75]

A Family Court judge expanded on the problem of the lack of context when sentencing for breaches:

> I guess sometimes a (District Court) judge is at a disadvantage...What the judge is sentencing for is a breach and the breach may be minor in the scale of things—it may amount to harassment, i.e. sending letters, obsessive phone calls, hanging around the locality rather than a physical assault...If all the judge has to go on is the description of some harassment, that's what judges punish for, not for the violence which was the cause of an order being made in the first place. And I guess some women feel dissatisfied with the criminal justice system for that reason, saying that it's not worth the bother.[76]

In a further discussion about whether victim impact reports should be obtained prior to sentences for breaches, the same judge continued:

> That would be helpful, yes. But I would think that if you put that to your average (courtroom) number one judge on a busy Monday, he'd say, "Oh no, this is of relatively minor importance; why waste the court's time by adjourning the matter for two weeks to get a Victim Impact Report and clog up the court two weeks hence?" I'm not saying that's the right response but I'm saying that, practically, that's the response you're likely to get. The judges are on a daily diet of very much more serious violence. When you've got a big list—in excess of 100-200 people—to deal with in a day and one of those cases happens to be a breach of a non-molestation order, you're not going to waste much time on it; it's not going to exercise your mind for long, put it that way.[77]

It is highly significant that certain judges are not "interested" in breach prosecutions and distinguish them from the "daily diet" of "serious violence" they deal with. The reasons for the trivialisation of breaches are clear. They include the fact that the maximum penalty for such breaches is only a $500 fine and/or three months in prison[78] and the predominance of family dysfunction models of understanding domestic violence. However, the consequences for victims of spousal violence of this approach are "serious" for several reasons. First, spousal violence represents the highest category of homicide in New Zealand.[79] In terms of lethality assessments, the likelihood of homicide is greater when there has been prior police intervention, threats of homicide or suicide, and other forms of separation violence.[80] Secondly, the judicial practice of not obtaining victim impact statements prior to breach sentencings (coupled with the fact that the sentencing judge does not have access to the material presented in the Family Court where the non-molestation order is granted) means that frequently, all that the District Court judge has before him or her for sentencing purposes are the abuser's justifications and excuses for his breach. The breach, therefore, is not placed within the context of the history of the spousal violence. Instead a specific violent or intimidatory incident will in all likelihood be interpreted as a unique, isolated act rather than as part of a pattern of abusive behaviour.

The trivialisation of breaches underestimates the cumulative effect of the abuse on the victim. For example, in one case in which a man was convicted 13 times in a four year period of breaching his former wife's non-molestation order, he was sentenced to prison for the breaches on only one occasion. On that day, the District Court judge sentenced him to two months imprisonment for six breach convictions as well as a conviction for wilful trespass.[81] One of the breaches had involved him breaking into his ex-wife's home at 4 am; the wilful trespass had been against the offices of her lawyer. The latter incident had entailed an armed offender's call-out and the evacuation of the firm's staff. One of the police officers familiar with her case described the long-term effects on the wife of the repeated breaches:

> (Esther) mentally deteriorated, became very paranoid to the point of unreasonableness herself. Initially, I worried for her health, but when the system was not operating the way she thought it should, then it was hard to have a conversation with her because she saw you as part of the system. She said, "I'm going to be killed before something is done." She wasn't like that initially. It was a total campaign. She must have got a sore neck turning around. He's clever and smart enough to keep his breaches in the "technical" category.[82]

The wife herself described the effects of the breaches on her and the children:

> This behaviour has a serious damaging impact on the lives of myself and the children. The fact that (Fred) appears constantly makes me nervous, causes me to become introverted because I know he will interfere if I seem to have formed any social contacts. I am reluctant to appear in a public place in case it results in a confrontation with him. I am uneasy about the fact that he may approach the children as they play outside. I am reluctant to go even out onto the verandah in the evening and always am apprehensive of being beset by him. The intrusion on my privacy is humiliating and socially I feel very low about having to call out to neighbours for help against him.

> The effect of the intrusions by (Fred) disturbs the children greatly. I can see how their happy, confident behaviour changes even after a sighting of (Fred). I feel they become insecure and definitely feel threatened by him. They definitely behave more erratically when (Fred) has made an appearance. They cannot walk to school as their friends in the street do. I am sure it is humiliating for them when he causes trouble at school. I know (daughter) was very upset the day she was taken out of school. It is bad enough for them not having a father, without having the insult and degradation of him interfering in our lives.

> (Fred) refers to me as having an appetite for vengeance. To the extent that I think he should have been imprisoned now for his behaviour I am vengeful. All I really want is a peaceful life for myself and the girls. (Fred) is incapable of giving us that because he is incapable of accepting that he cannot have what he wants and what he wants is to be affecting our lives. He did it when we were together by violence, physical and sexual, and the degradation of that violence, and the keeping us impoverished and completely controlled by him. Having escaped from him and continually asserted my independence of him I believe that (Fred's) agenda has become doing me and/or my children harm.[83]

Given the repetitive nature of domestic violence, it is an important issue if judges do not realise that the consequences for an abused spouse of breaches as well as instances of physical violence may be greater than—not less significant than—the consequences to a stranger of an isolated incident of violence. It is not less traumatic to be assaulted by someone you know and have loved and trusted, than by a stranger.

A summary of a second woman's experience with the criminal justice system is perhaps best encapsulated in a memorandum filed in her husband's police file:

> (Gavin) has been arrested seven times for breaching a non-molestation order held by his ex-wife. His print out shows four Court appearances and six charges. There have been more breaches but of a nature that did not warrant prosecution (sic). As can be seen by his history, (Gavin) is not deterred in the slightest by the Court and makes a mockery of the whole thing. A side result and most importantly, I feel, is that the effect all this had on the holder of the non-molestation order. In this instance, (Maureen) was advised to obtain the order as a means of protection from her ex-husband. She now feels completely disillusioned with the Court system. She does not feel that there is any sort of protection from this man who has hounded her for over three years. He has phoned her, followed her, prowled around her property at night, threatened and even attempted suicide after blaming her for his actions. This, I believe, is a prime example of the law being ineffective.[84]

Section 5 of the *Criminal Justice Act* 1985 (NZ): recent criminal court cases

Section 5(1) of the *Criminal Justice Act* 1985 (NZ) mandates that an accused shall be imprisoned if he is convicted of an offence which involves serious violence and is punishable by a term of imprisonment of two years or more. Judicial discretion to impose a non-custodial sentence for such an offence has been removed by section 5(1) unless the sentencing judge finds that there are special circumstances of the offence or of the offender which would make a custodial sentence inappropriate. The issue in cases to which section 5(1) applies involve two questions: has there been serious violence and do special circumstances exist?

In terms of what constitutes "serious violence", a Family Court judge interviewed by the author gave his perspective when discussing the criteria he uses in deciding whether to issue *ex parte* non-molestation orders:

> If I start at one end of the scale—kicking with shoes on or off, that is severe violence. Punching—there was a case where a woman was punched in the nose and the nose was broken. Plainly that's serious enough. I think some assistance is gained from the criminal area where you've got this serious violence category, as distinct from violence which is not categorised as serious violence for the purposes of section 5 of the Criminal Justice Act 1985 (NZ). I think that serious violence in terms of section 5 automatically warrants a

*non-molestation order or a non-violence order. Violence which is not cate-
gorised as serious has to be looked at a bit more carefully. I don't think that
necessarily every form of violence warrants an order. Pushing and shoving,
however unpleasant, might not warrant the intervention of the Court at that
stage.*[85]

Kelly v the Police[86] is a High Court decision which has looked at the issue of what
constitutes "serious violence". The charge was "male assault on a female"
under section 194 (b) of the *Crimes Act* 1961 (NZ). In that case, Doogue J on
appeal reduced a sentence of six months imprisonment to three months periodic detention coupled with a sentence of six months supervision. As part of his
judgment, Doogue J stated:

> *I find it difficult to accept the District Court Judge's categorisation of this
> (single) punch (as constituting serious violence).* **This punch appears to
> have arisen out of the instinctive reaction** *by the appellant to the
> argument that had arisen between him and the complainant. It was not part
> of a sustained course of violence.* **The consequence was a not uncom-
> mon black eye** *and no more. It was not the worst of black eyes.*[87]

In characterising the punch as "the instinctive reaction by the appellant", the
judge echoes the views expressed in *G v G*[88] and *Newlands and the Police*[89] that
this offender is somehow less than accountable for his actions. The cause of the
violence is "the argument between him and the complainant". The appellant
was simply unable to restrain himself. In terms of the distinction between
"common black eyes" and "uncommon" ones or how one knows which is "the
worst", one can only query the evidence before the court about these categories. Would Doogue J have responded differently if the single punch had broken her nose? Most importantly, did the complainant feel safer or more
protected as a result of the sentencing decision, the judge's perspective about
the cause of the violence, or his description of her injury?[90]

Thomas v Police[91] involves the second part of the section 5 test, that is the
definition of "special circumstances". In *Thomas*, Eichelbaum CJ described the
facts of the assault. He found that Thomas had reacted to coffee being "accidentally spilled on him" by his wife by pouring a kettle of boiling water over
her. She suffered first and second degree burns and was assessed as likely to
suffer on-going physical and emotional consequences.[92]

Eichelbaum CJ found that Thomas' conduct constituted serious violence but
he found that special circumstances existed which allowed him to substitute a
sentence of six months periodic detention for the District Court judge's sentence of four months imprisonment. These circumstances were the first offender status of the appellant, the steps he had undertaken to deal with his alcohol
problem, the out of character nature of the offence ("I think it is highly unlikely, given his background, that the offender will re-offend in a similar manner"),

the forgiveness shown by the victim, and the harshness of the consequences of imprisonment including its impact on the appellant's employment.

It's important to note that each of these "circumstances" is in fact rather ordinary in domestic violence related offences. Victims typically forgive their abusers, whether freely or out of fear, and the assailants are often "first offenders". This may simply mean that their spouses have not reported them to the police before. Typically their offences are seen as being out of character. Indeed in *Thomas*, the appellant's response to having coffee spilled on him accidentally would seem to belie the "out of character" nature of this violence. The *actus reus* of the offence seems too over-reactive in the circumstances to represent an atypical episode. It is comprehensible only as part of a pattern of conduct aimed at punishing "infringements" by the victim spouse. And of course, virtually all prison sentences will impact on an accused's employment.

Eichelbaum CJ did not rely solely upon any one "ordinary" factor. He found that "the (above-mentioned) combination of matters enables a finding of special circumstances to be made".[93] The question must be asked, however, whether the combination of several ordinary factors converts the whole into a case justifying the judge in imposing a non-custodial sentence. More importantly, what is the consequence of the "combination" analysis of Eichelbaum CJ in terms of sentencing for domestic violence related offences in general? Will this approach result in different sentences being imposed for the same act of violence depending on whether the complainant and the accused are related or strangers? In other words, will the status of the victim as wife or de facto spouse, rather than a stranger, be more relevant in sentencing than the *actus reus* of the offence?

A highly problematic "special circumstance" is discussed in *Police v Descatoires*.[94] In *Descatoires*, the accused was charged with assault with intent to injure for pushing his spouse to the floor, putting his hands around her throat, choking her and kicking her in the face. While Brown J characterised the attack as "serious violence", he found that the section 5 special circumstance criterion had been fulfilled because just prior to the assault, the accused had learned that his wife had formed a new relationship. Rather than imprisonment, the accused was sentenced to six months periodic detention and attendance at the Hamilton Abuse Intervention Pilot Project's men's education programme. While the judge stressed that he did not feel that the accused was "justified" in his assault, his willingness to characterise the new relationship as a special circumstance tended to legitimise the accused's view (expressed by him during the defended hearing) that his wife "deserved" what he had done to her.

In fact, during separation, it is a rather "ordinary" circumstance that former partners form new relationships.[95]

On the other hand, there are recent cases in which judges have refused to find the existence of special circumstances for factors which whether seen in isolation or in the aggregate can only be described as commonplace in domestic violence scenarios. Rather than focusing on the offender's victim-blaming rationales for the violence, these judgments have looked at the extent of the violence and its consequences for the victim. They have refused to minimise the actual violence and have emphasised the victim's need for safety and protection as well as the court's role in expressing the community's opprobrium towards domestic violence. For instance, in *T v NZ Police*,[96] Robertson J stated:

> It cannot be said that there is anything wrong in principle with a judge reasserting the community's abhorrence of the extent of domestic violence in this country. This man had gone to a place where he knew his wife would be. He had gone to a place where the child was going into school and a situation of stress was inevitably created…for my part I am of the view that there is a need for the Courts (on behalf of the community) to repeat the fact that violence in the home is every bit as serious as other forms of violence and that we should not fall into the tragedy of calling something domestic violence again as if it were less serious.[97]

In a recent Hamilton District Court case, *Police v Chambers*,[98] the judge rejected the argument that the special circumstances criterion was met because the complainant had sent a letter to the court stating that she had forgiven the accused. In that case, the offender was facing three charges under section 194(b). One charge involved a push which knocked the then eight months pregnant victim unconscious. A second incident—which had occurred when the victim was changing their baby's nappy—had involved head-butting which left the victim suffering from chronic headaches. The accused was sentenced concurrently to nine months prison on each charge. Likewise in *Police v Manihera*,[99] a case in which the accused had delivered at least 12 punches to the victim's face and head (causing bruising and swelling), the judge rejected defence counsel's argument that the offender had used some restraint (for instance, the blows were not as forceful as they might have been), that he had taken out most of his frustration on the wall and that the violence was a result of the couple's communication problems and financial stress.

In *Manihera*, Jamieson J rejected counsel's submissions, imposed a six month prison term, and ordered the offender to attend HAIPP's men's programme upon his release. In passing sentence, the judge observed that, "nine and a half offenders out of ten have financial stress at some time or other but do not resort to violence". He considered the attack to be a "prolonged beating", stated that the head is a delicate and vulnerable part of the body, and that repeated beating is liable to do serious harm. He also noted that there had been a history of violence by the offender against the victim.

In *R v Teinatoa*,[100] the wife was charged with attempted murder; she stabbed her husband while she "was in a frenzy, probably based on jealousy". McGechan J ultimately found that there were special circumstances under section 5 because of the extremely adverse impact a jail sentence for the accused would have on the survival chances of the couple's eight year old daughter (who suffered from Hodgkins lymphoma). However, he reviewed the usual special circumstances factors found in domestic violence cases and clearly stated that had it not been for the daughter's cancer, the other circumstances raised would not have saved the accused from a prison term. These circumstances included the "provocation" of the husband's extra-marital relationship, the accused's jealousy-induced depression at the time of the stabbing, her previous good character (she was a first offender), her "real prospects for rehabilitation through (the couple's) newly improved relationship", the lack of long lasting effects on the victim of the offence and the husband's forgiveness. McGechan J stressed that in domestic violence cases, "the Court must consider still the need for a deterrent, not only personally but to offenders elsewhere in the community. There are wider public interests which cannot be disregarded."[101]

In *Wright v Saunders*,[102] Williamson J also gave the respondent a clear message about the inappropriateness of his violence. The respondent had been charged with assault with a weapon and had been sentenced by the District Court judge to eight months periodic detention. The Crown had appealed the sentence on the grounds that the trial court judge had erred in finding special circumstances under section 5 and also that the sentence imposed had been manifestly inadequate. The maximum penalty for the charge is five years imprisonment.

The facts of the incident as set out by Williamson J were:

> [t]he respondent, in a crowded night club bar, bumped into the complainant and then held a broken glass against her throat; made threats; and then punched her causing her to double up with the force of the blow or the pain. The offence was carried out in the presence of other persons who apparently made no moves to intervene or remonstrate with the respondent. Later, the respondent, in the bar, had treated the matter in a jocular way.[103]

The first question on appeal was whether the threat inherent in the accused's conduct, namely holding a broken glass to the throat of the complainant in a crowded bar ("so crowded that persons are being prevented from coming in")[104] constituted "serious violence". Williamson J held that this threat when combined with his deliberate bumping, threatening and punching did entail serious violence. The judge stated that "threats by themselves may, in my view, constitute serious violence in some circumstances".[105]

The second issue was whether there were special circumstances to justify the periodic detention sentence. The argument made by counsel for the respondent in this regard is important as he relied upon commonly held views which serve to minimise the seriousness of domestic violence related incidents. First, the lawyer argued that "so far as the offence was concerned, no person in the bar who had witnessed it intervened, and the inference to be drawn was that they did not regard it in the serious light that the complainant did."[106] Secondly, he argued that "the cause of the respondent's offending over the previous eight months, including this particular offence, was his pathological jealousy stemming from his broken relationship with the complainant and that this pathological jealousy had ceased prior to November 1989 when the sentence was passed".[107]

Williamson J rejected the argument that the "improved stability" shown by the respondent as a consequence of his psychiatric counselling amounted to a "special circumstance". He concluded that a term of 12 months imprisonment was appropriate for the offence, reduced to nine months because of the periodic detention period already served and held that:

> this sentence was manifestly inadequate primarily because of the earlier offending in respect of which periods of periodic detention had been imposed and because an element of deterrence is required both by the nature of the Act itself and the prevalence of domestic violence. No person can continue to physically abuse another without expecting that the reaction of the community as envisaged by section 5 of the Criminal Justice Act will be a severe one.[108]

In *Police v Shortland*,[109] another case under section 5, Tompkins J refused to find that the existence of a five year old domestic relationship between the respondent and the complainant constituted a "special circumstance". Neither was the fact that the complainant might wish to re-establish a stable relationship with the respondent. This case involved an appeal by the Crown against a sentence of six months periodic detention for assault with intent to injure and threatening to kill. The respondent had a conviction for assault on a female six years previously and a four year old conviction for aggravated assault. The facts of the case included repeated punching and kicking, threatening the victim with a butcher's knife, striking her with a hammer, and threats to kill.[110]

At the trial, the complainant "was clearly reluctant" to give evidence against the respondent and was declared a hostile witness. Furthermore, when the respondent appeared for sentence and later at the appeal hearing, an affidavit was produced in which the complainant swore that:

> She did not believe the respondent was fully responsible for what had happened because they had got into an argument and a fight together. She says she cannot say how she was hurt, it happened very quickly. She was knocked about a bit, but wasn't severely hurt. She says because she was angry with the respondent at the time and was still when talking to the police, she exaggerated what had happened. In particular, she said that when she told the police that the respondent did things to her with a knife and hammer, she exaggerated. She thought once the police became involved the matter was blown out of proportion. She says she is now reconciled with the respondent,

that they are not living together, but they see each other quite often and he visits her and the children quite often. They are, she says, "getting along fine".[111]

The complainant's behaviour is typical of many battered women. She minimised the violence used against her, blamed herself for her partner's violence, said she could not remember what really had happened and/or she had exaggerated its import, and that everything was fine. From interviews conducted by the author with Family Court judges and women's refuge workers, fear of a violent abuser's retribution was cited as a primary reason why victims may not seek the prosecution of breaches of non-molestation orders. Fear of further violence is clearly a major reason why it may appear to the victim that the risks entailed in prosecuting an abuser outweigh the benefits that may be derived from calling the police or testifying against him. As one Family Court judge stated:

The women probably don't complain to the police (about breaches)...the complainants might be too frightened to complain and they think that the judicial system won't take any notice of them anyway. They may think to themselves, "Oh well, I've got to get on with my life and this is just something I've got to put up with."[112]

At the sentencing of Shortland, the trial court judge had stated that "he considered that the complainant was badly injured and despite her efforts to try and minimise what had occurred, he was not persuaded that she was exaggerating".[113] As related by Tompkins J, the trial court judge "had considered long and hard how the respondent should be dealt with. A factor that weighed with him was that to send him to prison would almost certainly be the end of his relationship with the complainant. He was conscious of the anxiety that the complainant had to have a stable family relationship."[114] No reference was made in the trial court judge's sentencing to section 5. Were the elements of the assault not seen by him as constituting serious violence?

Tompkins J rejected the trial court judge's approach, quashed the six month periodic detention sentence and sentenced the respondent to a term of 42 days prison on each charge, those sentences to run concurrently. He stated that the appropriate sentence would have been two months imprisonment but he credited the respondent with the 18 days he had spent remanded in custody prior to trial. In dealing with the respondent's previous convictions, Tompkins J stated (perhaps ingenuously in the light of the trial court judge's sentence) "I have been referred to the two previous convictions involving at least some degree of violence, although the degree could not have been substantial since non-custodial sentences were imposed."[115]

While the 42 day sentence may appear to be totally inadequate given the violence involved (the maximum penalty for threatening to kill is five years),

Tompkins J in fact made a clear and unambiguous statement about societal disapproval of domestic violence:

> In the past, the community and the Courts may have regarded domestic violence as less serious than non-domestic violence. I believe that is no longer the case. Now, not only the community but also the Courts recognise that domestic violence is at such a level of seriousness that where it is proved to have occurred, the Courts should impose sentences that are deterrent in nature and that would discourage both the offender and others from such conduct. Although perhaps not to the same extent as previously another factor with domestic violence is that it frequently goes unreported and therefore undetected.[116]

Finally, in *Harris v The Police*,[117] Robertson J in the course of his judgment addressed some cogent and strong comments to the appellant about his behaviour and spoke generally about the importance of treating domestic violence in as serious a manner as stranger violence. However, he then reduced the District Court's custodial sentence of 12 months for "assault on a female" to a prison term of six months. In terms of the sentencing in cases already analysed, one can only agree that despite his remarks, Robertson J was correct when he viewed the 12 month prison sentence imposed by the trial court judge as "excessive". If two months prison is adequate to punish Shortland and six months periodic detention is adequate for Thomas, then the result on appeal in *Harris* is not surprising. The issue is that sentences for domestic violence related offences are all too often inadequate.[118]

In *Harris*, the appellant went to the home of his former wife. She was there with a male friend of hers, her daughter and three teenage friends of her daughter. The appellant punched his wife's friend in the head several times and then:

> when Mrs Harris tried to intervene Mr Harris struck her on the jaw with his fist and she fell to the ground...The appellant went quite berserk, overturning a fridge, smashing a hole in the top of the dining table, pushing over the television, video, heater, chairs, and some ornaments. His daughter tried to calm the rampage while her teenage friends locked themselves in the bathroom...He told the Police that he was frustrated at the difficulties involved in resolving outstanding problems.[119]

About $600 damage was done. The victims did not seek medical attention.

In obiter, Robertson J made some of the strongest judicial statements encountered condemning the appellant's violent conduct. He stated:

> His behaviour that night was intolerable. This man is 41. He is a grown adult and this type of behaviour is abhorrent to any civilised community...This was unacceptable, inexcusable and cowardly violence.[120]

Foreshadowing his comments in *T v NZ Police*,[121] Robertson J also gave the appellant a clear message about domestic violence in general:

> Too often we use the phrase "domestic violence" to describe assaults which occur within families as if they are somehow less serious than other assaults. In my judgment they are probably more serious because the home is the one place where people ought to be secure. I reject any suggestion that because there had once been a relationship between this man and this woman, the matter should be viewed in a different way.[122]

He then continued:

> A custodial sentence in my view is required in a case such as this to act as a clear signal to other frustrated and inebriated men that this is not the way to resolve outstanding problems. When a person becomes so self-centred as to create the intolerable situation which this man did, not only for his ex wife who is entitled to the dignity of her freedom, but also for his teenage daughter and her friends, a need for condemnatory and deterrent penalties exists to mark the fact that this sort of behaviour can never be acceptable.[123]

Most praiseworthy about the *Harris* decision is that Robertson J focused on the appellant's behaviour rather than on his justifications for that behaviour. He did not excuse the behaviour because of the appellant's stated "frustrations". He did not analyse whether the respondent was having difficulties coping with jealousy or had reacted out of an instinctive response. Instead, Robertson J clearly stated that the appellant's conduct had been reprehensible and he affirmed the wife's right "to the dignity of her freedom",[124] the type of remark that is too rarely seen in other decided domestic violence cases.

Custody and access considerations

It appears to some judges that one can be an abuser, even a killer, and yet be a good parent. In terms of the legal criteria for custody and access, the question is whether it is in the best interests of children to be in the custody of a spousal abuser or to have access to him? This issue becomes especially critical in terms of "the gap" because of the risk of further exposure to violence experienced by many battered women during access changeover times.[125]

Family Court judges interviewed by the author expressed the view that violence from one spouse to another - even in the presence of children - was an insufficient reason to deny access to the abusive parent. The issue of custody appeared to be more problematic. As one Family Court judge stated:

> If the violence has been directed toward the child, that must be of great significance. If there is violence in the presence of a child, that must be of considerable relevance. If there is violence, but not in the presence of the child, well you wouldn't necessarily give that great weight from the point of view

of the custody/access situation. It's always a question of what's in the best interests of the children and it's impossible to generalise but I wouldn't rule out custody or access to a party because he had been violent in the presence of the children. I would tell him in no uncertain terms that he had acted very irresponsibly to have beaten up the mother or something in the presence of the child. He would be told from the child's point of view that it would have scared the child and that sort of thing but of itself I would not consider it to be a barrier or a bar to access. [126]

When asked whether he would consider denying access to a parent who had "backhanded a child across the room" because the child had tried to intervene to stop his mother being hit, the Judge responded:

No, because you might say that that violence was a result of the poor relationship between Mum and Dad. If they separate, there's less likelihood of that violence erupting and if Dad can establish that he has some good attributes and that there are some good things from the child's point of view in being with him, then access is appropriate. [127]

This judge differentiated between access and custody applications in terms of the relevance of spousal violence. As he stated:

I have some reservations about whether one could be a custodial parent and be violent toward the other spouse. I'd have to scrutinise that very carefully. If the husband is violent towards the mother that would not disqualify him from having access but it's a different thing if he's asking for custody. He would have a far harder job of getting custody if he was violent to the mother than getting access. [128]

Another Family Court judge had a similar view:

The approach is prescribed by law and that is the welfare of the children is of paramount concern. While the man is a poor partner, if he is a good parent it would be wrong to deprive the children of the father as a matter of moral condemnation of him in respect of his conduct toward his partner. Moreover, once the parties have separated, the problem of violence occurring in front of the children may no longer be present. The focus is on the children. All the facts need to be considered. It is usually in the interests of the children to have access to both parents. It is a dramatic thing and an extremist thing to deprive the children of one parent. [129]

A third Family Court judge distinguished between violence that the child may have witnessed prior to the separation of the parties and violence that the child might be exposed to during a court-ordered access visit. In the former case, the judge would not deny access to the spousal abuser. But if the violence were likely to occur during the access visit or during the access changeover time, then the judge would take another look at the access order. [130]

Similar attitudes have been expressed in various cases decided under the

Guardianship Act 1968 (NZ) . In some of these cases, the violence against one spouse seems to have been interpreted as part of a two-to-tango scenario and therefore was seen as irrelevant. For instance, in his decision in *N v N*,[131] a case involving an application in respect of a six year old child's (J) schooling, Inglis J stated:

> *A parent's performance as a parent is not to be judged by that parent's behaviour to a spouse in the stress of a collapsing marriage; now that it is accepted that the marriage is finished **the real question** is the quality of parenting each of these people will be able to offer in the future. As I have already indicated, there has been no suggestion that the father's qualities as a parent should be judged by the events between the husband and wife which led **to the recent crisis**.[132]*

"The recent crisis" alluded to by the judge was the rape of the wife by the applicant husband who made his application from prison, having been sentenced to three years in respect of the rape. The sentence was under appeal at the time the application was heard.

As part of his decision, Inglis J recounted that the parties had first separated approximately a year before and that an *ex parte* non-molestation order had been granted to the wife. She had alleged that she had been forced to have sexual intercourse with the husband "on more than one occasion". The parties had reconciled for a short time, separated again, and according to the wife, there had been further incidents where the applicant had raped her. When the wife was three months pregnant with their youngest child, another such incident occurred which the wife reported to the police. The husband was tried and convicted of rape.

In what can only be characterised as a trivialisation of the husband's sexual violence to the wife as well as an implicit view that that violence was at least partially the wife's responsibility, Inglis J found:

> *The result of **the parties' discord** has been devastating to say the least. With the benefit of hindsight it is sad indeed that **the parties became so out of tune with each other** that events were allowed to develop as they did.[133]*

In assessing the father's application to have J attend a Catholic school, Inglis J specifically stated that there were no educational advantages for the child in a Catholic school education. He also found that the wife (an Open Brethren) would be "inconvenienced" by the choice of a Catholic school as she would have to drive J together with his two pre-school siblings to that school twice a day while a state school was well within walking distance. But Inglis J concluded:

> *No one underestimates the difficulty of the mother's position. But when the welfare of J is placed as the first and paramount consideration, the impor-*

tance of his future relationship with his father must obviously be considered in any plans for him. **It cannot be assumed that the mother will necessarily have J's permanent custody;** but even if that were to be the case J's upbringing is vested by law in both parents and both must have a voice in it...I have already mentioned the further factor that the local state primary school is within easy walking distance from where the mother now lives in Wanganui, whereas car transport would be needed if J were to attend a Catholic school. However, these latter factors, based largely on convenience, must be placed in proper perspective: the mother was not required to move from the matrimonial home (although it can readily be understood why she might have wished to do so), and no reason has been suggested why she could not have obtained accommodation nearer to a Catholic primary school. It needs to be remembered that **circumstances** have placed (the mother) in a position in which she is virtually a trustee for the children's interests and despite the sympathy which her position must attract the fact remains that in dealing with matters affecting the children's upbringing her freedom of action is limited by the need to consider the father's position as a co-guardian. [134]

The judge concluded:

...the most compelling factor in this case is that the mother's present regime for J, if not counterbalanced, is likely to separate J from his father. [135]

He, therefore, decided that J should attend the Catholic school.

Inglis J did not address any of the issues involved in the alienation of J from his mother's religious tradition and minimised as matters of "convenience" the problems that the mother would have in transporting J to and from school. Throughout the judgment, the focus of Inglis J is on the father's needs. The judge appears to equate the best interests of the father with J's best interests and echoes the father's argument that:

When the time comes for the father to start his life again he and J will at least be on the same mental and philosophical wavelength. He (the father) hopes, in other words, that when he is able to resume full contact with J he and J will be able to share a common Catholic outlook. [136]

As stated previously, the view that a violent spouse can be a good parent represents one of the major reasons why access changeover times are so dangerous for battered women who have custody of their children. From interviews with spousal victims, there appears to be little attention paid to making access orders which incorporate safety provisions for previously battered custodial parents.

A final example of judicial treatment of guardianship issues within the context of domestic violence arises from the recent Court of Appeal decision of *R v Panoa-Masina*. [137] *Masina* is significant in terms of its assumption that a spouse can be homicidally violent to his partner and yet be a fit custodial parent. The trial court decision especially is a clear example of the irrelevancy of spousal violence in terms of custody decision making.

Masina involved an appeal by the Solicitor-General against a sentence of nine months periodic detention for the manslaughter of the respondent's de facto partner. The legal issue entailed an evaluation of the special circumstances found by Gallen J under section 5(1) of the *Criminal Justice Act* 1985 (NZ) which allowed him to impose a non-custodial sentence. It goes without saying that manslaughter by definition represents "serious violence".

In the Court of Appeal judgment, Holland J outlined the background to the homicide. He stated that there was an argument between Masina and his partner about money which:

> led to what Masina described as a fight during which he admitted grabbing her by the hair, throwing her around the room, punching her and pushing her against furniture. There was no evidence of any blows to him. The medical evidence showed extensive bruising over the arms and legs and face of the deceased and injuries to her head which had caused a subdural haematoma from which she subsequently [10 days later] died.[138]

The Court of Appeal reviewed the five special circumstances relied on by Justice Gallen. First, there had been an issue of whether Mrs Masina's life could have been saved had doctors diagnosed the subdural haematoma earlier. Gallen J found, however, that "no criticism, of course, could be made of the doctors in this regard".[139] Secondly, the trial court judge had found that:

> there was a strong element of provocation in regard to the deceit of the deceased in relation to the financial matters and particularly the fact that Masina had that night been substantially embarrassed when he was told that his cousin had not received the $50 for the cousin's son's 21st birthday which he had given to the deceased for that purpose.[140]

One would have assumed that Masina had already been "credited" with his spouse's provocation by the fact that he had been convicted of manslaughter. One might also query what the financial threshold for provocation should be. In other words, what quantum is sufficient to allow a judge to "understand" a homicidal assault in terms of provocation?

The third, fourth and fifth special circumstances are quite "ordinary" in domestic violence cases, namely that Masina had used no weapons during the assault and was not seriously affected by alcohol; "had not appeared previously before the Courts and was described as a helpful and kindly person"; and members of the deceased's family were "supportive" of him.[141] The third special circumstance is especially interesting as Masina's lack of a weapon simply proves that he was sufficiently strong to beat his partner to death. Likewise the casting of his sobriety in a positive light suggests that he is credited with knowing what he was doing during "the persistent and deliberate assault"[142] which resulted in his victim's death.

While not undercutting the importance of the five above-noted considerations in terms of the section 5 issue, Holland J in the Court of Appeal judgment stated:

> *The sixth and most important special circumstance relied on by the (trial court) judge was that Masina had a son who was then only eight years of age **who had lost his mother** and who would if (Masina) was sentenced to imprisonment, **temporarily lose the advantage of the guidance and companionship of his only surviving parent**.*[143]

The "sixth and most important special circumstance" is a clear example of "the gap". It demonstrates domestic violence being not just trivialised but indeed, rendered invisible. The trial court judge's choice of the word "lost" to describe what happened to the deceased is problematic. Was the deceased really "lost"? This linguistic characterisation becomes even more problematic with the judge's suggestion that by imprisoning him, the accused too may be (temporarily) "lost" to the child. Could this special circumstance be seen as valid if the sentence re-incorporated the "lost" violence and read in part "...temporarily lose the advantage of the guidance and companionship of his only surviving parent—his mother's killer"?

What is the message that a court gives about domestic violence when credit is given to a killer because he falls into the category of "sole surviving parent" when, in fact, he stands convicted of the manslaughter of the other (now dead) parent? Neither in the High Court nor in the Court of Appeal judgment is there any concern expressed that a man who has killed his partner of 12 years may be a questionable custodial parent. Where the eight year old boy was during the late night assault is not even mentioned in the judgment although there is a body of literature which underscores the serious developmental effects on children of witnessing one parent assaulting (no less killing) the other.[144] The High Court and the Court of Appeal decisions underscore the view that Masina —despite his violence—has an important custodial role to play in his son's life. Indeed, the Court of Appeal contextualises the high value that the trial court judge placed on Masina's fathering qualities by stating:

> *We share the judge's concern for the 8 year old boy but the evidence produced in support of Masina shows that there are 8 other children of the deceased and 5 of Masina. We are told that all are over 20 years of age. We are confident that the boy will be well cared for during any period of imprisonment of his father.*[145]

The "advantage" of Masina as a parental figure to the child led the trial court judge to refuse to impose a custodial sentence. Even though the Court of Appeal judgment found that "a sentence short of imprisonment was an option not open to the trial court judge" the decision concluded, "We agree with the Judge that this is a case which called for a compassionate sentence for the reasons expressed by him."[146] The Court allowed the Crown's appeal and sentenced Masina to 18 months imprisonment. How "compassionate" that sentence is must be seen in the light of the facts that the average prison term for manslaughter in New Zealand in 1990 was 46 months while in 1989 the average was 59.7 months. In fact, over the period 1981-1990, the lowest annual average prison term for manslaughter was 30.6 months.[147]

Conclusion

In the preface to *Protection From Family Violence*, the authors outlined the "costs" of the research for its writers:

> We never foresaw the consequences that the researching of the report would have for us. We did not anticipate the horrific details we would be exposed to, the fear we felt at times, the sameness of the stories told to us by women whose life experiences cut across racial, religious, and class backgrounds. Over time we became familiar with the "scripts" of battering and the commonplaceness of women's terror. In terms of what we least expected, we did not realise that by the end of our inquiry we could produce a manual for assailants on how to avoid the consequences of their spousal abuse...what we have learned easiest and best are the excuses and justifications for domestic violence which the justice system readily accepts, thus rendering spousal abuse consequence-free.[148]

Despite recent cases which indicate that certain judges are now giving appropriate recognition to domestic violence, an analysis of the case law underscores that the paradigms utilised to characterise domestic violence all too frequently fail to provide protection for spousal violence victims. Emphasis on reconstitution of the family and/or conciliation have sometimes overshadowed victims' needs for protection.

Judicial attitudes convey powerful messages to victims and abusers alike about the justice system's commitment to stopping domestic violence. While it may be that "there are sometimes some quite unreal expectations about what the Courts can do (in terms of providing protection)"[149] and clearly not all domestic homicides are preventable, it is essential that judges convey unambiguous messages that the existence of violence in a relationship is, in fact, a real problem of that relationship. Moreover, courts should give clear messages that violence or threats of violence will not work in any situation. The message to the respondent if the Court does engage in such placatory behaviour is that he can continue to threaten with impunity. In the face of such a message, how can protection be afforded?

The experiences of victims set a measure by which the appropriateness of the justice system's responses to domestic violence can be judged. We have called it "the gap"—that limbo between women's realities and the system's attitudes. It is only by closing the gap that the wide-ranging personal and societal consequences of domestic violence can be lessened. Changes in judicial attitudes will not alone result in this occurring. In the context of the present New Zealand government's cutbacks in spending on benefits, women's refuge funding, health care services, legal aid, accident compensation, education, and housing—can anyone believe that abused spouses and children will be enabled to more easily escape from their batterers?

Notes

1   The "Abridged" version has the following statement on its cover and title page: "Commissioned by the Victims Task Force and prepared for public release from an original report by Ruth Busch, Neville Robertson and Hilary Lapsley, University of Waikato."

2   Busch, R, Robertson, N and Lapsley, H, *Protection From Family Violence: A Study of Protection Orders Under the Domestic Protection Act* (1992).

3   See, for instance, Pence, E, *The Justice System's Response to Domestic Assault Cases: A Guide for Policy Development* (1986).

4   The power and control analysis of domestic violence (as well as a discussion about the domestic violence intervention protocols developed between the Hamilton Family Court and the Hamilton Abuse Intervention Pilot Project) has recently been utilised in a paper co-authored by a Hamilton Family Court Judge and the Hamilton Family Court Co-ordinator. See Twaddle, A J, and Wasey, J F, *Hamilton Abuse Intervention Pilot Project (HAIPP)*, unpublished paper delivered to the Family Court Judges' Conference, Wellington (April, 1993). For a discussion of the adoption of an intervention approach to domestic violence within the New Zealand context, see Busch, R and Robertson, N, "What's Love Got to Do with It? An Analysis of An Intervention Approach to Domestic Violence", (1993) 1 *Waikato LR* 109.

5   Pence, E, above n3 at 1-8.

6   See, for instance, Busch, Robertson and Lapsley, above n2 at 264-5.

7   Ibid.

8   See, for instance, *Redward v Redward* (1988) 4 NZFLR 528.

9   *N v N* (1986) 2 FRNZ 534.

10 *R v Panoa-Masina*, unreported, Court of Appeal, 7 October 1991 (CA 309/91).

11   See, for example, *W v W* (1985) 1 FRNZ 554 which involved an application
     for protection orders and interim custody. There had been a history of
     violence directed to the wife by the husband and the most recent outbreak
     had also entailed the husband's "serious mistreatment" of the couple's nine
     year old child (A), after which the wife and child fled to a women's refuge.
     At the time of the hearing, the Department of Social Welfare expressed
     concern that the wife might be induced to reconcile with her husband.

     Stating that "the first and immediate need is for protection," Inglis J
     continued:

     In terms of the occupation order...the applicant was driven out of her own
     home by the respondent's violent behaviour whether or not that was the
     respondent's intention. Why should she have to live away from her own
     home cowering in a Women's Refuge while the respondent, who has himself
     brought this whole situation about, has the benefit of the home to himself?
     There is no thought of punishment in what I say. The main question is pro-
     tection of Mrs W and A. By the making of an occupation order Mrs W can
     have the home to herself. By the non-molestation order she can keep the
     respondent away. That may well turn the matrimonial home into her matri-
     monial fortress but that is what in the meantime she needs for her and A's
     protection (at 556).

     The judge also denied access to the respondent.

     An interesting feature of this case is that Inglis J conditioned the wife's
     occupation order on her attending court-directed counselling "...and further
     that she does not return to cohabit with her husband until such time as the
     Court can be satisfied that any risk of further violence on Mr W's part has
     gone". As a justification for this extraordinary condition, Inglis J stressed,
     "Of course it is a very unusual thing for a Family Court to say that a wife
     cannot have her husband back, if she wants him to come back, but this is an
     unusual case and I have to think of A's welfare as well as that of Mrs W (at
     557); cf *N v N*, above n9.

12   Busch, Robertson, and Lapsley, above n2 chapters 3-8. There are basically
     three types of protection orders which can be obtained under the *Domestic*
     Protection Act 1982 (NZ): non-violence orders, non-molestation orders and
     occupation orders. Pursuant to section 6 of the DPA a court may award a
     non-violence order if it is satisfied that the respondent has used violence
     against or caused bodily harm to the applicant and is likely to do so again.
     A breach of a non-violence order occurs when the respondent, after the
     making of the order, does use violence against the applicant or threatens to
     do so. The non-violence order is the only protection order which can be
     held if an applicant continues to cohabit with her abuser. There is no
     criminal penalty for a breach of a non-violence order but on a finding that
     the order has been breached, the respondent may be held in police custody
     for a period of 24 hours. It is clear that a non-violence order is meant to
     "cool off" the situation by removing the respondent from the domestic scene
     for a short time.

Pursuant to section 15 of the *Domestic Protection Act* 1982 (NZ), a non-molestation order can be granted if the court is satisfied that an applicant is "in need of protection". Section 16 sets out the effect of the non-molestation order, that is, it is breached by the respondent entering or remaining on any land or building the applicant occupies without the latter's consent, molesting the applicant by watching or besetting the applicant's dwelling house, place of business, employment or residence or by following or waylaying her in any public place. Breaches of non-molestation orders are dealt with by the criminal courts and the penalty for a breach is a fine of $500 and/or imprisonment for three months.

Under section 19 of the *Domestic Protection Act* 1982 (NZ), an applicant can apply for an occupation order, the effect of which is to give her exclusive possession of the household residence. For an occupation order to be granted, the court must be satisfied that the applicant is in need of protection or that such an order would be in the best interests of a child of the family.

At present, protection orders are the fastest growing type of Family Court application. In 1989, there were 3,286 non-molestation applications compared with 2,104 in 1984; and 2,378 non-violence applications compared to 1.324 in 1984. (Department of Justice Statistics)

13 Id at 207.

14 Ibid.

15 Unreported, Napier Family Court, FP 041/079/90, 16 May 1990.

16 Id at 1.

17 Section 15 of the *Domestic Protection Act* 1982 (NZ).

18 Subsections 14(1)(a) and (b) of the *Domestic Protection Act* 1982 (NZ).

19 *P-W v P-W*, above n15 at 3, emphasis added.

20 Ibid.

21 Id at 3.

22 Ibid.

23 Unreported, Wellington Family Court, FP 085/1127/83, 8 October 1986.

24 Id at 3, emphasis added.

25 One example of these difficulties can be found in Pam's case study, in Busch, Robertson, and Lapsley, above n2 at 76. After giving examples of the violence in her relationship (on one occasion, Pam's husband held a shotgun to her stomach and pulled the trigger; fortunately she had previously hidden the bolt and ammunition), Pam stated that she "went before an elderly male judge who read her affidavit and said to her, 'No one can live under those circumstances; it has got to be lies.' It was only after Pam 'lost control', cried and shook, which she said was 'a typical helpless female response', that he seemed to believe her."

26 *G v G*, above n23 at 3.

27 Above n10 at 4. Masina was convicted for beating his wife in what the Court of Appeal characterised as a "prolonged and deliberate assault" which resulted in her death 10 days later.

28 *G v G*, above n23 at 3.

29 In *P-W v P-W*, above n15 at 3 Inglis J had noted: "The husband's acts have not been malicious or designed to annoy; they have come from desperation, enhanced by his illness (depression)."

30 See Peggy's case study in Busch, Robertson, and Lapsley, above n2 at 145-9 for an example of this perspective in terms of police practice. In that case study, one of the arresting police officers characterised as "pathetic," "blubbering", and "harmless" a husband arrested for breaching a non-molestation order who was found to have in his possession four live .303 shells. When questioned, the husband admitted that he had intended to leave the bullets in his ex-wife's letterbox. He was granted bail despite the fact that his former wife held a non-violence order against him and that his admission, coupled with the bullets in his possession, constituted a breach of that order in that they represented a threat to cause her bodily harm. After being bailed, the offender collected a rifle and more ammunition from his home, returned to his ex-wife's home, shot her dead and then killed himself. One of the arresting constables stated that while he believed that the offender was attempting to "terrorise" his wife, he was "not dangerous". The result of "the gap" in this situation is that the husband was seen both as a "terrorist" and still as "harmless". Clearly, the offender was not perceived as dangerous to the police officers and that view allowed them to grant him bail.

31 As an example, see *Thomas v Police*, unreported, High Court, Wellington, 13 November 1991 AP. 222/91, discussed below.

32 See *Newlands and the Police* [1992] NZFLR 74, discussed more fully below.

33 [1992] NZFLR 79

34 In this case, the approach of Inglis J is somewhat novel. The previous case law had indicated that pursuant to section 31(4) of the *Domestic Protection Act* 1982 (NZ), there could only be one extension of a non-molestation order granted on an *ex parte* basis. After that extension (or in the absence of such an extension), the *ex parte* (interim) order lapsed when the period for which it was made lapsed and only a final non-molestation order could be made in its place. Technically, the "final" order is known simply as a non-molestation order. In *Police v N* (1984) 1 FRNZ 156, Inglis J himself had stated that:

The provisions of subsections (1) and (4) are mandatory. When an interim order is made *ex parte* the court must prescribe a date for the hearing of the question whether a final order should be made in substitution for the interim order. On that date, the Court may do one of three things: first, it may discharge the interim order; or secondly, it may discharge the interim order and replace it with a final order; or thirdly, it may adjourn the hearing to a fixed date...If the third option—that is, adjournment to a fixed date on good cause being shown—is the option selected, the Court's options on the resumed hearing are limited exclusively to the first two. Effectively that means that the interim order must be discharged or a final order made (at 157).

Recommendation 36 in the Family Court section of *Protection From Family Violence* specifically called for the amendment of section 31 of the *Domestic Protection Act* 1982 (NZ) to allow for judges to make repeated temporary non-molestation orders. For a discussion of section 31 issues, see Busch, Robertson, and Lapsley, above n2 at 226-7.

35   *Titter v Titter*, above n33 at 80.

36   Id at 80, emphasis added.

37   Id at 80-1, emphasis added.

38   Ibid.

39   See Fanslow, J, *The OASIS Protocol: Guidelines for Identifying, Treating and Referring Abused Women* (1993), at 13, 28-32. See also Hart, B, "Assessing Whether Batterers Will Kill", Appendix A to *Accountability: Program Standards for Batterer Intervention* (1992) at A-1 to A-3.

40   *Titter v Titter*, above n33 at 82.

41   Examples of these cases are found in Busch, Robertson, and Lapsley, above n2 at 198-206.

42   *Titter v Titter*, above n33 at 82, emphasis added.

43   Ibid, emphasis added.

44   As discussed above n12, Section 15 states that a non-molestation order may be granted if the Court is satisfied that the applicant is in need of protection. There is no provision in section 15 (as there is in section 21 in respect of occupation orders) for making a non-molestation order "on such terms and subject to such conditions as the Court thinks fit".

45   *Titter v Titter*, above n33 at 82.

46   For a critical analysis of current Family Court counselling and mediation practices, see Lapsley, H, Robertson, N and Busch, R, "Family Court Counselling, Part I" (March 1993) 3 *Butterworths Family Law Bulletin* 152 and Lapsley, H, Robertson, N and Busch, R, "Family Court Counselling, Part II" (June 1993)1 *Butterworths Family Law Journal* 9. See also *The Review of the Family Court: A Report for the Principal Family Court Judge* (April 1993) at 119, in which Boshier J and the other committee members agreed "that where domestic violence is evident, joint counselling and/or mediation is not appropriate. This should only be cautiously considered if there is informed and free agreement by both parties". The Committee went on to state, "Domestic violence, as a reflection of power, is obviously an important concept when it comes to considering how a Court process should operate when domestic violence exists. **We believe that mediation should be avoided by the judicial process as a legitimate means of dispute resolution in such circumstances**." (emphasis in the original).

47 A sample of overseas critiques are found in Lerman, L G, "Mediation of Wife Abuse Cases: The Adverse Impact of Informal Dispute Resolution on Women" (1984) 7 *Harvard Women's Law Review* 57; Adams, D., "Counselling Men who Batter: A Profeminist Analysis of Five Treatment Models" in Yllo, K and Bograd, M (eds), *Feminist Perspectives on Wife Abuse* (1988) at 176-99; Walker, L, "Psychology and Violence Against Women" (1989) 44 *American Psychologist* 695; and Buzawa, E S and Buzawa, C G, *Domestic Violence: The Criminal Justice Response* (1990) at 127-9.

48 Above n8.

49 Pence, E and Paymar, M, *Power and Control: Tactics of Men Who Batter* (1986) at 30.

50 *Redward v Redward*, above n8 at 530.

51 Id at 529.

52 Ibid, emphasis added.

53 Id at 530.

54 Busch, Robertson, and Lapsley, above n2 at 211.

55 Ibid.

56 Id at 212.

57 Busch, Robertson, and Lapsley, above n2 at 200-9. See also Moore, J, *Is a Non-Molestation Order Enough? Women's Experiences of the Family Court*, unpublished Master of Arts (Applied) in Social Work Thesis, Victoria University of Wellington, (1989).

58 For numerous examples, see Busch, Robertson, and Lapsley, above at n2 at 51-155.

59 Unreported, High Court, Auckland, A.P. 16/86, 24 February 1986.

60 Id at 2.

61 Id at 3, emphasis added.

62 Above n32.

63 Id at 75.

64 Ibid.

65 Busch, Robertson, and Lapsley, above n2 at 168-9 and at 174-5.

66 *Newlands and the Police*, above n32 at 77.

67 Ibid.

68 Id at 77-8, emphasis added.

69 *Newlands v the Police*, unreported, High Court, Timaru Registry, AP 30/90, 6 July 1990.

70 Id at 1.

71 Ibid, emphasis added.

72 Busch, Robertson, and Lapsley, above n2 at 197.

73   Ibid.

74   While there is no statutory authority for the classification "technical breaches", such breaches involve conduct which contravenes the provisions of the *Domestic Protection Act* 1982 (NZ) but does not involve physical violence. For a more detailed discussion of judicial and police approaches to such breaches, see Busch, Robertson, and Lapsley, above n2 at 202-6.

75   Id at 266.

76   Id at 277-8.

77   Ibid.

78   See above n12.

79   See Fanslow, J, above n39 at 13. For a more detailed discussion of the incidence of domestic homicides in New Zealand, see Fanslow, J L , Chalmers, D J and Langley, J D, *Injury from Assault: A Public Health Problem* (1991).

80   Above n39.

81   Busch, Robertson, and Lapsley, above n2 at 67.

82   Id at 73. Note also that the names in parentheses are pseudonyms.

83   Id at 67.

84   Id at 137.

85   Id at 210.

86   Unreported, High Court, Rotorua Registry, AP 29/91, 15 May 1991.

87   Id at 5, emphasis added.

88   See above n23.

89   See above n32.

90   In *Police v Wilson*, unreported, Hamilton District Court, CRN 3019013810, 4 August 1993, Jamieson J held that there was a distinction between "force" and "violence". The assault consisted of one open handed slap across the head which had not resulted in any injury to the complainant. The judge stated that while an assault had occurred, the incident was not a violent one. The issue is significant because under section 5(2) of the *Criminal Justice Act* 1985 (NZ), an accused convicted twice under section 194(b) within a two year period shall be sentenced to a term of imprisonment unless special circumstances can be found. There is no requirement of "serious violence" in section 5(2); "violence" however must be used.

91   Above n31.

92   Id at 1-2.

93   Id at 3.

94   Unreported, Hamilton District Court, CRN 3019010743, 13 May 1993. The author has discussed the conduct of the trial as well as the judgment with the court advocate for the Hamilton Abuse Intervention Pilot Project. The HAIPP Court Advocate attends District Court domestic violence hearings daily, monitoring court proceedings and providing support for complainants.

95 Penlington J considered the relevance for sentencing of the separated wife's new relationship in *Martens v The Commissioner of Police* unreported, High Court, Tauranga Registry, AP 14/91, 24 June 1991. *Martens* involved the case of a man who assaulted his wife twice within an eight day period. On the first occasion, he struck the complainant several times around the head and face, pushed her to the ground, ordered her into a motor car ("She complied because of fear of the appellant"), repeatedly punched her on the arms and shoulders, and while she was on the ground after the car had stopped, he pulled her hair and grabbed her neck. In the second assault, he struck her and forced her to the floor, grabbed her by the throat and kicked her in the upper legs and punched about her body. While not finding that the wife's new relationship constituted a special circumstance, the judge accepted defence counsel's submission that:

When the appellant acquired knowledge of this fact he said that he became provoked and that his outburst which followed was as the result of gaining this knowledge. The appellant now readily accepts that he emotionally lost control of himself. It is contended that at the time he was deeply upset at the breakdown of his marriage. He was trying hard to restore the marriage. Knowledge of his wife's association with another person was a bitter blow to him at that time.

Penlington J clearly attributes the two assaults to the new relationship. As he says, "The appellant was provoked when these assaults took place. He was plainly in a highly emotionally charged state at that time."

96 Unreported, High Court, Dunedin Registry, AP 94/91, 13 September 1991.

97 Id at 2-3. The assault had entailed punching the complainant on the side of her face. It had occurred at the children's school.

98 Unreported, Hamilton District Court, CRN 3019008149251, 12 May 1993.

99 Unreported, Hamilton District Court, CRN 3019010032, 3 May 1993.

100 Unreported, High Court, Wellington Registry, T 16/93, 4 June 1993.

101 Id at 4.

102 (1990) 5 CRNZ 234.

103 Id at 235.

104 Id at 236.

105 Ibid.

106 Ibid.

107 Ibid.

108 Ibid.

109 (1989) 4 CRNZ 155.

110 Id at 156.

111 Ibid.

112 Busch, Robertson, and Lapsley, above n2 at 266.

113 *Police v Shortland*, above n109 at 157.

114 Ibid.

115 Id at 159.

116 Id at 158-9.

117 Unreported, High Court, New Plymouth Registry, AP 15/91, 2 July 1991.

118 Some appellate court judges have recently been indirectly alluding to the same issue. In *Paki v The Police*, unreported High Court, Rotorua Registry, AP 23/93, 17 May 1993, Anderson J deals with the issue of the appropriate sentence for an appellant convicted of assault on his wife under section 194(b) of the *Crimes Act* 1961 (NZ). The summary of facts stated that "the defendant punched the complainant heavily in the mouth, splitting her top lip. He then punched her on the left upper arm. Both blows caused major bruising and swelling....The complainant was treated at Whakatane Hospital for her injuries." While stating that the appellant had already had supervision and periodic detention for violence related convictions and that a full time custodial sentence was warranted, Anderson J continued:

> *Having said that I am troubled by the severity of the sentence. I cannot recall a sentence of 12 months imprisonment for this type of case, except in the case of Lucas, AP 38/92, where Fisher J declined to intervene on appeal with a sentence of 2 months imprisonment where the conduct of the appellant was significantly worse than in this case. In Lucas the appellant pushed the complainant on to the floor causing her to strike her head; he then came at her with "a flurry of arms, fists and hands". He punched her twice in the head giving her a black eye; then he pushed her again and shook her and then threatened her with a mug of boiling beverage which he seemed about to pour over her.*

> *This case is not in that category but the sentence imposed was the same. There is an understandable concern by judges to make it plain to bullying males that they will not get away with a slap on the wrist for bashing women, but there is also a need for some general uniformity and some consistency in sentencing, as I generally observed in Rongonui, AP 5/92, Gisborne Registry....In all the circumstances I have come to the view that the sentence imposed here was appropriately imprisonment but was 50 per cent too severe and accordingly I allow the appeal and substitute a sentence of eight months imprisonment for the 12 months imposed.*

119 *Harris v The Police*, above n117 at 2.

120 Id at 3-4.

121 Above n96.

122 *Harris v The Police*, above n117 at 3.

123 Id at 5.

124 Ibid.

125 See Busch, Robertson and Lapsley, above n2 at 245-6.

126 Id at 239.

127 Ibid.

128 Ibid.

129 Id at 339-40.

130 Id at 240.

131 (1986) 2 FRNZ 534.

132 Id at 537, emphasis added.

133 Id at 534, emphasis added.

134 Id at 536, emphasis added.

135 Ibid.

136 Id at 536.

137 Above n10.

138 Id at 1.

139 Id at 4.

140 Id at 4-5.

141 Ibid.

142 Id at 6. In another paragraph on this page, Holland J stated, "A life has been taken as a result of his violence and, although the violence might not have been expected to have led to death, it was violence of quite an extreme and prolonged nature."

143 Id at 5, emphasis added.

144 See, for instance, Bowker, L H, Arbitell, M and McFerron, J R , "On the Relationship Between Wife Beating and Child Abuse", in Yllo and Bograd (eds), above n47 at 158-66.

145 *R v Panoa-Masina*, above n10 at 6.

146 Id at 6-7.

147 Minister of Justice, written reply, Order Paper 8/8/91 as cited in *The Capital Letter*, Vol 14, no. 32 at 4.

148 Busch, Robertson, and Lapsley, above n2 at vi.

149 *D v N*, unreported, Napier Family Court, FP 041/277/92, 22 March 1993, at 1.

7

Swimming Against the Tide: Keeping Violent Men Out of Mediation

Hilary Astor*

The writer gratefully acknowledges the research assistance of Katrina Budrikis and the financial support of the Law Foundation of New South Wales Legal Scholarship Support Fund and the Faculty of Law, University of Sydney.

Introduction

The increasing use of mediation and related alternative dispute resolution processes for family disputes is one of the most significant changes presently taking place in family law in Australia. Matters which would have been resolved by negotiation or dealt with in the formal justice system are being referred to informal dispute resolution processes and it appears likely that this trend will continue. A wide range of family disputes are being mediated. Disputes consequent on separation and divorce are strong candidates for referral to mediation, especially disputes concerning custody and access. Property and maintenance disputes also go to mediation. Mediation of disputes between parents and children, especially parent/adolescent mediation, is a growth area. Women who need protective orders because of violence in the home may also find themselves referred to mediation. In such cases mediation may be offered in addition to protective orders, as a method of resolving disputes arising out of separation. However it is sometimes offered as an alternative to protective orders.

The focus of this chapter is the use of mediation for that significant proportion of family disputes which involve violence against women.[1] It will be argued that mediation cannot provide protection for women who are the target of male violence. It is an inadequate and unsuitable mechanism for almost all family disputes where there has been violence. It is highly likely to produce inequitable results and may place women and the children in their care in danger.

In order to understand the dangers of mediation where there has been violence, it is necessary to understand the nature of the mediation process. Mediation procedure is therefore briefly outlined below, and the reasons for excluding disputes involving violence are considered. If mediation is such a dangerous dispute resolution mechanism where there has been violence it is necessary to explain why such disputes presently go to mediation, whether they find their way there through referral or because of party choice. The dynamics which direct such disputes into mediation are complex and powerful ones which may prevail despite the best efforts of those seeking to exclude them. The second part of this chapter is substantially devoted to an analysis of the forces which propel disputes involving violence into mediation. This analysis is presented in the hope that, if we understand what propels these cases into mediation, we may better understand how to keep them out.

Mediation: Its nature and capacity to deal with violence

Mediation procedure

Mediation is a procedure where the parties to a dispute meet and negotiate about the matters in dispute between them. They are assisted in this endeavour by a "neutral" third party, the mediator. The role of the mediator is to assist the parties to isolate the matters about which they disagree, and to develop options and consider alternatives for a consensual settlement which will accommodate the parties' needs.[2] Consensuality is seen as a key element of mediation. The parties are assisted to resolve their dispute in a co-operative fashion. The parties are said to control the content of the mediation. They define the nature of the problems they have brought to the mediation, deciding for themselves what is relevant or irrelevant. The parties are also said to control the outcome of the mediation.[3] They formulate any agreement and decide on its terms. The mediator strives to retain a neutral position, controlling only the procedure of the mediation. The parties should bargain as equals, the mediator creating procedural equality.

It is difficult to make generalisations about the procedure followed in mediation, since there will be variations not only between different mediation schemes but also between individual mediators.[4] The description below should be read with this caveat in mind. The term "mediation" is sometimes used inaccurately to describe perfunctory and unstructured attempts to achieve settlement or even to describe directive third party intervention. The nature of any procedure described as mediation should always be investigated.

When the parties to a dispute decide to use, or are referred to, mediation they will generally go through an intake procedure which may be more or less rigorous. Intake may involve a carefully considered process administered by trained staff designed to explain the nature of mediation to the parties and allow them to make an informed choice as to whether they wish to continue. It may filter out disputes which are unsuitable for mediation and provide effective and appropriate referrals. Such an extensive procedure can be resource intensive. However intake may involve little more than a telephone call to make an appointment for the mediation session. It may consist of anything between these two extremes, depending on the individual scheme or mediator.

At the commencement of the mediation session the mediator or mediators will meet with the parties. Co-mediation is frequently used for family disputes. In co-mediation two mediators, often one female and one male, work together. Sometimes mediator expertise in family law and in counselling is combined.[5] The mediators will explain their role and the process of mediation to the parties. Ground rules about issues such as confidentiality or behaviour in the mediation may be agreed upon.

The next stage of mediation is aimed at establishing the nature of the dispute. The mediators will encourage each party in turn to explain the issues as they see them in full and without interruption. The mediators will listen carefully and may take notes of what is said. Mediators are likely to summarise what each party has said to check that they, as well as the other party in mediation, have heard and understood. This feedback also confirms to the party who has stated their view of the dispute that they have been heard as well as providing an opportunity for correction and elaboration. Once all of the issues, including the parties' feelings about them, have been raised the mediators will assist the parties to decide which issues will be dealt with in the mediation and the order in which they will be dealt with.

The issues in dispute will be discussed in turn and options for their resolution will be considered. The mediator will encourage the parties towards agreement. The nature of that encouragement varies according to the mediator. Mediators have many techniques.[6] They are likely to be persistent in keeping the parties directed towards their task. They may suggest that the parties consider an option or options to resolve an issue. To keep the parties motivated to agree in mediation, mediators may remind the parties of the costs and hazards of alternatives such as litigating the dispute. They may take more coercive steps such as threatening to terminate the mediation.[7] The mediator should, however, maintain an impartial position towards outcome and should not attempt to induce the parties to adopt a particular option or persuade them in a particular direction.

At some stage in the mediation there may be a private caucus when a mediator meets with each party privately. Private caucus may be the opportunity for a party to reveal an issue they wish to be kept confidential from the other party. It may be an opportunity to vent strong feelings or to consider options for settlement.[8]

Some disputes may need more than one mediation session. The parties may be referred to, or encouraged to seek, legal or other advice between sessions. At the end of the process the parties may have reached agreement on some or all of the matters in dispute between them. Agreements should be "reality tested" so that the parties understand and concur about the details of the implementation of their agreement. An agreement reached in mediation may be put in writing. It may later be embodied in a court order.

Mediation is sometimes described as assisted negotiation. The parties in mediation bargain with each other to attempt to reach a mutually acceptable solution to their problems. The mediator's role is to assist them to do this by creating a framework for their negotiations whilst remaining impartial as to the nature and outcome of their dispute. Where both parties have the capacity to negotiate a consensual solution to their dispute, are roughly equal in power, and are motivated to resolve their dispute, mediation can be an effective, speedy, inexpensive and fair way of resolving disputes. However some parties and some disputes are not suitable for mediation. It will be argued here that mediation is not a suitable method of resolving disputes where there has been violence. It is unsuitable because violence creates an extreme power imbalance between the parties, because the parties do not have the capacity to mediate and because mediation does not provide for the needs of the person who has been the target of violence.

The parties in mediation: Violence, power and control

There are many problems associated with the mediation of disputes involving violence.[9] One fundamental problem is that violence creates an extreme imbalance of power between the parties. It is important to emphasise that it is not only violence which creates such an imbalance. There is likely to be some inequality of power between any two parties who come to mediation. Sources of interpersonal power available to any individual in mediation have been usefully analysed by Mayer.[10] Applying Mayer's analysis to family disputes, a party in mediation may be empowered, for example, by having access to expert advice, such as legal or financial advice. Power may accrue from greater economic security such as the ability to maintain an acceptable standard of living without resolving those issues of family finances which may be at stake in the mediation. Power may exist simply in greater self assurance, the conviction that one is in the right, that one will be heard and believed. Power may also consist of what Mayer calls "sanction power", the ability to inflict harm upon the other party. This may involve depriving them of access to needed resources, harassing them, or inflicting physical or emotional violence. In Australian society sources of power are unevenly allocated. In relationships between men and women power is usually disproportionately allocated in favour of men.[11] The use of violence—the exercise of sanction power—is also usually exercised by men and produces an extreme imbalance of power.

Mayer's analysis of sources of power is extremely useful, especially in elaborating and calling attention to those sources of interpersonal power which are perhaps less readily apparent or measurable. Elements of personal power such as confidence and self esteem may be especially important when an individual is engaged in bargaining for their needs and interests. However people do not simply come to mediation as independent units, the bearers of more or less of any of the sources of power. They come to mediation (perhaps most particularly to family mediation) in the context of a relationship which has its own history, habits and patterns, including patterns of the exercise of power and control. Violence against women is characterised by determined measures by the perpetrator to control the actions of the target. This control is exerted in many ways. It is not confined to physical brutality. It includes emotional abuse, sexual abuse, forced social isolation and economic deprivation.[12] A relationship where there has been violence is very far from a relationship of equals. It is a relationship where the perpetrator has used violence to ensure compliance by the target of his violence. This relationship, with its habits of coercion and compliance, is brought to mediation.

Mediation requires the parties to have the capacity to negotiate with each other.[13] There must be at least some capacity for consensual decision making; a willingness to be honest; a desire to settle the dispute; some capacity to compromise. These types of behaviours are very unlikely to be within the repertoire of behaviours of perpetrators of violence, at least not in relation to the targets of their violence.[14] The relationship between perpetrator and target is not characterised by consensuality, honesty, mutuality and compromise. It is characterised by coercion by the perpetrator and, almost certainly, by compliance to avoid violence by the target.[15] This is not to say that all relationships where there has been violence are identical. There are differences in the degree to which the perpetrator has been and is able to exert control. There will be differences in the resources available to the target of violence and thus the extent to which she has had to comply with the controlling behaviour of the perpetrator. Nevertheless the imbalance of power and the dynamic of control in the relationship mean that the target of violence does not have the capacity to negotiate freely and fairly.

It is one of the characteristics of men who are violent towards their partners that their violent attempts at control escalate at the time of separation.[16] It is often soon after separation has occurred that mediation to determine issues of custody, access and support takes place. Mediation may thus take place at a time of particularly aggressive efforts by the perpetrator to control the target of his violence, a time when the perpetrator is particularly likely to exercise his "sanction power".

Mediation places severe burdens on a woman who has been the target of violence. It may require her to negotiate face to face with the perpetrator, and this in itself may put her in fear and in danger.[17] It is the practice of some mediators to keep the parties separate when there has been violence and to mediate by a process of shuttle negotiation between them. Whatever physical arrangement is adopted, mediation still requires a woman who is the target of violence to assert, and negotiate for, her own needs and interests.[18] This may be precisely what has resulted in her being beaten in the past. Mediation requires her to negotiate effectively on her own behalf when she is likely to have had to concede or adapt her needs in an attempt to avoid violence in the past. There must be a strong likelihood that she will negotiate for what she thinks she can get, rather than for what she is entitled to or what is just and equitable.[19] The perpetrator may determine the outcome of mediation through violence or threats. Mediation may also place a woman who is the target of violence in danger: by providing an opportunity for contact the mediation may also provide the opportunity for violence.

However, the parties do not negotiate unassisted in mediation. They negotiate with the assistance of the mediator who controls the procedure of the mediation. The question which must be addressed, therefore, is whether or not mediators can balance power in mediation so as to create the possibility of a fair outcome. In particular it is necessary to question whether mediators can address severe power imbalances such as those created by violence.

The role of the mediator: Neutrality and power

Before the mediation itself commences measures may be taken to balance power between the parties. Intake may provide the opportunity for the parties to be referred to legal or other advice. The effectiveness of intake in providing needed support and referrals will, however, depend on the resources of the mediation scheme and the availability of legal and other advice for those who cannot afford to pay for it. During the mediation itself the mediator should strive to be as neutral as possible. The mediator's role is confined to control of procedure and, in theory, does not extend to input into the content of the dispute or the agreement. Mediators should not make decisions for the parties, persuade them in any particular direction or judge whether their agreements are fair or equitable. However, in practice it would appear that there is some variation in the extent to which mediators will stray beyond procedural interventions.[20]

Procedural control gives the mediator some ability to balance power between the parties. For instance, at the beginning of the mediation the mediator will specify the ground rules for the mediation and ask the parties to agree to them. These rules can include prohibitions on verbal abuse, undertakings to listen to the other party, promises of confidentiality. The mediator will enforce the ground rules during the mediation, for example by insisting that both parties are allowed to put their views without interruption, or by enforcing equal participation. Private caucus may provide the opportunity for the mediator to discuss the provision of support for a weaker party, such as legal or financial advice. Terminating the mediation where there are strong inequalities between the parties which cannot be addressed, or where one party is not competent to mediate is also an option within the control of the mediator.[21]

There are those who argue that mediators can balance power in the mediation of disputes where there has been violence by procedural interventions such as insisting that each party is given equal time to speak, insisting on respectful behaviour in the mediation, making meaningful and supportive referrals.[22] Other mediators acknowledge the powerful dynamic of control by the perpetrator but assert that the mediator can often address the perpetrator's attempts to control the mediation and assist the parties to an acceptable negotiated agreement.[23] However, whilst striving to address power imbalances the mediator should remain neutral. There is a limit to the procedural support that a mediator can offer a woman who has been the target of violence without sacrificing neutrality and creating at least the appearance of being partisan. If the mediator does provide support to a disempowered woman in mediation and is perceived by the perpetrator to be other than impartial it is possible that the perpetrator may either terminate the mediation or refuse to comply with any agreement reached. On the other hand, if the mediators' procedural interventions are confined to treating the parties equally, then it must be remembered that the consequence of treating unequal parties equally is inequality. Even if it is accepted, for the purposes of argument, that the mediator can create an island of procedural equality in a grossly unequal relationship, it must be doubted whether this can alter entrenched patterns of relating sufficient to create the possibility of equality in the substance of the negotiation. It is doubtful if substantive justice will be done in any resulting agreement or that any just agreement, achieved in the context of a relationship marked by injustice and coercion, will last long beyond the mediation session.

What mediators perceive to be an equal hearing is inevitably affected by their values. We know, for instance, that the way we judge equal participation is strongly affected by gender;[24] that our reactions to the expression of emotions such as anger or assertiveness differs according to whether it is expressed by a man or a woman.[25] Mediators strive for neutrality, but it is impossible for any interaction to be entirely value free. It is perhaps not surprising that there is already considerable evidence that mediators do have some impact on the content and outcome of disputes.[26] Research in the United Kingdom, for instance, has shown that mediators ignore some issues raised by the parties but pursue others so that the parties are steered in directions favoured by the mediator.[27] Participants in mediation have alleged that mediators put pressure on them to make all of the compromises in the face of intransigence by the other party.[28]

The values held by mediators about violence must affect the way in which they behave in mediation as well as their policies and protocols.

Strong concerns have been raised in the United States about mediators who fail to protect the interests and safety of women who are the target of violence.[29] It is necessary to be careful in applying conclusions from the United States to Australian conditions. Some of the critiques from the United States, for instance, have been developed in relation to court connected compulsory mediation. However, many mediation schemes in Australia are court connected or have close links with the formal justice system. Whilst compulsion to mediate may be rare in Australia, a "choice" to mediate may be profoundly affected by referral from a person in a position of power or influence, or by the fact that mediation is a condition of legal aid. We should not reject all American critiques, but should apply them selectively. There is presently very little Australian research on mediation. It would facilitate the development of policy, as well as the protection of those affected by violence, if there were Australian research on mediator practice in relation to violence as well as explanations from mediators about their understanding of violence and the impact of this understanding on their practice.

Why are disputes involving violence being mediated?

The weight of the arguments canvassed above is clearly in favour of the exclusion of disputes involving violence against women from mediation. Nevertheless many such disputes continue to be dealt with in mediation. The forces which will propel them into mediation are powerful ones, and to resist them is to swim against the tide. If there is to be any realistic possibility of effectively excluding disputes involving violence against women from mediation it is necessary to understand the nature of the forces which will operate to direct them there. Disputes where there has been violence will go to mediation because of the rapidly increasing popularity and availability of mediation; because of the high level of violence against women; because it is the policy of many mediators to accept such disputes; and because mediation uses and supports an idealised notion of the family which does not easily incorporate the notion of the family as the locus of violence.

Increasing availability of family mediation

Mediation as a method of resolving family disputes acquires more supporters daily. It has found favour with governments and court administrators. There is strong pressure to save money on the formal justice system, and mediation appears to be both a promising and caring way to achieve this. Court connected mediation schemes are increasing; referrals from the formal justice system to mediation are developing; community and neighbourhood schemes which handle family disputes are growing; private practitioners of mediation are increasing in number.[30] Developments in this area are moving so rapidly that it is not possible to provide an overview which is up to date.[31]

The Family Court of Australia has, since its inception, emphasised alternatives to litigation in the resolution of family disputes. Order 24 Conferences, where the parties negotiate with the assistance of a Registrar, are used primarily for property matters.[32] Conciliation counselling is available for a wide range of disputes. Its most frequent use is for disputes concerning children.[33] The parties may be compelled to attend conciliation counselling in relation to certain disputes concerning children.[34] Conciliation counselling is not mediation, although it has some similarities.[35] The Family Court set up a pilot mediation project in three Registries in 1992. Amendments to the *Family Law Act* 1975 (Cth) provide for voluntary and court ordered mediation.[36] Following the pilot scheme mediation has been extended to the Sydney Registry. Further extension has been recommended and appears to be dependent on the availability of funding.[37] The differences between the various dispute resolution mechanisms used by the Family Court are not always easy to differentiate in practise.[38]

Specialist family mediation schemes have proliferated throughout Australia. Some, such as the Noble Park Centre have been in operation for many years.[39] Organisations such as the Marriage Guidance Counsels in all States provide mediation of family disputes and receive some federal funding for their work.[40] Church and charitable organisations also provide mediation services. In New South Wales for instance, Unifam, the marriage and counselling service of the Uniting Church in Australia, operates Family Mediation Centres and provides a service in fifteen different centres.[41] Specialist schemes to deal with parent/adolescent conflicts are also being established, sometimes in conjunction with existing counselling services.

In addition to specialist family mediation schemes, generalist mediation providers do a great deal of family work. The *Annual Report* of the New South Wales Community Justice Centres for 1990-91, for instance, shows that the Centres dealt with 2,128 disputes which they characterised as family disputes. These disputes included disputes about residence in the family home, division of property and custody and access.

Some private practitioners specialising in family law have trained as mediators and use mediation as part of their family law practice.[42] As court connected mediation schemes proliferate the legal profession will perforce acquire greater contact with mediation. Courses in dispute resolution are increasingly being offered as part of law degrees.[43] It is likely that it will become a more significant part of legal practice.

In addition to the burgeoning in the availability of mediation schemes, disputes are increasingly likely to be referred compulsorily to mediation. Even if mediation is not mandated it may be very difficult for individuals to refuse. In New South Wales, where there is an application for legal aid in family matters the Legal Aid Commission refers the matter to mediation.[44] In addition the Commission has introduced a pilot scheme of mediation based "conferencing" for family matters.[45] A scheme for referral of applicants for legal aid in family matters to mediation operates in Victoria.[46] It may be difficult for applicants to refuse mediation if it is offered as a condition of receiving legal aid, or if they are strongly encouraged to use mediation.[47] Where referral is made by anyone in a position of power or authority in relation to the disputant, such as a legal aid provider, a magistrate, or a lawyer, it may be difficult for the parties to decline.

The incidence of violence

The incidence of violence against women in the family is high, and it is especially high in the divorcing population. If a substantial percentage of family disputes are referred to mediation, many disputes involving violence will inevitably be referred to mediation.

Available statistical estimates of the incidence of violence in the general population are problematic as a measure of the incidence of violence in Australia for a number of reasons. There is no Australian study of the general incidence of violence. Incidence studies which are sometimes cited originate from other countries such as the United Kingdom[48] and the United States[49]. It is necessary to be cautious in assuming their applicability in Australia. Incidence studies also have problems of inconsistencies caused by the methods of research and the variations in the definitions of what constitutes violence used by different studies. Measuring the incidence of violence is also extremely difficult because of the many disincentives to reporting violence.[50]

However the available data clearly indicates that the incidence of violence is high, however measured, and the problem one of great seriousness. Its seriousness is confirmed by research on homicide: 43 per cent of all homicides in New South Wales between 1968-1986 were committed within the family. Approximately one quarter of all homicides were spouse killings. Men were responsible for three times as many spouse killings as were women.[51] Those homicides where women killed men were very likely to be related to violence by the man against the woman.[52] We know that violence in the home consumes more police time than any other call on them except traffic[53] and, further, that most incidents of violence are not reported to the police.[54]

Refuge studies provide further data. A study of the 40 refuges operating in New South Wales in 1984-5 showed 5,605 women and 6,949 children accommodated that year. A further 23,000 had been turned away because of overcrowding.[55]

In a recent telephone survey one in five Australians admitted that they believe violence by a man against his female partner to be acceptable, and one in twenty thought that more extreme forms of violence such as kicking, beating and threatening to or using a weapon can be justified against either a wife or a child. Nearly half of the population knew either a victim or a perpetrator. A large proportion of the population thought that violence was a private matter for families and would ignore it if they found out about it.[56]

However mediators of family disputes are often not dealing with a simple cross section of the Australian population. Frequently those people who use family mediation will be recently separated and seeking a resolution to disputes associated with the end of the relationship. The incidence of violence in the divorcing population is much higher than in the general population. In Australia nearly half of the women who were killed by their spouses were either separated or in the process of separating at the time they were killed.[57] Estimates of violence in the divorcing population in the United States are as high as 36-60 per cent.[58] Mahoney in the United States has suggested renaming domestic violence "separation assault" because of the escalation of violence at the time of the decision to separate and during the period of separation itself.[59] The results of research coincide with anecdotal evidence from conversations with family mediators, who report that there has been violence in a high percentage of the disputes they mediate.

Why do the perpetrators and targets of violence go to mediation?

If an increasing number of disputes are being referred to mediation and the incidence of violence is high, many perpetrators and targets of violence will be amongst those referred to mediation. One pertinent question is why they consent to go to mediation. If mediation is so problematic for family disputes where violence has been perpetrated it is necessary to explain why violent men and (perhaps most pertinently) women who are the target of violence will agree to go to mediation.

The perpetrators and targets of mediation will be attracted to mediation for many of the same reasons as anyone else. There is no Australian research which gives a clear picture of the reasons why people go to mediation. However, mediation is attractive for a number of reasons.[60] If it is successful it will almost certainly be quicker and less expensive than more formal alternatives. If the expense of lawyer/lawyer negotiations is mounting, legal aid is unavailable, or litigation is threatened, cost will be a powerful incentive to try mediation. The promise of a speedy resolution to an emotionally stressful dispute is also likely to be important. The possibility of greater party control and a consensual outcome is no doubt also very appealing. A sample of couples using the Marriage Guidance Council's Couples Mediation service in New South Wales appreciated the opportunity to have "a forum and a framework" to discuss matters in dispute and reach agreement.[61] Those people who fear the intrusion of the welfare services into their lives may also be strongly motivated to avoid court proceedings.[62] However, at this stage in the establishment of mediation as a dispute resolution option, the reason most people go to mediation is not because they are aware of a range of dispute resolution options and make a free and informed choice to use mediation. Most people are referred to mediation by someone they have approached for advice or assistance. Often the person who makes the referral is in a position of authority, trust, or influence in relation to them.[63]

In addition to the reasons which might propel anyone into mediation, why would the perpetrators of violence go to mediation? Given the paucity of information which would answer this question directly it is necessary to extrapolate from what we know of perpetrators and what we know of mediation. If perpetrators were making a free and informed choice of a dispute resolution mechanism, mediation is likely to be a very appealing procedure. It involves negotiated decision making, rather than the imposition of enforceable decisions by a third party. To a perpetrator used to getting his own way by violence, mediation may appear to offer a significantly better opportunity for control of the target of his violence.[64] In court the content of what is said is governed, restricted and tested by rules of procedure and evidence. In mediation content and outcome are negotiated by the parties. The target of violence may have legal representation or other support in court. She is not likely to be allowed representation in mediation. Protective orders are available from courts. If the parties do not go to court but seek a settlement negotiated through lawyers, the lawyer should be a buffer between the target and the perpetrator's violence and attempts at control. Her decisions will be informed by legal advice about available protections and just and equitable outcomes.

Logically, therefore, mediation should be much more attractive to perpetrators. It places fewer barriers between the perpetrator and the target of his violence. It offers opportunities for continued contact with the target of his violence where she may be unprotected and where violence and coercion can continue. The perpetrator who understands the nature of mediation will know that his partner is unlikely to be represented, that no-one will cross examine him, that he has to negotiate with someone who, in the past, has done what he wanted or paid the price. Mediation may appear to offer an extended opportunity for him to continue his likely patterns of denying the abuse, or minimising it and projecting the blame for the matters in dispute onto his partner.[65]

It is perhaps fortunate that few perpetrators understand the nature of mediation and the opportunities it could offer them and even more fortunate that some mediators do understand these things. The importance of exclusionary rules and appropriate protocols for dealing with violent men is made manifest when considering the potential advantages of mediation for perpetrators.

The disadvantages of mediation for a woman who has been the target of violence have been canvassed above. Mediation requires her to negotiate for her own needs and interests with someone who is accustomed to getting what he wants by violence. Why then would a woman who has been the target of violence go to mediation? There are a number of reasons which, alone or in combination, will mean that a woman who has been the target of violence might choose or consent to mediation.

The first reason relates to poverty. Mediation is likely to be very appealing to those people who cannot afford to litigate, and women are disproportionately poor in our society - a phenomenon which has been referred to as the feminisation of poverty. In the post-separation period, the time of mediation, women are a great deal poorer than men.[66] Faced with a determined perpetrator offering mediation or an alternative of extended litigation, which will use her limited financial resources and which may include challenges to her custody of children, many women will feel constrained to try mediation. Women who have no financial resources may be especially vulnerable to referral to mediation since mediation may be a condition of access to needed services such as legal aid.

Mediation may be especially appealing to women who fear going to court because they fear the involvement of the welfare services in their lives. This may be the case, for example, for Aboriginal women. Welfare involvement is still disproportionately high in Aboriginal families and disputes with the state more frequent than individual disputes.[67] The dynamic of state racism is very important for Aboriginal women and may lead them to avoid the formal justice system when they have disputes about their children. State racism also affects the levels of protection from violence which Aboriginal women can expect from the formal justice system. Any tendency to recommend mediation for disputes involving Aboriginal women should take careful cognisance of issues such as whether the models of mediation are culturally appropriate and how issues of violence are to be dealt with. Judgments about appropriate mediation services for Aboriginal women must be made by Aboriginal women.

Women who have been the targets of violence may go to mediation because they are induced to go by threats or violence from their partner or his relatives or associates. Women who are the target of violence and those who work with them are familiar with the phenomenon of "car park violence", where the perpetrator issues instructions and writes the script for the mediation by threats or beatings in the car park. The instruction not to tell the mediator about the violence is, of course, part of the content of the violence. Even if there are no immediate threats or violence, a woman who has been the target of violence may have become accustomed to complying with the wishes of the perpetrator in the hope that this will prevent his violence. Agreement to use mediation at the perpetrator's behest may be a consequence of this pattern of compliance rather than a consequence of free and informed consent. A woman who is the target of violence may believe that, because mediation does not involve court proceedings and is less coercive, it will placate the perpetrator. Other women may go to mediation because they are desperate to separate themselves quickly from a violent man. They may be prepared to bargain away almost anything in the hope that this will bring an end to the violence and harassment.

Some women, perhaps especially those who have recently left a long-term relationship with a violent man, are likely to have had their confidence in their own judgment severely eroded. Knowing her own needs and interests and asserting them against the wishes of a violent partner may have been made impossible. Thus some women will be unable, at the time they need to resolve issues of property custody and access, to make an informed decision about whether they wish to be in mediation or using another dispute resolution mechanism. Separation from a violent man is highly likely to have the effect of exacerbating his violence. The stresses he is causing to the woman may well be enormous. Any woman who has just separated from her partner, whether violent or not, is in an extremely high-stress situation. If she has care of children who are also traumatised by violence or disturbed by the separation the stresses on her will be even greater. Making clear and informed decisions in a situation of high stress, and possibly immediately following traumatic incidents, is extremely difficult. The temptation to acquiesce with a course of action recommended by a respected adviser must be strong.

It is likely that the response of some mediators to these arguments will be that they have the qualifications, training and experience to detect any lack of capacity to mediate. They may also respond that they will exclude the dispute from mediation if they are told about these effects of violence and separation. However, the difficulty that mediators face in detecting a lack of capacity to mediate caused by violence is the silence which surrounds violence.

Women may go to mediation, even when they have strong doubts about it, because they do not want to admit the violence, either to themselves or to other people. The experience of telling other people about violence is often a destructive experience. Women who reveal violence to others are often not believed; are not taken seriously; are accused of causing the violence themselves by their actions or inadequacies; are told that it cannot be as bad as they allege; are encouraged to return to their husbands. After such experiences women become hesitant to speak of it again, may blame themselves or be ashamed. Many women have actively concealed the fact of violence from family, friends and others, during the course of the relationship.[68] They may continue to do so when they go to mediation. Some women may not count what has happened to them as violence. One mediator recounts the case of a woman whose husband forced her against her will to return to the matrimonial home every day at lunch time so he could have sex. She was surprised that the mediator regarded this as violence.[69] Other women may strongly resist seeing themselves as a "battered woman", a "victim".[70]

It is also very important to remember that the silence of individual women who are the target of violence occurs in the context of societal silence about, and denial of, violence.[71] Social attitudes about the private nature of this violence persist. There is also an astonishing acceptance amongst a substantial proportion of the population that violence against women in the home is acceptable.[72] A woman who wishes to speak out about the violence perpetrated against her must deal not only with her own denial, but with the denial and silence of the society in which she lives.

Mediator policies on violence

Given the high incidence of violence and the dangers of mediating disputes involving violence it might be expected that mediators would have strong reservations about mediating these family disputes and highly developed protocols to exclude them. Indeed some mediators do have exclusionary policies. However reservations about the mediation of these disputes have so far been asserted most strongly by feminists and those working with women who are the target of violence.[73] For instance, in 1991, the National Committee on Violence Against Women became concerned about the referral of disputes involving violence against women and commissioned a position paper on the issue.[74] The policy adopted by the National Committee is that disputes involving violence against women should not be in mediation. They should be excluded, so far as it is possible to do so, by rigorous intake procedures designed to identify and exclude any disputes where there is violence. Nevertheless the Committee recognised that, even with the most careful and rigorous exclusionary measures, it would not be possible to exclude effectively all disputes involving violence because of the extreme difficulty of reliable identification. Women who have been the target of violence have many reasons not to reveal the fact of violence. The reasons for this are considered below.

Because some disputes will inevitably go to mediation despite the best efforts of all concerned, the National Committee recommended that mediators should have training to deal with them in a way which protects women and the children in their care. The Committee also developed *Guidelines for the Mediation of Cases Involving Violence Against Women*[75] and an explanatory booklet *Women and Mediation*.[76]

The Position Paper and Guidelines have been used and adapted by some mediation schemes.[77] Other mediators, whilst not necessarily adopting the position of the National Committee, nevertheless would exclude disputes involving violence.[78] However, some long-standing mediation schemes have protocols which permit the mediation of disputes involving violence. Community Justice Centres (CJCs) in New South Wales, for instance, have such a policy which has been adopted by many other neighbourhood mediation schemes in Australia.[79] CJC Guidelines provide that mediation should not be an alternative to a court protection order, nor should Community Justice Centres make representations for the withdrawal of any police or court action. CJCs will not be a party to negotiation on continuing violence, nor will they mediate on the "victim" returning to violent circumstances. However they will accept cases where there has been violence for mediation. They believe that violence can be separated from issues such as custody and access which remain "mediable issues". Mediators are instructed by CJC Guidelines to address issues of violence openly and in detail and are warned against accepting promises that the perpetrator will not do it again. Mediators are instructed to look for clear indications that the violent "disputant" will carry out promises and be capable of a change of behaviour.

One of the reasons for the divergences of opinion and uneven development of policy may be that this is a time of policy development. Family mediation is of relatively recent provenance in Australia. Inevitably an understanding of the best methods of practice must develop over time. However this cannot be a sufficient explanation. It does not account for the resistance of some mediators to a policy which would exclude disputes involving violence. Nor does it explain why so much of the opposition to the mediation of disputes involving violence has been voiced by those outside the mediation movement. Nor does it account for the fact that the same debates and dynamics in policy development have been identified in other jurisdictions where the resurgence of interest in family mediation occurred rather earlier.[80]

It could be argued that the reluctance of some mediators to exclude cases involving violence, or to institute rigorous procedures to identify such cases, stems from the fact that effective exclusion would mean that mediators would lose a great number of clients. Given the high incidence of violence in the general population, especially in the separating and divorcing population, effective exclusion would mean that a great many cases would be turned away. Mediation is in a development stage and must prove its utility and its success to clients and to funding bodies. It is also true that many people have made great personal commitments to family mediation. They have given their time, money and work, as well as directing their careers, to the development of family mediation. They desire the establishment and acceptance of mediation and the recognition of their skills and professionalism.

However it would be excessively cynical to believe that loss of business and personal ambition would be significant factors explaining the resistance of some mediators to turn violent disputes away. Many mediators give substantial amounts of time to mediation, selflessly and for almost no remuneration. They pay for training and continuing education from their own pockets. They are strongly committed to assisting people to find an inexpensive and consensual way to resolve their disputes; to empowering ordinary people; to resolving family disputes with the minimum of bitterness and distress; to supporting the interests of the children of divorce. Ironically, however, it may be exactly these admirable qualities and commitments which make some mediators reluctant to deal effectively with issues of violence in the family.

The promise of family mediation—rescuing the intact family

The group of people who support family mediation have been described as strange bedfellows. They come from different disciplines and professions and have widely varying interests and identifications. The observation made by Silbey and Sarat about the ADR movement in the United States holds true in Australia;

> *Professional and institutional support for ADR comes from all positions along the political spectrum; it has produced, nonetheless, a recognisable, if not fully coherent political movement.* [81]

One of the characteristics of this movement has been almost unquestioned support for the mediation of family disputes. Even those who would be selective about which commercial disputes should be referred to mediation, support family mediation unreservedly.[82] Indeed the support for family mediation is not only unreserved, it is sometimes passionate.[83]

Undoubtedly mediation is an excellent dispute resolution mechanism for some family disputes. However, there are a considerable number of family disputes where there is violence, a marked imbalance of power, or other reasons why the parties lack the capacity to mediate. Logically mediation should be presented as a useful method of resolving only a proportion of family disputes. On the contrary, however, family mediation is greeted with almost unreserved and uncritical enthusiasm.

One important reason why family mediation has such a powerful, indeed emotional, appeal is because mediation is a process which appears to rescue the values of the intact family at the point when the family is, in fact, disintegrating. It can be represented as having this capacity for a number of reasons. First, mediation itself embodies the qualities of the private. It is intimate, confidential, consensual, caring; it is credited with preserving relationships; it is described as making continued parenting possible. It has the capacity to make the family look like the ideal image of the family,[84] and to do so at the very point at which this image is most threatened.

The claimed utility of mediation for family disputes because of its capacity to preserve the fantasy of an ideal intact family is pervasive in the literature on family mediation. It is exemplified by this passage from a leading Australian family law textbook.

> It is implicit in any adversary court proceedings that they will be conducted by adversaries, in other words, by people who are opposed or hostile towards one another. That again means that the opposing sides approach one another in a spirit of opposition, in which each wants to gain the upper hand over the other. While the court system is designed to ensure that the contest is conducted fairly, the process is not designed to see the parties, at the conclusion of the case, leave the court arm in arm and the best of friends.
>
> This does not perhaps matter very much in commercial or ordinary civil litigation, as it does in running down or industrial accidents. In the case of family disputes, on the other hand, where the parties usually remain in some kind of family relationship to one another, particularly as regards their children, a great deal of damage can result. Whole families may be polarised.[85]

It is interesting to examine this (perhaps somewhat polemical) statement carefully. In fact divorce precisely concerns the "polarisation" of the "whole family" in that it involves the consequences of the termination of an ideal nuclear family. Separation and divorce are events almost inevitably attended by conflict and distress. For some people mediation will provide a useful, productive and appropriate way to resolve the disputes attendant on separation and divorce. However it is highly unlikely to allow the parties to avoid the rupture or distancing of relationships which is the usual consequence of divorce, or to ensure that the divorcing parties will leave "… arm in arm and the best of friends".

The realities of separation and divorce are distressing whatever dispute resolution method is used. It must be desirable for society to continue to seek better ways of resolving the disputes attendant on divorce. It is perhaps especially important to seek ways to ameliorate distress to the children of divorce, whatever dispute resolution mechanism is used. However, the source of the distress is the interpersonal issues between the parties, the conflict and pain attendant upon loss and disrupted relationships. Whilst the parties may be assisted by a method of resolving disputes which is appropriate to their needs, dispute resolution mechanisms cannot remove the pain or recreate the intact family. Mediation does appear, however, to be able to conjure comforting images of the continuation of the intact family, even at the point of divorce. It is perhaps this promise of rescuing the family at the point at which it is most threatened which accounts for the extraordinarily fulsome nature of some of the praise heaped on mediation. As one mediator enthused "There seems to be an undeniable power, if not magic, to mediation. It almost seems heaven sent." [86]

The assertion that family mediation has the role of preserving an ideal image of the family is supported by the way in which the literature on family mediation uses the public/private dichotomy to argue for the location of family disputes in mediation. The formal justice system is invariably described by the proponents of family mediation as having all the qualities of the public - it is hard, it is adversarial, dispassionate, coercive, formal and does not deal well with the needs of children.[87] Mediation is soft, private, consensual, deals well with emotions, is therapeutic, and is protective of the needs of children. Family disputes therefore, of course, belong in the private domain of mediation. Even the most measured advocates of family mediation rely upon such dichotomous characterisations of litigation and mediation.

> For (family) lawyers, mediation is an alternative to an agreement negotiated with the opposition, or decided in litigation. It can focus on what is really at issue between the parties by using a neutral, exploratory but structured approach, worked out by collaboration rather than hard bargaining.
>
> Mediation ... has provided the means of recognising the joint social and legal aspects of divorce, very particularly with regard to establishing and ensuring the needs of children.[88]

The promise of mediation to preserve the illusion of an intact and idealised family is most evident in the assertions about its capacities in relation to children. One element of this has been the commitment of many family mediators to shared parenting.[89] The ideological commitment of family mediators to shared parenting has been clearly identified and analysed by Fineman in the United States[90] and also identified in the United Kingdom by Davis.[91] It is in fact highly questionable that the pursuit of shared parenting in mediation serves the interests of children unless both parents actively pursue that arrangement.[92] It is also questionable whether children are any better represented in mediation than they are in adjudication. We know very little about mediator practice in Australia with respect to involving children in mediation.[93]

Mediation is asserted to be of particular importance in family disputes because it is supposed to have a therapeutic effect, absent from the formal justice system, which acts to preserve the family unit for the children. This argument is evident in the following quotation from Canadian mediators:

> As mediation continues to develop, integrative work is being done that is blending family therapy objectives with family mediation. The awareness that there really is no such thing as "a single parent family", in the sense that both parents from broken marriages continue to function in important ways in the lives of their children, has resulted in continued innovative approaches....[94]

The assertion that there is no such thing as a single parent family is necessarily a statement of what is desirable rather than what is real. There are in fact a significant number of single parent families following divorce. In a significant proportion of those families both parents do not continue to function in important ways for their children and the children have little or no contact with one of their parents, usually their father.[95] For some children this is regrettable and is the source of unhappiness.[96] It must be desirable to seek ways in which this unhappiness can be ameliorated. One element of this project may be to find more creative ways in which the needs and wishes of children can be heard in mediation and litigation.[97] However it is questionable whether mediation, or any other dispute resolution mechanism, can change parenting patterns after divorce at either an individual or a social level.

Mediation assists people who are trying to resolve disputes attendant on divorce or separation. It does not set out to achieve personal change or improve the relationships of the parties to one another or to their children. Whilst some mediation schemes blend mediation with family therapy[98] these are exceptional schemes. Most mediation schemes do not offer family therapy, or any other sort of therapy. Despite some early optimism the evidence that mediation can effect personal change or the improvement of relationships is very slim. Kelly reports from a longitudinal survey comparing people using mediation with those using litigation. Mediation appears to have a greater capacity to reduce conflict for some divorcing couples. However, this effect is short-term and disappears between one to two years after divorce. Kelly concludes that

> The research demonstrates that some of the claims made on behalf of media-
> tion have been overly enthusiastic, particularly with regard to the power of
> mediation to effect more substantial change in the psychological adjustment
> or personality attributes of the participants. Given the brief, task-oriented,
> problem solving and agreement-focused nature of the divorce mediation
> process, it is clear that too much power to effect change was imputed to, or
> hypothesised for, this alternative method for resolving disputes.[99]

Because mediation is so closely identified with the values of the private, any challenge to the view of the intact family as the haven in a heartless world threatens the existence of mediation. Consequently mediators are resistant to adopting any analysis which seeks to make the issue of power relationships in the family central. In particular an analysis which seeks to deal seriously with the issue of violence against women and abuse of children and consider their implications for mediation not only challenges the propriety of a high percent-age of disputes going to mediation, but challenges the ideological base of medi-ation.

Feminist commentators insist on pointing out that for a significant number of women and children, far from being a site of caring and nurturing, the fam-ily is a place of violence and exploitation. They also insist that such violence does not only occur in a few pathological families, but that it is common. These are not messages to which mediators are immediately receptive, and it is not surprising that this is so. If they are to maintain the image of the family with which mediation is identified mediators must deny, or at least de-emphasise, the exploitation which occurs in the family. To acknowledge the presence, level and severity of violence in the family does not simply threaten potential client numbers. The appeal and future expansion of mediation is justified by arguments and rhetoric which associate mediation with the preservation of the idealised intact nuclear family. Mediation is to be supported because of its supposed capacity to preserve that family, at least for the children of divorce. To challenge this view of the family may be to challenge the foundations upon which the justifications for family mediation are built.

Conclusion

Disputes involving violence against women are likely to continue to go to mediation for a number of reasons. The current enthusiasm for mediation is fuelled by its promise to governments that it can deliver inexpensive dispute resolution. The level of violence against women, especially in the divorcing population, is high. The social denial of violence, as well as the nature of violence itself, make it difficult for women who are the target of violence to reveal it or to reject mediation. Mediators will find it very difficult to effectively exclude disputes involving violence. This is not so much because they are ambitious to colonise the area of family dispute resolution as it is because their model of the family makes them resistant to admit the violence which is found there.

The view of the family which is adopted by mediators is a strongly appealing view. It excludes from the picture a great deal which is bloody and frightening and exploitative. However, unless that part of the picture is included and brought into sharp focus there can be no change. Women, and the children they care for, will continue to be endangered and exploited. Mediators might, with perfect justification, claim that an idealised view of the family is not confined to mediators. However the pervasiveness of the problem does not exempt them, or anyone else, from efforts to change their practice and develop their policy and theory.

Notes

1 It is recognised that there are some instances where men are the target of violence in the home and also that there is sometimes violence between gay men and between lesbians. Such violence is not the focus of this chapter.

2 For definitions of mediation see Astor, H and Chinkin, C, *Dispute Resolution in Australia* (1992); Folberg, J and Taylor, A, *Mediation: A Comprehensive Guide to Resolving Conflict* (1984); Moore, C, *The Mediation Process: Practical Strategies for Resolving Conflict* (1987).

3   See Astor and Chinkin, id at 96-112; Gribben, S, "Mediation of Family Disputes" (1992) 6 *Aust J Family Law* 126.

4   Chisholm, R, "Mediation Services for the Family Court: Something New Under the Sun" *(1991) 5 Aust J Family Law* 277 at 278-9.

5   Gribben, above n3 at 129.

6   Moore, above n2 at Chapters 13 and 15.

7   Kressel, K, "Clinical Implications of Existing Research on Divorce Mediation" (1987) 15 *Am J Family Therapy* 69 at 72.

8   See Moore, above n2 at 263-71.

9   For a more detailed account of these issues see Astor, H, "Violence and Family Mediation Policy" (1994) *Aust J Family Law* (forthcoming).

10 Mayer, B, "The Dynamics of Power in Mediation and Negotiation" (1987) 16 *Mediation Q*75.

11 Astor, H, "Feminist Issues in ADR", (1991) 65 *Law Inst J* 69.

12 For a more extended discussion of the nature of violence see National Committee on Violence Against Women, *Position Paper*, May 1991: Astor, H, *Position Paper on Mediation*, National Committee on Violence Against Women, December 1991, especially at 12-17.

13 Gribben, above n3.

14 National Committee on Violence Against Women, above n12; Dobash, R E and Dobash, R P, *Women, Violence and Social Change* (1992).

15 For an account of the attempts at appeasement by women who are the target of violence, see McGregor, H and Hopkins, A, *Working For Change: The Movement Against Domestic Violence* (1991) at 118-21. Perpetrator behaviours of control of the target, denial of violence and blaming the target are considered in Ptacek J, "Why Do Men Batter their Wives" in Yllo, K and Bograd, M (eds), *Feminist Perspectives on Wife Abuse* (1988) 133 at 139; see also Queensland Domestic Violence Task Force, *Beyond These Walls: Report of the Queensland Domestic Violence Task Force* (1988); Gondolf, E, *Men Who Batter: An Integrated Approach for Stopping Wife Abuse* (1985).

16 Mahoney, M, "Legal Images of Battered Women: Redefining the Issue of Separation" (1991) 90 *Mich L R* 1.

17 Gagnon, A, "Ending Mandatory Divorce Mediation for Battered Women" (1992) 15 *Harv Women's L J* 272.

18 Hart, B J, "Gentle Jeopardy: The Further Endangerment of Battered Women and Children in Custody Mediation" (1990) 7 *Mediation Q* 317.

19 Gagnon, above n19; Weitzman, L J, *The Divorce Revolution: The Unexpected Social and Economic Consequences for Women and Children in America* (1985) especially at 311.

20 Moore, above n2 at 39-43.

21 Marthaler, D, "Successful Mediation with Abusive Couples" (1989) 23 *Mediation Q* 53 at 65.

22 Davis, A and Salem, R, "Dealing With Power Imbalances in the Mediation of Interpersonal Disputes" (1984) 6 *Mediation Q* 17.

23 Marthaler, above n21.

24 Spender D, *Invisible Women: The Schooling Scandal* (1982) especially at 54-7.

25 Grillo T, "The Mediation Alternative: Process Dangers for Women" (1991) 100 *Yale L J* 1545 at 1574-81.

26 Ray, M, *Divorce Settlements: Comparing the Outcomes of Three Different Dispute Resolution Mechanisms*, Unpublished Doctoral Dissertation, Cornell University, 1988; Fineman, M, "Dominant Discourse, Professional Language, and Legal Change in Child Custody Decisionmaking" (1988) 101 *Harv LR* 727; Davis, G, *Partisans and Mediators* (1988).

27 Greatbatch, D and Dingwall, R, "Selective Facilitation: Some Observations on a Strategy Used by Divorce Mediators" (1989) 23 *Law and Soc Review* 613.

28 Davis, above n26.

29 Germane, C, Johnson, M and Lemon, N, "Mandatory Custody Mediation and Joint Custody Orders in California: The Danger for Victims of Domestic Violence" (1985) 1 *Berkeley Women's LJ* 175; Lerman, L, "Mediation of Wife Abuse Cases: the Adverse Impact of Informal Dispute Settlement on Women" (1984) 7 *Harv Women's LJ* 57; Stallone, D, "Decriminalisation of Violence in the Home: Mediation in Wife Battering Cases" (1984) 2 *Law and Inequality* 493.

30 Family Law Council, *Family Mediation Report* (1992) at 13-17.

31 Id at 15-16.

32 *Family Law Act* 1975 (Cth) s79(9) and Family Law Rules O 24.

33 *Family Law Act* 1975 (Cth) s62.

34 *Family Law Act* 1975 (Cth) s64(1B-D).

35 It has been described as most like therapeutic family mediation; see Browne, C, "Dispute Resolution Services: Family Court of Australia" in Fisher, L (ed) *Dispute Resolution in the 90's,* Proceedings of the Conference of the Australian Dispute Resolution Association (1990) at 69.

36 *Family Law Act* 1975 (Cth) ss19A-M, O25A Family Law Rules; see also Chisholm, R, above n4.

37 Joint Select Committee on Certain Aspects of the Operation and Interpretation of the Family Law Act, *Report, The Family Law Act 1975: Aspects of its Operation and Interpretation* (1992).

38 Chisholm, above n4.

39 Donnelly, L, "Establishing an Alternative Dispute Resolution Centre with a Community Based Philosophy" in Mugford, J (ed), *Alternative Dispute Resolution* (1986) Seminar Proceedings No 15, Australian Institute of Criminology 251.

40   Gribben, above n3.

41   Stevenson, E, "The Use of Community Mediation in the Family Mediation Centre (NSW)" (1990) 1 *Aust Dispute Resolution J* 24.

42   Wade, J, "Lawyers and Mediators: Learning From and About Each Other" (1991) 2 *Aust Dispute Resolution J* 159-78; Coddington, B, "Mediation in Private Legal Practice" in Fisher, L (ed), *Dispute Resolution in the 90's: Proceedings of the Conference of the Australian Dispute Resolution Association*, 94.

43   Astor, H and Chinkin, C, "Dispute Resolution as Part of Legal Education" (1990) 1 *Aust Dispute Resolution J* 208.

44   Legal Aid Commission of New South Wales, Guidelines 4.19.

45   Letter from the Legal Aid Commission to the Chairperson, New South Wales Domestic Violence Advisory Council, August 1993.

46   Joint Select Committee on Certain Aspects of the Operation and Interpretation of the Family Law Act, above n37 at 73 para 4.26.

47   The operation of such schemes deserves to be further reported. Available information on their operation is confusing. For instance the Victorian scheme is described in the Joint Select Committee Report, ibid, as "mandatory for suitable parties" at para 4.26. However it is later reported that in the first six months of the operation of the scheme two hundred and seventy nine "offers of mediation" were made, with seventy nine taken up by the applicant but only forty accepted by the other party (at para 4.31).

48   Dobash, R and Dobash, R, *Violence Against Wives: A Case Against the Patriarchy* (1979).

49   Straus, M, Gelles, R and Steinmetz, S, *Behind Closed Doors: Violence and the American Family* (1980).

50   For further discussion of the incidence of violence see Stubbs, J and Powell, D, *Domestic Violence: Impact of Legal Reform in New South Wales* (1989).

51   Wallace, A, *Homicide: the Social Reality* (1986); Bonney, R, *Homicide II* (1988).

52   Ibid.

53   Avery, J, *Police—Force or Service?* (1981).

54   Stubbs and Powell, above n50 at 4, refer to studies in Australia which show reporting rates varying from 27 per cent to 47 per cent, and overseas studies showing reporting rates from 27 per cent to 2 per cent.

55   Noesjirwan, J, *Evaluation of Women's Refuge 1985: Ten Years On* (1985).

56   Public Policy Research Centre, *Community Attitudes Towards Domestic Violence in Australia* (1988) at 23.

57   Wallace, above n51.

58   Levinger, G, "Sources of Marital Dissatisfaction Amongst Applicants for Divorce" 26 *Am J Orthopsychiatry* 803, reprinted in Straus, M and Steinmetz, S, *Violence in the Family* (1974).

59   Mahoney, above n16.

60   For a general review of the advantages of mediation and comparisons between mediation and litigation see Astor and Chinkin, above n2 at 30-57.

61   Fisher, L and Blondel, M, *Couples Mediation: A Forum and a Framework* (1993).

62   Astor, H, "Mediation of Family Disputes in Australia", in Stark, B (ed), *Family Law and Gender Bias: Comparative Perspectives* (1992) 4 *Int'l Review of Comparative Public Policy* 107 .

63   Astor and Chinkin, above n2 at 47-9; Ingleby, R, *In the Ball Park: Alternative Dispute Resolution and the Courts* (1991).

64   The more skilled and informed the mediator concerning the dynamics of violence and the characteristics of perpetrators, the less likely the perpetrator is to be correct in his assessment that he can control the process of mediation; Marthaler, above n21.

65   On perpetrator behaviour see references above n15.

66   MacDonald, P (ed) *Settling Up: Property and Income Distribution on Divorce in Australia* (1986); Weitzman, L J, *The Divorce Revolution: The Unexpected Social and Economic Consequences for Women and Children in America* (1985).

67   Graycar, R and Morgan, J, *The Hidden Gender of Law* (1990) at 258-62.

68   Family Violence Professional Education Taskforce, *Family Violence: Everybody's Business, Somebody's Life* (1991) at 65-6.

69   Marthaler, above n21 at 58.

70   Mahoney, above n16.

71   Ibid.

72   Public Policy Research Centre, *Community Attitudes Towards Domestic Violence in Australia* (1988). One in five Australians think that physical violence by a man against his wife is acceptable in some circumstances.

73   See for example Astor, H, *Position Paper on Mediation*, above n12; Lerman , above n29; Sun, M and Woods, L, *A Mediator's Guide to Domestic Abuse* (1989).

74   Astor, above n12.

75   Astor, H, *Guidelines for Use if Mediating in Cases Involving Violence Against Women*, National Committee on Violence Against Women, 1992.

76   Astor, H, *Women and Mediation: Information About Mediation for Women* (1992).

77   For instance the Queensland Community Justice Project and the Australian Dispute Resolution Association.

78   Gribben, above n3.

79   Community Justice Centres, *Annual Report 1988-9* at 31-2.

80 For example in the United States see Lerman, above n29; Sun and Woods, above n73; Germane, C, Johnson, M and Lemon, N, above n29; Stallone, D, above n29: In Canada see Bailey, M, "Unpacking the 'Rational Alternative': A Critical Review of the Family Mediation Movement Claims" (1989) 8 *Canadian J Family Law* 61.

81 Silbey, S and Sarat, A, "Dispute Processing in Law and Legal Scholarship: From Institutional Critique to the Reconstruction of the Juridical Subject" (1989) 66 *Denver ULR* 437 at 445.

82 Pears, G, *Beyond Dispute: ADR in Australia* (1989) at 66, "Adversary law and its courts have limited ability to achieve equity in many cases of human dispute. The adversary system reinforces the emotional stress to which any dispute is likely to give rise. These two features are major motivators in the move towards alternative forms of dispute resolution. They have particular importance in those interpersonal disputes in which the emotions are most strongly involved and it should come as no surprise that the move towards ADR in the Western world generally has gone further for longer in the family field than in any other area."

83 See, for instance, Melamed, J, "Attorneys and Mediation: From Threat to Opportunity" (1989) 23 *Mediation* Q13 at 18: "The hostility that accompanies many interpersonal disputes can almost always be communicated and managed in mediation. The ability to compartmentalise hostility and move beyond anger to consider constructive alternatives for the future is part of the magic of the mediation process."

84 Olsen, F, "The Family and the Market: A Study of Ideology and Legal Reform" (1983) 96 *Harv LR* 1497 especially at 1450-2; Hilton, N Z, "Mediating Wife Assault: Battered Women and the `New Family'" (1991) 9 *Canadian J Family Law* 29.

85 Finlay, H and Bailey-Harris, R, *Family Law in Australia* (4th ed 1989) at 39.

86 Melamed, J, above n83 at 14. Although Melamed's article covers mediation in general it is clear, from the research he relies upon to support his claims for mediation, that his subject matter is predominantly family disputes.

87 Court proceedings have been described as " ... an unhealthy, warlike process that tends to damage a sense of community between people". Micka, C, "From Litigator to Mediator" (1989) 23 *Mediation Q* 85 at 88. A leading Canadian text on family mediation asserts that "There is a general consensus that adversarial proceedings in divorce are both traumatizing and alienating .... Forced to say and do things they may later regret, many emerge from the experience with an unsavoury taste in their mouth ...." Irving, H and Benjamin, M, *Family Mediation: Theory and Practice of Dispute Resolution* (1987) at 39.

88 Charlesworth, S, Turner,J and Foreman, L, *Lawyers, Social Workers and Families* (1990) at 222.

89 The term shared parenting is used to describe the arrangements sometimes referred to in the United States and elsewhere as joint custody.

90 Fineman, above n26.

91 Davis, above n26.

92 Wallerstein, J and Blakeslee, S, *Second Chances: Men, Women and Children a Decade After Divorce* (1989).

93 De Biasi, F, "Children's Rights and Children's Participation in Litigation and ADR", report of an address by Richard Chisholm to the Family Mediation Division of the Australian Dispute Resolution Association (1992) 6 *ADRA Newsletter* 8.

94 Landau, B, Bartoletti, M and Mesbur, R, *Family Mediation Handbook* (1987) at 183.

95 Gibson, J, *Non-custodial Fathers and Access Patterns*, Research Report No 10, Family Court of Australia, 1992.

96 See Gibson, ibid; McDonald, M, *Children's Perceptions of Access and their Adjustment in the Post-Separation Period*, Research Report No 9, Family Court of Australia, 1990.

97 De Biasi, above n93 describes the suggestions of Richard Chisholm; cf Maloney, L, "Beyond Custody and Access: Post-separation Parenting in the Nineties", (1993) 34 *Family Matters* 11 at 13-14.

98 Benjamin, M and Irving, H, "Towards a Feminist-Informed Model of Therapeutic Family Mediation" (1992) 10 *Mediation Q* 129.

99 Kelly, J, "Mediated and Adversarial Divorce Resolution Processes: A Comparison of Post Divorce Outcomes" (1991) 21 *Family Law* 382 at 387.

8

Battered Woman Syndrome: Developments in Canadian Law After R v Lavallee

Elizabeth Sheehy

Traumatic events call into question basic human relationships. They breach the attachments of family, love, and community. They shatter the construction of the self that is formed and sustained in relation to others. They undermine the victim's faith in a natural or divine order and cast the victim into a state of existential crisis.[1]

Introduction

The recognition of "Battered Woman Syndrome" (BWS) by the Supreme Court of Canada in *R v Lavallee*[2] has facilitated the mitigation of sentence for women who have survived violence and who have themselves been charged with the commission of particular criminal offences. While an unascertainable number of homicide prosecutions against battered women have been declined or derailed by virtue of *Lavallee,* it has not yet prompted either a wholesale review of the cases of women who are already serving sentences for their offences or a searching public inquiry into the nature and extent of male violence, the long-term, ripple effects of that violence in the lives of the children and adult women who survive it, and the appropriate response by the criminal justice system to the offences committed by those women.

In this chapter I begin by outlining the ways in which defence counsel in Canada have utilised *Lavallee*, both successfully and unsuccessfully, on behalf of their clients as evidenced in reported cases. I then turn to an examination of the cases of women whose actions and lives have yet to be understood in light of their experience of traumatic violence, and I then identify several directions in which feminists might lead change.

Case review

In 1990, the Supreme Court of Canada decided *Lavallee* and, for the first time, gave explicit recognition to the legal relevance of evidence of BWS to the defence of self-defence where a woman has killed her violent partner. The case was ground-breaking not only because it reversed precedents that had hereto-fore precluded such evidence and arguments,[3] but also because the majority opinion, written by a feminist judge, crafted a wide and flexible understanding of self-defence in the context of a battering relationship that left open doors already closed by some case law from the United States. In *Lavallee*, the Court upheld a trial judgment permitting a psychiatrist to testify both as to BWS gen-erally and as to his opinion that Ms Lavallee in fact suffered from the syn-drome. The trial judge had allowed the jury to use this testimony in their interpretation of the statutory defence of self-defence, specifically relating it to the issue of whether the accused reasonably apprehended "imminent death or grievous bodily harm" and whether she believed, on reasonable grounds, that she could not otherwise preserve herself from this anticipated harm.[4] The jury had returned a verdict of not guilty to the charge of second degree murder.

The particular ways in which *Lavallee* offers a broad defence to women are that: 1) the accused's situation did not meet the traditional paradigm of self-defence in that the deceased apparently threatened to get her "later", after their guests had gone home, and the accused fired the gun at the back of the deceased's head as he was leaving the bedroom; 2) the judgment clearly stated that women who are in violent situations are entitled to use self-defence when they have acted in anticipation of violence threatened in the future, that they need not wait to face the "uplifted knife" before taking action;[5] and 3) the woman need not fit some stereotype of passivity or "helplessness" to receive the benefit of BWS evidence, since the Court recognised that such a woman may have fought back or attempted to leave while still being victimised and desper-ate to save herself.[6]

In the period following *Lavallee*, 1990 to August 1993, I have been able to find only ten reported cases in which counsel has relied upon BWS. These num-bers do not include the cases where prosecutors have dropped charges because evidence suggesting self-defence has surfaced[7] or where the case was not reported in the legal reporting services.[8] In eight of the cases that I did find, the evidence was used in support of a plea for mitigation of sentence; in the ninth, the accused was acquitted of the charge on the basis that BWS affected her *mens rea*; and in the tenth case, the accused's defence of self-defence failed because the court held that she could have called for assistance in fending off a threatening advance rather than resort to self-help. I discuss these decisions in more detail, with emphasis first upon the positive, then the negative aspects of the cases.

A first positive development is that in the one case where the accused suc-cessfully used BWS as a defence rather than a mitigating factor, *R v Eagles*,[9] the evidence was not narrowly interpreted in the context of a specific pre-existing defence, but rather was used in the broadest manner possible to make out a "no *mens rea*" defence. Resort to this general defence means that the accused did not have to "fit" within the criteria of a specific defence, and that the case provides a flexible precedent for other accused women.

The charge in this case was that of knowingly uttering a threat to cause death or bodily harm, and the accused had made the threat by telephone to her ex-husband, after two prior calls in which she had suggested reconciliation or payment by him of money owed to her, and had been rebuffed by him. Lilles J accepted the evidence of the accused and her children as to a 25-year pattern of extreme physical and emotional abuse by the husband of the accused, and the evidence that the man continued to control the accused's life by denying her share of the marital assets after separation, verbally abusing her, and threatening to expose her as an alcoholic in the community if she fought him:

> The facts conjure up elements of reflex action, provocation and self-defence while not being clearly any of these three. Yet at the same time, it is with considerable certainty that I have concluded that there is a total absence of the kind of moral guilt which would justify a finding of criminal responsibility.[10]

A second expansion upon *Lavallee* is also evident in *Eagles*. The judge placed great emphasis on the BWS evidence in spite of the fact that the accused was no longer living in the same home as the abuser and seemingly was not being physically threatened by him:

> [I]t was apparent that her act was that of a desperate woman, cornered, and barely hanging on to threads of self-esteem and self-worth. She was powerless. Even while separated from her husband, he was significantly impacting, if not controlling her life. In the result, I am not satisfied that Mrs Eagles state of mind was such that she could be said to have intended the threat to be taken seriously. I am not satisfied that she was in the position of making or exercising any real choice....[11]

A third positive development can be found in the sentencing cases and is a further enlargement of the scope of *Lavallee*: several of these cases involve charges that do not involve an assaulted woman striking back at her abuser. In *R v Bennett* [No 2],[12] the accused had already pleaded guilty to manslaughter with respect to the killing of her violent mate, Lonnie Shaw, (*R v Bennett* [No 1][13]) and then pleaded guilty to robbery and conspiracy to commit robbery in relation to two armed robberies committed in between the time of her partner's death and the laying of the murder charges against her. Jocelyne Bennett's role in these two robberies included planning the offence and counselling the actual perpetrators, although she apparently did not receive any proceeds. Nicholas J heard evidence regarding a lifetime of abuse endured by the accused, including the violence from her deceased partner Shaw, her resultant addictions to drugs and alcohol, and the fact that Bennett was apparently operating under the direction of another psychologically abusive and controlling man, John D'Amico, when she arranged the robberies.

Although the judge did not explicitly list BWS among the mitigating factors, in imposing a sentence of imprisonment for 10 months in addition to time served (nine months), her remarks near the end of her judgment indicate that not only was BWS evidence pertinent to the armed robbery charges, but also that conformity with a stereotype of the "battered woman" is legally unnecessary:

> Lastly, I wish to comment on the cynicism repeatedly expressed by the Crown, about Ms. Bennett's experience as a battered woman, belittling and trivialising that trauma by stating, on a number of occasions, that she is no longer a victim and not the same person as portrayed in the manslaughter sentencing hearing. The tapes speak volumes about the abuse reaped on this accused by Shaw [the victim in the manslaughter case]. They also reveal the accused to be verbally aggressive and abusive and one tough woman by anyone's standard. One does not negate the other, in my opinion. I have no difficulty accepting that the real Jocelyne Bennett is both: a woman who for reasons of emotional dependence, love and low self esteem was brutally abused by Lonnie Shaw, yet also a woman who is a player in the underworld of this city, capable of being aggressive and reckless. Those who would disregard or mock her portrayal as a victim in her intimate relationships, given her subsequent and violent criminal behaviour for which she is being severely punished, suffer, in my opinion from a rather myopic view of what is a victim, and fail to fully appreciate the battered wife syndrome. In this case, it certainly does not excuse her behaviour, but it does go a long way in explaining how her life took a wrong turn with the result that she stands before me today. All victims of abuse, not only those who are sweet, meek and conform to the stereotyped acceptable behaviour for a female, are deserving of some compassion and an opportunity to break the cycle through rehabilitation and counselling. [14]

Examples of reference to BWS in mitigation of sentence where the accused has not struck back at her abuser are found as well in *R v Phillips*,[15] where the accused pleaded guilty to manslaughter with respect to the death of her partner and was sentenced to incarceration in a provincial institution for two years less a day, and *R v Bradbury*,[16] where the accused pleaded guilty to trafficking in a narcotic and was sentenced to 90 days' imprisonment, to be served on weekends.

In *Phillips*, Watt J heard lengthy evidence regarding past abuse of the accused by other men, but it was "no part of the defence case that [the victim] was abusive towards Gloria Phillips. No evidence [was] adduced of any reported incident of, a fortiori any pattern or series of incidents of physical, sexual, emotional or financial abuse".[17] The only evidence of conflict between the deceased and the accused related to the accused's jealousy regarding the deceased's contact with a former partner and their children; at trial the accused stated that she had no memory of the events that led to the stabbing on the night of the killing, although there was medical evidence regarding bruises on the accused's thigh, breast, shoulder, and bicep.

The evidence that documented abuse of the accused in foster homes and in prior relationships, as recent as 1990, was used by the judge to affirm that the accused did not pose a serious danger to the community and to mitigate her sentence:

> Here, a battered woman has caused the death of another, a non-battering partner. She did so, in part at least, as a result of an emotional state produced by previous battering relationships. Some penalty must, nonetheless, be paid for having caused the death of another. The nature of the punishment imposed, however, ought to take cognizance of the realities of the battered spouse or battered woman syndrome, more accurately the sense of utter helplessness and emotional turmoil it is said to create in the mind of the battered person who causes death. [18]

In *Bradbury*, the evidence was in effect that the accused had suffered an abusive and tragic upbringing. Counsel argued that she committed the offences at the instigation of the main perpetrator of the offence, with whom she was involved in an abusive relationship, on the understanding that the man would abandon her if she did not comply. Although Bruser J did not specifically use BWS evidence, it was invoked by way of analogy to mitigate the sentence:

> [Defence counsel] says that Bradbury was a "patsy" which is a somewhat cruder way of expressing what I have said, and that she is close to a compulsion defence. That may be so. Defence counsel says the matter parallels the Battered Woman Syndrome. I find a better parallel in the area of those who live off the avails of prostitution. Those people, men and women alike, who have women or men dependent upon them for stability and who use them for the purpose of prostitution are guilty of the most heinous sort of crime. The facts in this case are close to that sort of fact pattern. [19]

A fourth positive aspect, found in both *Eagles* and in several of the sentencing cases, including *Bennett* [No 2], is a relaxation of the kind of evidence required to demonstrate BWS and the fact of abuse itself. For example, in *Bennett* [No 2], the Crown objected vigorously to the testimony of two defence witnesses, one a crisis counsellor for battered women and the other a lawyer who had represented over one hundred assaulted women, who Judge Dianne Nicholas permitted to testify as to the relationship of power and control by D'Amico over Bennett and as to "the issue of battered women, how they behave and what can best help them". [20] While in some ways it might be said that *Bennett* [No 2] does not provide a very compelling precedent given that a traditional "expert", psychiatrist Fred Shane, was employed in the earlier manslaughter sentencing hearing, and thus both the sentencing brief by the defence and the judgment from *Bennett* [No 1] were available to the judge, *Eagles* does provide a stronger case.

In *Eagles* the judge explicitly stated that in the circumstances, expert evidence as to BWS generally or in relation to the accused specifically was unnecessary:

> Lavallee *held that the opinion evidence of an expert witness was admissible and could be heard, not that the witness was a necessary precondition to hearing factual evidence which could impact upon the accused's state of mind. Further, it is open to this trial court to refer to and rely on the scholarly authorities cited by Justice Wilson in the majority decision.... It would be both absurd and wasteful to require expert witnesses to attend court for the purpose of describing the generic battered wife syndrome. Such experts may not be available in remote and isolated communities....*
>
> *That is not to say that expert evidence may not be helpful in assisting the trier of fact to better understand the impact of the battering on the accused's state of mind at the critical time. In some instances, the effect of the battering may be apparent without the assistance of experts.*[21]

The negative implications of the post-*Lavallee* jurisprudence emerge from the majority of the sentencing cases.

In the cases involving resort to BWS evidence regarding violent behaviour by the victim in mitigation of sentence by women who have wounded or killed them, *R v Dunlap*,[22] *R v Whitten*,[23] *R v Howard*,[24] *R v Catholique*,[25] *R v Bennett* [No 1], and *R v Eyapaise*,[26] it would appear that in fact the accused had strong grounds for self-defence such that acquittals may have been appropriate. Instead, in *Eyapaise* the defence was rejected and the accused convicted of assault causing bodily harm, and all of the other accused entered guilty pleas, relying on BWS evidence in mitigation. These are not the results that a generous reading of *Lavallee* would produce.

In *Dunlap* the accused's evidence was that she and the deceased were drinking, that an argument developed, that he raised his arm, which was in a cast, and threatened to hit her with it, and that she grabbed the nearest item, a knife, to defend herself and stabbed him with it. The trial judge reviewed the evidence that indicated a history of violence by the deceased against the accused and stated that "there is ample reason to accept her statement that she was in fear that the deceased was going to attack her and cause her serious harm".[27] He accepted her plea of guilty to manslaughter, and imposed a one year sentence of imprisonment with two years probation, which was upheld against a Crown appeal.

The court in *Whitten* also accepted a plea of guilty to manslaughter; it suspended the passing of sentence and put the accused on probation for three years, on the basis of the following facts:

> She said that they drank a bottle and a half of a 40 oz. bottle and Mr Sampson was verbally abusing her with insults and calling her a whore and, as she described it, they started to struggle and the coffee table went flying. He kicked it across the room and he was very angry. He had a steak knife in his hand and she had one in hers and she put her knife into his side. She thought it was a slight injury and claims that she had not intended to injure him or hurt him but was trying to stop his verbal abuse.[28]

Glube CJ took into account these facts as well as the lengthy history of violence by the deceased against the accused, her unsuccessful attempts to terminate the relationship (the deceased not only threatened her with death but also broke into the home to resume living there), her efforts to secure medical assistance after the stabbing, and the accused's remorse and work towards rehabilitation.[29]

In *Howard* the accused was originally sentenced to five and a half years imprisonment after a sentencing hearing for a plea to manslaughter in which no evidence of abuse or BWS was introduced. Because the accused asserted on appeal that she did not wish to challenge her plea of guilty, the court declined to accept the psychologist's assessment of the accused made after the original sentencing hearing.[30] The court refused to reduce the sentence to time served because the accused had been the one to leave the bedroom where a physical struggle was taking place and to bring the knife back into the room. The appellate court nonetheless reduced the sentence to two years purportedly on the basis of the accused's progress in rehabilitation, the fact that she was the mother of five children, and "[t]he background of this marriage and this appellant".[31] Thus it appears that the BWS evidence may have influenced the sentence on appeal.

In *Catholique* the accused pleaded guilty to aggravated assault for an assault with a broken bottle that caused the near death of her defacto partner. De Weerdt J heard evidence with respect to prior violent assaults by the victim upon the accused, including an attack two months before that resulted in the accused requiring stitches in her forehead.[32] The conduct by the accused that brought her before this court was in reaction to violence by the "victim":

> They had a barbeque and were consuming liquor when an argument flared up between them, in the course of which "the victim" began to push "the offender" physically around. The latter was, in fact, thrown to the ground by her spouse who proceeded to slap her vigorously and repeatedly with his open hand so that she reacted, or better, overreacted, with an overwhelming rage actuated as much by fear for her personal safety as by her being again physically abused and by her consequent anger. Picking up a broken beer

> bottle "the offender" slashed at "the victim's" chest and arm, drawing blood, following this with a jab or thrust into "the victim's" abdominal region.[33]

Despite this strong evidence of self-defence, the judge mentioned only provocation, which is not available for offences other than murder, and "emotional pressure sensing herself to be genuinely in real peril".[34] He stated that "[t]he guilty plea is a clear acknowledgment, furthermore, that use of the broken bottle to severely wound 'the victim', as was done, was use of excessive force by 'the offender' which cannot be justified as self defence in all the circumstances",[35] and accepted the guilty plea. The elements mitigating against incarceration were said by the judge to include the fact that the accused was of Aboriginal descent and a woman, such that prison facilities would have a harsher impact upon her, and that although "[i]t is difficult, in the circumstances of the present case, to gauge with any hope of accuracy the degree to which 'the battered woman syndrome' truly applies",[36] that prison would serve no purpose. In the result, he gave the accused a suspended sentence of two years, accompanied by a probation order.

In *Bennett* [No 1], the accused did not testify at trial, and the defence relied on the evidence of other witnesses as to past violence by the deceased against the accused and an expert who testified that Ms Bennett met the criteria for BWS. Ample evidence was introduced as to the nature and extent of the violence inflicted upon the accused, including recent death threats by the deceased, and some of the statements made by the accused to police after the killing, such as "I was defending for my life."[37] In light of the fact that self-defence was clearly raised by the facts, Ratushny J had to consider whether it was appropriate to accept a guilty plea to manslaughter, given that defence counsel stated that his client did not wish to argue BWS as a defence, but rather to have the court "recognize the reality of her experience".[38] Ratushny J decided to accept the plea on the basis that the accused and her counsel had carefully considered her options and that it would be unfair to force her to trial. Ms Bennett received a sentence of a suspended sentence and probation for a period of three years for the manslaughter.

In this case, counsel may have declined to plead self-defence with respect to the manslaughter charge for several reasons. First, the accused may not have been able to sustain self-defence had the facts gone to trial. For example, there was abundant evidence of the accused's own aggression against the deceased, which, although labelled by Ratushny J as "pathetic compared to the scale of the violence Mr Shaw inflicted upon her",[39] takes on more significance when considered along with testimony by a babysitter who received a call from the accused minutes before the killing in which she stated that the deceased was asleep, that she couldn't take it any longer, and that she was going to kill him. However, in the end Ratushny J seems to have been more sympathetic than may have been expected, for she emphasised the positive statements from

Lavallee that indicated that women need not wait until an attack is in progress to defend themselves, and she also highlighted testimony from the deceased's former wife in which she described a particular violent attack where she believed Shaw to have been asleep and he suddenly sprang up and began choking her.[40] Second, in light of the subsequent charge of armed robbery, counsel may have hoped that Ms Bennett would receive a reduced sentence for both sets of charges rather than risk a public and judicial backlash when she was later sentenced for the armed robberies.

In *Eyapaise* the accused and her cousin had brought a man with whom they had been drinking at a bar to the cousin's home . While all three continued to drink, the man sexually assaulted Ms Eyapaise by placing his hands on her breasts and legs several times, in spite of the fact that she not only objected but also struck him in the face on each occasion. When the man grabbed her around the waist as she tried to leave the room, she broke free of his grasp, took a kitchen knife, and stabbed him in the neck.

McMahon J accepted that the accused had endured a life of sexual and physical abuse and acknowledged that, as a woman who had been repeatedly battered, she *may* have been under a reasonable apprehension of grievous bodily harm from "even" a stranger: "Given the realities now recognised by *Lavallee* it may be that the exterior source of that perceived threat, namely someone other than the long-term abuser, may not itself preclude a plea of self-defence."[41] However, he did not accept that she, on reasonable grounds, believed that she could not otherwise preserve herself from that harm,[42] as is required by s.34 of the *Criminal Code*, which governs the defence of self-defence:

> Her cousin Donald Ironbow was present and could have intervened, as in fact he eventually did. Mrs. Ironbow was in an adjacent room and apparently sober. Boutin was a stranger. Had the accused left in a taxi as she had arrived, he could neither follow nor find her. A phone was close at hand to call the police or her husband. She struck Boutin twice and twice he stopped his objectionable conduct at least for a while. There is no evidence that he was violent in the usual sense of the word. The accused's actions belie the feeling of helplessness or the paralysis of fear that is more typical of a battered woman in an abusive domestic situation.[43]

He convicted the accused of the offence of assault causing bodily harm, and remitted the matter for sentencing.

These three cases illustrate how deeply entrenched the requirement of women's gender role conformity is for both judges and perhaps, defence lawyers: women who respond to violence with aggression may not receive the same recognition as "battered women". In the other cases where the women have fared better than these three women, the reader will have noticed that the judges have described the women in ways that reinforce the pathological focus on the "syndrome" as the cause of the women's criminality: the accused are described as powerless, paralysed, and under the control of men. Sheila Noonan has analysed the legal significance assigned to reliance on BWS as the denial of both women's agency and rationality and as universalised, professional accounts of what are otherwise individual experiences and responses. This analysis suggests that not only is there a price attached to successful invocation of BWS, but also "the more rational and reasonable the woman's actions seem, the more likely they are to warrant criminal sanction".[44]

For example, Ms Dunlap was apparently not eligible for self-defence in spite of the trial judge's recognition of the threat she faced, because, according to the appellate court, "[t]he trial judge recognized that more force was used than was necessary by the respondent in warding off the deceased".[45] It should be noted that the use of such a purely objective test in fact constitutes legal error under the terms of s. 34 of the *Criminal Code*. Glube J never explained why the actions of Ms Whitten did not raise the issue of self-defence, although she accepted as fact that the accused was confronted by a raging partner who himself held a knife as he advanced. Ms Howard was faulted for bringing a knife into an otherwise unarmed altercation, but we have no information as to the context in the sense of the kind of physical risk the accused faced given past violence from her partner.

While the evidence is unclear as to whether Ms Bennett was confronted with a situation fitting traditional notions of self-defence, her acts were within the defence articulated by Madam Justice Wilson in *Lavallee*, in that a woman need not wait until her life is in imminent danger, but is entitled to act to preserve her own life when she can.[46] Furthermore, both Ms Catholique and Ms Eyapaise were in obviously dangerous situations that posed the risk of grievous bodily harm within the meaning of self-defence. Each had "reasonable grounds" to believe that nothing short of the actions taken would preserve them from the threatened harm, not only because women can rarely match men's physical strength without a weapon like a broken bottle or a knife, but also because Ms Catholique had already experienced extreme violence from her partner and, in the case of Ms Eyapaise, nothing seemed to deter the man's assaults upon her, including the presence of her cousin.

These latter three cases, *Howard, Catholique*, and *Eyapaise* can also be understood in light of racism within both the criminal "justice" system's construction of Aboriginal women and the articulation of the "battered woman syndrome" by feminist and non-feminist activists, academics, and lawyers. While the violence of white women is pathologised as unwomanly, and rendered explicable through BWS and the re-characterisation of the women as stuck in the cycle of violence, paralysed, and helpless, the violence of Aboriginal women in Canada may be seen, through the lens of racism, as consistent with stereotypes of Aboriginal women, and thus not requiring rationalisation through syndromisation.

The work of Julie Stubbs and Julia Tolmie[47] pulls together Australian and United States research on the lack of fit between feminist accounts of violence and the experience of Aboriginal (Australian) and Black women, as well as the stereotypes of Aboriginal women perpetrated by the criminal justice system. They use this research to analyse the ways in which BWS might fail to serve Aboriginal women, for example by its narrow focus on self-defence rather than defence of their children or other kin members, or striking out at persons other than a male partner;[48] by the fact that Aboriginal women may not have sought criminal justice or social work intervention because these institutions themselves replicate relations of dominance and racism and their intervention may put not only the men but also the women themselves at greater risk of state violence;[49] because Aboriginal women may see alcohol as playing a significant role in the violence not recognised by accounts of battering that focus singularly upon patriarchy;[50] and because not only stereotypes about Aboriginal women and criminality may undermine the presentation of a passive "victim", but also because Aboriginal women are more likely than white women to be subjected to extreme violence and may be more likely to respond to violence with force,[51] again weakening reliance upon the paradigm of the "battered woman".

The judgments in *Howard*, *Catholique* and *Eyapaise* contain little by way of overt racism, with the exception of the remark in *Eyapaise* that the accused's cousin's wife was "apparently sober", implying that we could otherwise assume that she was intoxicated because she was Aboriginal. At play in these cases may be a judicial preoccupation with the fact that the women themselves were drinking and were thus not perfect "victims", that these women did not seek the intervention thought to be appropriate, that Ms Eyapaise struck back at a man not her partner, and that these women's self-defensive violence was at least as consistent with their Aboriginality as with BWS. Furthermore, at a more general level, the extraordinarily high rates of incarceration of Aboriginal women in Canada[52] and the brutal treatment that federally sentenced Aboriginal women have experienced at the hands of various components of the criminal justice system,[53] suggest that those who participate in constructing offenders for sentencing, such as social workers, police, probation and parole officers, lawyers, prison guards, therapists, and judges, may not readily view Aboriginal women as fitting within BWS.

Finally, these cases do not expose either the widespread nature of violence against women and children or the systemic failures of the various systems to intervene or provide the support necessary to transform relations of dominance. The judges frequently do not describe or comment upon the women's efforts to seek help or the results of attempts to bring police or courts into the "private" sphere. The precipitating violence itself may be completely submerged as in *Phillips*, where it seems highly implausible that the deceased was in no way violent toward the accused, and as in *Eyapaise* (the man was not "violent" "in the usual sense of the word") and in *Whitten* and *Catholique*, where real evidence of danger was minimised by the judges. The judges in *Bennett* [No 2] and *Bradbury* acknowledged that the women were, in some ways, under the control of domineering men, but failed to recognise that psychological abuse itself may be perceived as one or perhaps even the most destructive, form of violence.

The use of gender neutral language in several of the cases, "battered spouse" (*Phillips*) and "men and women alike" "who live off the avails of prostitution" (*Bradbury*), suggests that judges may be equally willing to accept a "battered man" defence, thus further hiding the reality of violence in the lives of women. For example, an Ontario Provincial Court judge, Bark J recently gave a conditional discharge to a man who pleaded guilty to assault by throwing a garbage can at his wife, but argued that he was "provoked" by her "taunting". The judge stated, without revealing his sources, that "he was reminded of a statistic, one that is 'not very well publicized, and not likely to be: there are far more husbands abused by their wives than the other way around.'"[54] The fact that judges in cases like *Eagles* and *Bennett* [No 2] have not required a great deal of evidence to make out the argument that the accused experienced BWS may further support such flagrant assertions of "truth" by judges to deny both men's and the state's responsibility for violence against women and children.

Beyond *Lavallee*

The limitations identified in the cases decided since *Lavallee* are, to some extent, inherent in the individualistic, narrowly-focused, too little, far too late nature of criminal law adjudications of innocence, guilt, and punishment. These constraints can be challenged through three different avenues.

The first strategy, which has been undertaken by the Canadian Association of Elizabeth Fry Societies (CAEFS), is that of calling for an *en bloc* review of the cases of women currently serving sentences in connection with the deaths of their partners. This approach has been taken in several states in the United States and has resulted in the release of women prisoners.[55]

Researchers for CAEFS have identified and interviewed at least fifteen women serving federal sentences who they believe ought to benefit from a generous interpretation of *Lavallee*.[56] These cases cover a range of circumstances, including cases decided since *Lavallee* where lawyers have declined to even raise the issue of prior abuse on behalf of their clients. CAEFS's request has been formally denied by the current Minister of Justice, who asserts that he cannot proceed without a statutory basis for this remedy.[57] CAEFS's response has been to create a national campaign to create the pressure to force the government to act.

CAEFS is pursuing this strategy for several reasons: 1) many women serving time were tried and convicted prior to *Lavallee* so that they may not be able to rely on the new interpretation of self-defence; 2) not all of the women can use the appeal process to open this issue either because an adequate evidentiary basis was not established at trial and the evidence would not qualify as "fresh" evidence, or because their lawyers entered guilty pleas on their behalf in exchange for a deal on sentencing; 3) pardons and judicial inquiries into alleged miscarriages of justice are discretionary, extraordinary remedies that will not be equally available to all of the women; 4) these legal remedies require access to legal services, which again are not equally available; 5) individual adjudications would fail to reveal the systemic features shared by these cases such as institutionalised racism, and the justice system's failure to respond to violence against women and children; and 6) without such an exposure and the accompanying public and judicial education, feminists will be in a weaker position to demand the allocation of resources to **prevent** violence and to reshape the legal understanding of BWS.

A second avenue for challenging constraints is for legal researchers, lawyers, and activists to educate lawyers and judges about the impact of traumatic violence upon the lives of women and children and the role that social, economic, and political institutions play in perpetuating this violence. This task can be accomplished by expanding the range of cases in which BWS is raised as an issue, enlarging the understanding of the forms and consequences of violence, and creating links between cases that are otherwise viewed as isolated tragedies.

The cases reviewed indicate that some Canadian lawyers are clearly presenting background information with respect to accused women's traumatic pasts; some of the cases also focus, appropriately, I would argue, upon the batterer's pattern of violence as part of demonstrating the "reasonableness" of the accused's fear and her reaction of defensive force. The work of activists and lawyers could also be to document and argue the relevance of not only the women's efforts to change their partner's behaviour or to secure effective intervention, but also information about the availability and appropriateness of criminal law remedies and social services for women from the accused's community, and statistics and expert evidence regarding the escalation of violence and danger that women who do leave abusive men face.[58] The value of this kind of evidence may be to expand judicial understandings of what violence looks like and women's appraisals that no one but themselves will protect them from violence.

I also think that we must look beyond the cases of women who kill violent men to the much larger group of women who were victimised as children or as adults, who are either vulnerable to control by men who involve them in other forms of criminal activity, or who act out the violence against others who are not necessarily their abusers. The cases of *Bennett* [No 2], *Phillips*, *Bradbury*, and to a lesser extent, *Eyapaise* offer opportunities to expose the wide-ranging and long-term repercussions of trauma in the lives of women; there is no question that if one examined the cases of women charged for failure to protect their children from abuse by their partners[59] and women charged with other offences of violence against the person[60] that one would discover women who have been traumatised by violence and who have been coerced in one way or another to refrain from intervening in their partners' violence against others or to become involved in criminal activity.

The work of Dr Judith Herman on the impact of traumatic violence is particularly important in this regard. Through her research and therapy, she has looked at the effect of traumatic events. Her point is that none of us is immune from the effects of a severe enough trauma such as witnessing atrocities or the deaths of family members, or being repeatedly subjected to the risk of death: "Traumatic events are extraordinary, not because they occur rarely, but because they overwhelm the ordinary human adaptations to life."[61] She argues that the experience of **repeated** trauma through **captivity**, whether as prisoners of war, soldiers in combat, political hostages, children who are abused in their families, or women who are battered over a period of time, produces qualitatively worse damage that is profound and long-term, including loss of will to live, robotisation, and erosion of the personality.[62] I think that her account is significant, for the analogy she draws between the experience of prisoners of war, who may be forced to participate in the degradation or even killing of others and that of battered women who fail to prevent harm to their children or whose partners require them to injure others, may assist in making palpable to lawyers and to judges what it is we are asking of women, such as Hedda Nussbaum,[63] whose personalities have been substantially destroyed by trauma in captivity, when we propose to hold them criminally responsible for their (in)action.

A third direction that feminists might take is to use these legal developments since *Lavallee* to mount public education campaigns about the systemic nature of violence, to stake claims to allocation of resources to prevent violence and to assist women and children who are escaping, and to broaden the debates on reform of the criminal law. For example, one risk presented by the developing case law in Canada is that the government will codify the trends we see in plea bargaining and jury trials of the reduction of murder to manslaughter in battering situations, thus rendering acquittals based on BWS less compelling for jurors. We need to publicly challenge the appropriateness of plea bargains on behalf of these women, and resist codification of these practices.

Furthermore, it is clear from Dr Herman's work that the **recovery** of those who have been affected by traumatic violence, and particularly those who have, as a result, participated in inflicting violence upon others, is absolutely dependent upon having their histories understood and accepted by the wider community.[64] In this connection, it is not enough to secure lenient sentences or acquittals for women who have been traumatised, for without the resources needed for these women to work through the damage and a supportive community that also takes responsibility for dismantling the structures that facilitated the violence, we risk repetition, self-destruction, and the futures of these women's children.

Notes

1   Herman, JL, *Trauma and Recovery* (1992) at 51.

2   (1990), 55 C.C.C.(3d) 97 (S.C.C.).

3   See, eg, *R v Whynot (Stafford)* (1983), 37 C.R.(3d) 198 (N.S.S.Ct.) and *R v Lavallee*, [1990] 4 W.W.R. 1 (Man.C.A.).

4   Section 34(2) of the *Criminal Code*, R.S.C. 1985, c. C-46 reads: "Every one who is assaulted and who causes death or grievous bodily harm in repelling the assault is justified if a) he causes it under reasonable apprehension of death or grievous bodily harm from the violence with which the assault was originally made or with which the assailant pursues his purposes; and b) he believes, on reasonable grounds, that he cannot otherwise preserve himself from death or grievous bodily harm."

5   Above n2 at 120.

6   Id at 125.

7   For example, see MacQueen, K, "Justifiable Homicide" *The Ottawa Citizen* (3 May 1991) A1, A2 (The Crown Attorney dropped charges of second degree murder against Roxanne Murray for killing Doug "Juicer" Murray after the RCMP investigation revealed a string of charges and a long history of extreme violence against the accused and others).

8   One such example is provided by the case of Jean Millar, who was acquitted of second degree murder charges but convicted of manslaughter by a jury after relying on BWS evidence in her defence: Mike Blanchfield, "Millar Convicted of Manslaughter" *The Ottawa Citizen* (30 October 1992) A1, C3.

9   [1991] Y.J. No. 147 (Yukon Terr. Ct.).

10   Id at 14-15.

11   Id at 14.

12   [1993] O.J. No.892 (Ont. Prov.Ct.).

13   (Ont. Prov.Ct.). (Ottawa, 28 January 1993), [unreported].

14   Above n12 at 41-2. See also the judgment in Bennett [No 1], above n13 at 42, where the accused's own aggression is detailed and the judge comments:

> [S]ociety, in the process of becoming more enlightened and accepting that women do find themselves in these situations, nevertheless could fall back into stereotyping these women as having to be credible, sweet and helpless victims who are brutalized by tyrannical men. With this I disagree.

15　[1992] O.J. 2716 (Ont.Ct.J. Gen.Div.).

16　[1992] N.W.T.J. No.178 (N.W.T. Terr. Ct.).

17　*Phillips*, above n15 at 4-5.

18　Id at 23-4.

19　*Bradbury*, above n16 at 15.

20　*Bennett* [No 2], above n12 at 21.

21　Above n9 at 12-13.

22　(1991), 101 N.S.R.(2d) 263 (S.Ct. App.Div.).

23　(1992), 110 N.S.R.(2d) 149 (S.Ct. T.Div.).

24　(1992), 8 B.C.A.C. 241 (C.A.).

25　[1990] N.W.T.J. No.164 (N.W.T. Sup. Ct.).

26　(1993), 20 C.R.(4th) 246 (Alta.Q.B.).

27　Above n22 at 266.

28　Above n23 at 151.

29　Id at 157.

30　*R v Howard* (1992), 8 B.C.A.C. 249 (C.A.). The court also stated that it would not hear the fresh evidence because it contradicted the statements made by the accused immediately after the stabbing and accepted at the original sentencing hearing.

31　Above n24 at 248.

32　Above n25 at 4.

33　Id at 2-3.

34　Id at 4.

35　Id at 6.

36　Id at 20.

37　Above n13 at 39.

38　Id at 7.

39　Id at 43.

40　Id at 44.

41　Above n26 at 250-1.

42　Id at 251.

43　Ibid.

44   Noonan, S, "Strategies of Survival: Exploring the Limits of the Battered Woman Syndrome", in Currie, C and Adelberg, E, *Too Few To Count*, (3rd edn, 1993).

45   Above n22 at 266.

46   *Lavallee*, above n2.

47   Stubbs, J and Tolmie, J, "Women Out of Context: Battered Woman Syndrome and the Australian Experience" (1994) 8 *Canadian J Women and Law* (forthcoming).

48   Atkinson, J, "Violence in Aboriginal Australia: Colonisation and Gender" Part I (June 1990) *Aboriginal and Islander Health Worker J* 5, and Part II (September 1990) *Aboriginal and Islander Health Worker J* 4, and "Violence Against Aboriginal Women: Reconstitution of Community Law—The Way Forward" (1990) 2 (46) *Aboriginal Law Bulletin* 6, discussed in Stubbs and Tolmie, id at note 102, and at 15.

49   See the reference cited in Stubbs and Tolmie, id at 15, notes 122- 7.

50   See Stubbs and Tolmie, id at 18, note 149.

51   Stubbs and Tolmie, id at 14, notes 118-19 refer to statistics suggesting that Aboriginal women are killed at a rate ten times higher than white women, and at 21, note 170 cites a study indicating that while the male:female ratio of homicide offenders was 3:1 generally in Australia, it was 1:1 for Aboriginal offenders.

52   Sinclair J reports that in the provincial institutions, 70-90 per cent of women incarcerated are Aboriginal: "A Presentation to the Western Workshop of the Western Judicial Education Centre" (14 May 1990) in Abell, J and Sheehy, E, (eds), *Criminal Law & Procedure: Cases, Context, Critique* (1993) 51 at 52.

53   See Sugar, F and Fox, L, "Nistum Peyako Seht'wawin Iskwewak: Breaking Chains" (1989-90) 3 *Canadian J Women and Law* 465.

54   "Taunted Husband Lashes Out at Wife" *Cobourg Daily Star* (22 July 1993) 2.

55   See for example the review that took place in the state of Ohio: "Clemency Granted to 25 Women Convicted for Assault or Murder" *New York Times* (22 December 1990) 1.

56   The initial research was conducted by Felicity Hawthorn, "Interviews with Four Battered Women at the Prison for Women who are Serving Life Sentences for Murder" (27 April 1992), unpublished. Noonan, above n44 has completed more interviews and refers to her general findings in her article "Strategies for Survival"; Kim Pate, Executive Director of CAEFS has also conducted some of these interviews.

57   Letter from Pierre Blais, Minister of Justice (8 September 1993).

58   See for example the work of Mahoney, M, "Legal Images of Battered Women: Redefining the Issue of Separation" (1991) 90 *Mich LR* 1. See also Sheehy, E, Stubbs, J and Tolmie, J, "Defending Battered Women on Trial: The Battered Woman Syndrome and its Limitations" (1992) 16 *Crim LJ* 369.

59 See *R v Urbanovitch and Brown* (1985), 19 C.C.C.(3d) 43 Man.C.A. and, for recent but common examples see "An Inexplicable Double Standard" *The [Halifax] Chronicle Herald* (28 September 1993) C1 (a mother was jailed for six months failing to prevent physical abuse of her two children by her boyfriend, while the boyfriend received a suspended sentence for inflicting the injuries); Nadine Fownes, "Woman Pleads Guilty to not Reporting Abuse" *The [Halifax] Chronicle Herald* (1 October 1993) A16 ("Each time the girls asked their mother for help, usually in the form of handwritten notes, the woman would confront her husband. He made repeated promises to stop abusing the girls but resumed his assaults soon afterward.").

60 See for example *R v Robins* (1982), 66 C.C.C.(2d) 550 (Que.C.A.), battered woman denied duress defence to kidnapping charges because threats to kidnap child not sufficient and Fine, S, "Woman Seeks to Use Coercion as Abuse Defence" *The [Toronto] Globe and Mail* (31 December 1992) A4, battered woman denied duress defence regarding forced participation in sexual abuse of children.

61 Above n1 at 33.

62 Id at 83, 86.

63 For an account of the case see Ehrlich, S, *Lisa, Hedda & Joel* (1989).

64 Above n1 at 70.

9

Battered woman syndrome in Australia: A challenge to gender bias in the law?

Julie Stubbs and Julia Tolmie*

* Katrina Budrikis and Lynda-ann Blanchard provided valuable research assistance for this chapter, which was also supported by a grant from the NSW Law Foundation Legal Scholarship Support Fund.

Domestic violence, predominantly committed by men against women, is a prevalent problem in Australian society. It is no surprise then that some women commit crimes under threat of this type of violence. These women may either engage in criminal activity outside the domestic situation in order to appease their violent partner or, in more extreme circumstances, they may kill their partner in order to protect themselves or their children from his violent behaviour.

This chapter examines the use of the battered woman syndrome in Australian cases where women have been charged with an offence committed in response to, or under the influence of, domestic violence. It outlines the rationale for using battered woman syndrome, and questions whether evidence concerning the syndrome has been effective in challenging gender bias within the law. The chapter places particular emphasis on homicide and defences to homicide, since it has been in that context that much of the literature concerning battered woman syndrome has developed.

The rationale for the use of the Battered Woman Syndrome evidence: The failure of conventional defences

In the past women who committed homicide in response to domestic violence, and who wished to defend a criminal charge, had most success in offering a defence which relied on their own mental infirmity or emotional volatility, for instance diminished responsibility[1] or provocation.[2] These are partial defences, which reduce the charge from murder to manslaughter. Until recently in Australia, women who had killed in the context of domestic violence had not been successful in raising the defence of self-defence which depends on establishing that their perceptions and reactions were reasonable in response to the circumstances in which they found themselves. Self-defence provides a complete defence to a charge of murder and results in the acquittal of the accused.[3]

This historical failure by courts to understand women's resort to lethal self-help as self-defence has been explained by numerous commentators largely in terms of the many levels on which such women's life experiences are either not heard or are distorted by the legal system. For example, it has been suggested that the perceptions and actions of battered women have been taken out of context by the courts, that legal rules and standards of reasonableness tend to reflect male rather than female life experiences and that women, particularly battered women, are subject to a number of damaging stereotypes. The section which follows examines each of these issues in the context of women prosecuted for killing a violent partner (or ex-partner).

Decontextualisation of the offender's actions.

A finding of self-defence involves recognition that a person's defensive behaviour was a necessary response to the circumstances in which they found themselves. The reported Australian cases evidence a double failure on the part of the courts to realistically locate women's defensive behaviour within its surrounding circumstances.

First, the courts have frequently minimised the deceased's violence towards the accused. Research indicates that significant sections of the broader community also normalise or trivialise criminal assaults in the home,[4] and that this occurs despite evidence that domestic violence is widespread and extremely dangerous or life-threatening for many women.[5] Nevertheless such attitudes survive and function to downplay both the immediate threat a particular woman may have faced as well as the cumulative experience of living through past violent incidents.[6] The result is that her final resort to defensive action may seem manifestly unnecessary or excessive as a response to the threat she faced.

This dynamic is illustrated in *R v Whalen*.[7] In that case the judge minimised the long history of physical and emotional abuse the accused had received at the hands of her husband by labelling it "matrimonial discord". The judge described more "provocative" conduct by the husband on the night on which the accused ultimately killed him with an axe and knife as he slept. However, the judge made it clear that this provocation was not to be viewed as "mistreatment by violence" or "actual physical violence", being more in the nature of "mistreatment by humiliation" or "psychological torture". This is an extraordinary perspective on the facts which were that the deceased had "gone berserk", locking the accused in a cupboard, hitting her over the head, holding a knife to her face and threatening to kill her, verbally abusing her and eventually throwing her on the bed to urinate on her. The judge's sanitised descriptions of "marital discord" can be contrasted with his condemnation of the accused's crime as one "committed with the utmost savagery upon the deceased while he was helpless in bed".

Secondly, the courts typically have not given due regard to the broader social and political context in which a woman who has killed an abusive man may have acted. Women's claims that it was necessary for them to resort to lethal self-help in response to domestic violence are supported by research in Australia which suggests that peaceful and effective avenues for self-protection are not readily available to many women.[8] Their vulnerability to violence within an intimate relationship stems from well documented social realities such as failures by police[9] and the criminal justice system[10] to provide them with adequate protection, separation assault,[11] economic dependence or financial hardship,[12] a crisis in refuge accommodation,[13] a shortage of safe and affordable housing,[14] social isolation, a reluctance to leave children in the custody of a violent partner[15] and cultural constraints and pressures. The latter include sex role expectations, the ideology of the family and community attitudes which serve to deny, trivialise or normalise the violence.

Prior to the advent of the battered woman syndrome in Australia there are no reported cases which explore the implications of the social and political factors listed above for the woman on trial.[16] In order to accurately assess whether or not the accused's claim that lethal self-help was necessary in her **circumstances** was reasonable, it would be appropriate to ask some or all of the following questions: What was the nature and extent of the violence which she had suffered in the relationship? How many times had she called the police and with what result? How had she tried to enlist the protection of the criminal justice system, or other agencies and what was the result? How many times had she tried to leave? If she returned what were the factors which influenced her decision? Did she have a safe and affordable place to go? Was it reasonable to expect **her** to be the one to leave the family home? How had he responded to her efforts to protect herself in the past? Had he intimated what he might do to her in the future? Was there anything about her cultural circumstances that made it particularly difficult for her to detach from him, negotiate the relationship or seek outside help?[17]

These sorts of issues are rarely given adequate attention in the Australian courts, and where they are raised the presumption seems to be that leaving the relationship would have been an effective and available way of terminating the violence and should be the woman's responsibility. As a substitute for investigating or crediting the circumstances surrounding women's killings the courts have found explanations for their behaviour in the women themselves.[18] Women tried for homicide have tended to be either pathologised or constructed as "out of control" in order to receive partial legal recognition under the defences of diminished responsibility, insanity or provocation.[19]

Practical and procedural difficulties also limit and shape the nature of the account of the homicide which can be presented to the court. [20] For example, the hearsay rule has the potential to exclude statements made by the accused to her doctor. If there had been incidents of prior violence by the deceased against the accused, this may be important in establishing the context in which she resorted to violent self-help. However, domestic violence often occurs in private and without witnesses. Statements to a doctor about the violence may provide corroboration of her account of past violence where no other corroboration is available. [21]

The legal rules.

There is a well established literature which argues that some of the legal rules which traditionally gave shape to the doctrine of self-defence were designed (or interpreted) by the courts to tailor the defence to a factual paradigm involving a one-off confrontational encounter between two strangers of roughly equal size and strength.[22] Such a paradigm may describe many homicides in which both parties are men, but is not typical of homicides which occur in the context of domestic violence and is particularly inappropriate where the offender is a woman.[23] The courts have had difficulties in recognising and fitting women's stories into the conceptual framework provided by this paradigm, and the rules relating to imminence, proportionality, serious harm and the duty to retreat have provided particular obstacles for female defendants.[24]

Since 1987 in Australia these concepts have no longer had the status of legal rules which must be complied with if self-defence is to be successfully raised. In that year the High Court in *Zecevic*[25] reformulated the law to place the focus of the legal test for self-defence on the question of whether or not defensive action was necessary in the circumstances. Nevertheless the concepts of imminence, proportionality, serious harm and the duty to retreat remain as informal considerations in deciding that question and, as such, continue to exert influence in the application of the law to the facts of any particular case.

The requirement of an imminent attack has presented particular problems for women who use lethal defensive force in response to domestic violence. Many of the women in the reported Australian cases seem to have been judged to have acted other than in self-defence because they protected themselves in advance by pre-emptive attacks,[26] armed themselves before being attacked,[27] or killed during a lull in violence in the course of a battering incident,[28] thus failing to satisfy the imminent attack requirement.

This requirement is based on a number of assumptions: that a person cannot be absolutely sure that a threat made by someone else is serious or inevitable until the attack commences; that someone with advance notice of an attack can always deal with it by peaceful means; and that if the worst comes to the worst and a confrontational situation develops, then he is still left with a good chance of successfully using defensive physical force. The consequence of relying on such assumptions is that it is only in respect of attacks actually or almost underway that violent defensive action might be seen to be necessary.

However, these assumptions are likely to be invalid when considering the behaviour of battered women. Women in battering relationships often do not have access to effective peaceful mechanisms for retreat or avoidance even when they do have advance notice of an attack, and they are unlikely to be able to defend themselves physically without resort to a weapon once an attack has commenced.[29] Furthermore, their intimate understanding of their assailant and their past experience of his violence may enable them to predict the inevitable and, or, immediate nature of an attack long before it commences and in circumstances where this is not obvious to others.[30] Some commentators have suggested that the concept of imminence is wholly inappropriate because the danger that women who are habitually and seriously abused face is not so much embodied in a single attack as in the day to day experience of living under continuous threat.[31]

Standards of reasonableness

Where a battered woman is brought to trial, a standard of "reasonableness" is used to "objectively" measure the accused's perception that her defensive actions were necessary in self-defence.[32] Legal and cultural constructions of rationality are not gender neutral. Notions of reasonableness have been based on the experiences, perceptions and actions of the hypothetical reasonable man.[33]

MacCrimmon[34] is one of many commentators, for example, who argues that women often make psychological choices based on a moral framework that values connectedness. They may therefore choose to expose themselves to situations in which they are vulnerable, not because they accept the violence or forfeit the right to defend themselves if necessary, but because they place importance on the goal of developing and preserving relationships, including the relationships their partners have with the children.[35] Within a moral framework that places primary importance on individual self-sufficiency, the choice to place other considerations (or people) before one's self may appear inherently irrational.

Stereotypes and dichotomies in legal thought.

Legal rules and standards typically embody dichotomised and simplistic structures according to which the complexity of human thought and experience must be ordered and understood. Within such an approach conduct is informed by reason or emotion, it is either normal or abnormal. If perceptions are not objectively real then they are subjective, if decisions to respond physically to a violent attack are not made under the pressure of immediate threat then they are revenge. If a subject is not active and self determining (an actor or agent) then they are acted upon (passive, victimised, determined).[36]

Women as a gender are rewarded for complying with, and are most easily constructed according to, gender stereotypes that view them as passive, victimised, subjective, emotional, abnormal (the "other"). This creates a real problem for women who seek to rely on self-defence, since self-defence requires that they be recognised as rational, normal and active agents who have made self determining and objectively valid choices given their circumstances.

The Battered Woman Syndrome

Expert evidence on the battered woman syndrome is traditionally given by a psychiatrist or psychologist.[37] The syndrome is based on a body of research[38] which suggests that domestic violence is of a cyclical and escalating nature and that the cumulative effect of surviving such violence for the women concerned may be a particular state of mind characterised by features such as "learned helplessness" and "chronic fear". These features mean that a woman is psychologically unable to escape a violent relationship, or particular incidents of violence, even when the opportunity is ostensibly open to her to do so.

The battered woman syndrome is not a defence in itself but is introduced in support of one of the established criminal defences. It was first developed in America as a feminist defence strategy designed to support self-defence in respect of women who had killed their tormentors,[39] although it has long since ceased to be confined to this scenario. The aim of using evidence concerning battered woman syndrome is to overcome the difficulties women had in demonstrating that, given the circumstances of violence in which they found themselves, their perceptions and actions were reasonable for the purposes of the various defences.

Whilst the battered woman syndrome has been accepted by courts in many US jurisdictions for over two decades, it was a recent Canadian case which was significant in the introduction of battered woman syndrome as a defence strategy in Australia. In *Lavallee*[40] battered woman syndrome evidence was first ruled admissible by the Supreme Court of Canada. In that case the accused shot her abusive partner in the back of the head when he was leaving the room after assaulting her and threatening to kill her later if she did not kill him first. The Supreme Court restored her first instance acquittal on the basis that she had been correctly allowed to introduce evidence of the syndrome in support of her self-defence plea.

Lavallee is a significant decision because Wilson J, with whom the other judges concurred, explicitly articulated the strategic aims of using battered woman syndrome evidence to support self-defence. In a powerfully worded judgment she made it clear that such evidence is necessary in order to challenge gender bias in the law, in this case the law on self-defence.

The judge presented the syndrome as reforming each of the different levels on which women's stories are distorted by the trial process or do not fit within the legal rules. She said that the syndrome challenges the configuration of legal rules[41] and extends the reasonableness standard to accommodate women's experiences.[42] It counteracts existing mythology about domestic violence and battered women.[43] She made it clear that evidence concerning the battered woman syndrome is necessary not because domestic violence is special or unusual but because it has been condoned by society until very recently. She also expressed the view that the battered woman syndrome avoids setting up new stereotypes about battered women to replace the old ones it counteracts. In relation to the latter point she said that syndrome evidence is neither intended to provide battered women with a defence because of who they are,[44] nor to be definitive of all women's experiences of domestic abuse.[45] She pointed out that environmental factors can also make women vulnerable to relationship violence.[46] Further, the judge stressed that it is not for the jury to pass judgment on the fact that the accused stayed in the relationship or to conclude that she forfeited her right of self-defence by having done so.[47]

Lavallee was cited by the South Australian Court of Criminal Appeal in *Runjanjic and Kontinnen*[48] as an authority supporting the introduction of battered woman syndrome evidence into Australia. *Runjanjic and Kontinnen* was the first Australian case to rule as to whether evidence concerning the battered woman syndrome was admissible and the only case which discusses the issue of admissibility in any detail. Unfortunately in that case King CJ stripped the battered woman syndrome of its feminist agenda in the very act of accepting it. He suggested, contrary to most indications,[49] that such evidence is admissible because domestic violence, at least when it is habitual and severe, is so special and unusual that it is outside common knowledge or ordinary experience. As a consequence he found that jurors could benefit from the testimony of experts on the subject.[50]

The use of battered woman syndrome evidence in *Lavallee,* and more generally, has been criticised on a number of grounds. Criticism has been directed towards the research and methodology supporting the syndrome,[51] and towards using the syndrome as a defence strategy.[52] It is the criticism of battered woman syndrome as a defence strategy that we wish to address.

Using battered woman syndrome in support of a defence carries with it a number of dangers. These are well canvassed in the literature and include, *inter alia*, an over-emphasis on the psychology of the defendant and a consequent under-emphasis on the context in which the offence took place, reinforcing the notion that the accused's behaviour was not objectively reasonable, but perhaps only reasonable (if at all) in the light of some psychological state which resulted from her experience as a victim of on-going violence, reinforcing notions of women's irrationality or emotional instability, the danger of developing a new stereotype by which the battered woman is to be measured in such cases, and reinforcing the notion that battered women as a group share certain psychological characteristics.

These concerns can be reduced to the proposition that it is both dubious and dangerous to explain how a person's reactions and beliefs are reasonable in their **circumstances** using bodies of expertise that locate problems in, and work with, **individual psyches**. In other words, there is a tension between what the syndrome describes, that is the psychological state of the defendant, and the legal requirements for the defence of self-defence, a reasonable belief that the defensive action was necessary. There are good grounds for concern about the manner in which this tension is resolved within the courts, after all the battered woman syndrome has to be applied within a criminal justice system that produced the very bias that the construct is designed to redress. Utilised by agents of the justice system, most of whom do not share Wilson J's agenda for feminist reform or her sensitivity to gender issues, this tension has the potential to be resolved in a way that endorses rather than transforms the status quo. In particular, it has the potential to be used more in support of those defences which stress emotional response (provocation) or mental instability (diminished responsibility), rather than in transforming self-defence.

A further criticism can be directed at the battered woman syndrome as it was outlined in *Lavallee*. The case itself involved an indigenous woman but nowhere did the feminist framework employed by Wilson J address the intersectionality of race and gender in exploring the circumstances the particular accused found herself in.

Following a brief review of the Australian cases in which evidence concerning the battered woman syndrome has been introduced, this chapter will examine the manner in which the tension identified above has been evident in those cases, and will explore the particular problems which arise for Aboriginal women defendants seeking to rely on evidence concerning battered woman syndrome.

The Australian cases to date

Expert evidence on the battered woman syndrome has now been accepted in South Australia, New South Wales, Tasmania, Queensland, the Australian

Capital Territory, Western Australia and the Northern Territory. It has been introduced in support of the defences of duress, self-defence, provocation and diminished responsibility. It has been raised in mitigation of sentence, formed the basis of decisions by the Director of Public Prosecutions not to proceed against accused persons and has been influential in setting aside a conviction on the basis of a miscarriage of justice. The following is a synopsis of those Australian cases which have raised the battered woman syndrome and which have come to the authors' attention at this point in time.

Duress

Runjanjic and Kontinnen[53] was a case arising out of a domestic triangle between two women, Runjanjic and Kontinnen, and their joint (and violent) de facto, Hill. Both women appealed against their conviction for false imprisonment and causing grievous bodily harm to a third woman. They argued that their will had been overborne by fear of Hill's violence. The South Australian Court of Criminal Appeal ruled that the trial judge had erred in not accepting evidence of the battered woman syndrome in support of their defence of duress. The Court ordered a retrial.

Battered woman syndrome evidence has also been accepted in support of a defence of duress in two other cases each of which related to property offences —breaking, entering and stealing in *Webb v R*,[54] and defrauding the Department of Social Security in *Winnett v Stephenson*.[55]

Self-defence

Kontinnen[56] was the second case to arise out of the domestic triangle described in *Runjanjic and Kontinnen*. Kontinnen admitted shooting Hill while he was asleep and after he had threatened to kill her, Runjanjic and a child. The South Australian Supreme Court accepted self-defence, as supported by battered woman syndrome evidence, and acquitted Kontinnen of murder.

In *Hickey*[57] evidence concerning the battered woman syndrome was introduced in support of a successful plea of self-defence before the Supreme Court of New South Wales. In that case the accused stabbed her violent ex de facto after he had refused to allow her to leave his house with their children and had attacked her. Although he was sitting with his back to her at the time that she stabbed him, the accused testified that she did not believe that his attack on her was over.

Self-defence or provocation

In *R v Muy Ky Chhay*[58] the facts were unclear although the sentencing judge expressed the opinion that the accused had killed her violent husband "when he was resting on the lounge room floor either asleep or dozing and only hours after he had acted aggressively and in a violent manner towards the prisoner". The accused unsuccessfully raised both provocation and self-defence at her murder trial. The Supreme Court of New South Wales sentenced her to 12 years imprisonment with a minimum term of six years. This "reduction in the minimum term in favour of a longer additional term" was justified by her unfortunate background and experience, both in Cambodia (she had fled from that country as a refugee) and in the violence she had suffered in her marriage to the deceased. This case was appealed on the basis of the directions given by the judge concerning provocation. The appeal was allowed, the conviction quashed and a re-trial ordered.[59]

In *R v Gilbert*[60] the accused had stabbed her violent de facto during an angry exchange. Battered woman syndrome evidence was run in support of both self-defence and provocation before the Supreme Court of Western Australia. The jury acquitted the accused of murder but convicted her of manslaughter. The sentencing judge expressed the opinion that the jury verdict of manslaughter was reached on the basis of provocation. He sentenced her to three years probation and 150 hours of community service.

In *R v Buzzacott*[61] the defence raised both self-defence and provocation and chose not to have the facts put to the jury. Bollen J of the South Australian Supreme Court accepted that the accused had been abused by the deceased on the night of the incident and over a period of months, and that she did not intend to kill her abusive partner. However, the judge did not accept that the accused manifested the battered woman syndrome: "I do not think that any situation of battered woman arises in this case. There was not sufficient battering."[62] The judge rejected both self-defence and provocation and convicted the woman of manslaughter. She was sentenced to four years imprisonment with a minimum term of two years.

Mitigation of sentence following a guilty plea

In *R v Woolsey*[63] the accused stabbed her husband after he had threatened to kill her intellectually disabled son and had assaulted her. Her son had barricaded himself in his bedroom and was attempting to leave to seek help via the window. The Crown accepted a guilty plea to manslaughter on the basis of provocation and did not proceed with a murder charge. Battered woman syndrome evidence was run successfully in mitigation of sentence and the Supreme Court of New South Wales imposed a suspended sentence. Newman J made it clear that in his opinion domestic violence, no matter how extreme, would not justify leniency in cases involving manslaughter due to provocation. However in this case the prisoner's plea to manslaughter was more properly founded on an unlawful and dangerous act.

In *R v Spencer*[64] the Crown accepted a plea of guilty to manslaughter on the basis of provocation and "possibly also diminished responsibility". The Supreme Court of New South Wales sentenced the accused to three years periodic detention. While the Court did not use the label "battered woman syndrome", it accepted expert evidence from a psychologist and a psychiatrist which amounted to the same thing.[65]

In *R v Taylor*[66] the accused pleaded guilty to manslaughter before the South Australian Supreme Court. She was given a five year suspended sentence and a good behaviour bond. Over the years Taylor had her teeth broken up to a dozen times, her nose smashed with an iron and handfuls of her hair ripped out by her violent husband. After enduring an assault the accused shot her husband in the head as he sat in front of the television. The Crown argued unsuccessfully that she had not been subjected to enough violence to qualify for the battered woman syndrome. The judge accepted that she was suffering from the syndrome at the time of the offence. He commented that she had put up with "a nightmare situation...in a manner and with a degree of stoicism which would have been unthinkable in the case of most other people". He also placed part of the blame for the shooting on an "unimaginative social security officer" who had failed to provide enough assistance when Taylor had sought a restraining order against her husband.

In *R v Gunnarsson Weiner*[67] the accused pleaded guilty to counts of perverting the course of justice, breaching the Tasmanian Companies Code and dishonestly obtaining a financial advantage contrary to the Tasmanian Criminal Code. The Supreme Court of Tasmania accepted evidence of the battered woman syndrome in mitigation of sentence and imposed suspended sentences.[68] The judge stated that "had it not been for the conduct of the husband towards the accused it would have been appropriate to send the accused to prison immediately".

Runjanjic and Kontinnen were set down for re-trial following the appeal decision reported above. However before re-trial, the appellants agreed to plead guilty to the charge of false imprisonment and all other charges were abandoned by the prosecution. Both women were given suspended sentences.[69]

Prosecutorial discretion

Sherrie Seakins was charged by the Northern Territory DPP with murdering her violent de facto husband.[70] She refused to plead guilty to manslaughter, indicating that she intended to seek a complete acquittal on the basis of self-defence, as supported by the battered woman syndrome. The facts were that she had pretended to be unconscious after four hours of beatings and threats by her de facto husband. She had then killed him with a tomahawk, the same weapon which he had threatened to use to cut off their baby's head. The DPP exercised prosecutorial discretion in deciding not to proceed to trial.

Miscarriage of justice

In *R v Kina*[71] the appellant had left the room where she was under attack by her violent de facto and returned with a knife with which she stabbed him. At her trial she did not give or call evidence. She was convicted of murder and was sentenced to life imprisonment.

Almost four and a half years later, her petition for a pardon was referred by the Attorney General to the Supreme Court of Queensland as an appeal. The Court allowed the appeal and ordered a retrial. The President and Davies J A relied on the fact that her Aboriginality, the battered woman syndrome and the shameful nature (to her) of the events which characterised her relationship with the deceased[72] had interacted to produce exceptional difficulties in communication between herself and her lawyers. The result was a miscarriage of justice due to inadequate legal representation. McPherson J A found a miscarriage of justice on the basis that evidence suggesting self-defence or provocation, and thus of a nature likely to produce acquittal, was not available at the original trial. This evidence was to the effect that the deceased's history of violence towards the accused included frequent anal rape, that he had demanded anal intercourse on the night in question and had threatened to anally rape the young niece of the accused who was living with them at the time. The DPP in its exercise of prosecutorial discretion announced that it would not proceed with the retrial.

A Feminist Critique

Recent cases have demonstrated a possible shift in the court's response to women charged with a criminal offence in the context of domestic violence. The cases reviewed above indicate that whilst three women have been acquitted where evidence of battered woman syndrome has been introduced,[73] others have received non-custodial sentences. These outcomes differ markedly from those in apparently comparable cases in the recent past.[74] Prior to the introduction of evidence concerning the battered woman syndrome there had been no reported cases in which women who had killed their violent partners had been successful in gaining a complete acquittal.[75] That possibility is now raised by *Hickey* and *Kontinnen*. The cases *Gilbert*, *Woolsey* and *Taylor* demonstrate that there is now a significant possibility of a non-custodial or suspended sentence following a verdict of manslaughter. The *Kina* case also raises the possibility of the review of the sentences or convictions of those women already serving long sentences for killing their violent partners.[76]

We should be cautious however about proclaiming the success of the battered woman syndrome for a number of reasons. First, it is not clear to what extent the above outcomes can be attributed solely, or in part if at all, to the use of evidence concerning the battered woman syndrome in court. Over the same period in which these cases were determined, that is since early 1991, there have been major on-going community education campaigns concerning domestic violence. There have been successive rounds of law reform in all Australian jurisdictions providing for enhanced protection orders and addressing domestic violence related offences. There have been several controversial decisions which have generated a public debate about gender bias in the law and the need for judicial education concerning bias. There have also been public inquiries concerning gender bias and the law[77] and the adequacy of existing defences to charges of homicide.[78] Each of these factors, singly or in combination, may have contributed to changing attitudes of juries, and/or lawyers and judges in dealing with domestic violence related matters.

Secondly, there is the concern that the results in at least some of the above cases suggest that any improvement in outcomes may be partial. One reading of the above cases suggests that there remains a real reluctance by courts to acquit in domestic violence related homicide cases, and also a reluctance by counsel to argue self-defence. In the three cases in which the defendant raised both self-defence and provocation, *Muy Ky Chhay*, *Gilbert* and *Buzzacott,* the courts found the defendant guilty of manslaughter. A reading of the facts in *Woolsey* and *Taylor*, in which each defendant entered a guilty plea, suggests that self-defence may have been a more appropriate plea. [79]

While we applaud any improvement in result for these women, our concern is that the battered woman syndrome does not appear to have presented many challenges to the patterns of gender bias informing the law and legal practice. It remains possible to see each of the levels at which women's stories were distorted by the legal system prior to the advent of the syndrome in operation in the cases using battered woman syndrome evidence.

Decontextualisation of the offender's actions

From its inception in Australia the battered woman syndrome has been used to explain the psychology of the offender rather than locating her in the broader context in which her actions took place.[80]

Runjanjic and Kontinnen[81] and *Kontinnen*[82] both emphasised that expert evidence on the battered woman syndrome is directed towards explaining the responses of ordinary and reasonable women to circumstances of domestic violence.[83] However, in both cases the syndrome evidence did not focus directly on what it was about the **circumstances** of domestic violence that could produce a criminal response in reasonable women but rather on the transient **psychological state** occurring in otherwise normal women as a result of surviving such abuse. As a consequence both cases mention the actual circumstance of the violence survived by the women concerned but neither do more than partially locate that violence within the broader set of circumstances in which it took place. Furthermore, those surrounding circumstances that do receive mention are stripped of "objective reality" by the focus placed on the offender's psychology. The suggestion is that these circumstances form a part of the "subjective" impressions of a mind temporarily affected by an abnormal experience of violence.

For example, in *Runjanjic and Kontinnen* King CJ describes how as a consequence of violence battered women develop a "perceived" (and by implication not real) "inability to escape the situation". They have an "all pervasive feeling" (as opposed to a belief based on reasonable grounds) "that it is impossible to escape the violence and domination of the mate". While he mentions some of the socio-economic factors (financial dependence, children and separation assault) which might prevent women from escaping violent circumstances, his reference to them is a brief notation that they might reinforce the inaccurate belief patterns he is describing. In *Kontinnen* the expert comments on the "catch 22" situation the accused and other women like her face when they are unable to continue living with the violence and unable to leave because of the limitations of police protection, the lack of a safe place to go and the fear that, if they leave, the batterer will find them and the violence and brutality will be worse than before. Just one page later the expert discounts the social reality of this catch 22 situation he has described by labelling battered women's inability to leave, and their fear that if they do they will just exacerbate the violence, as a symptom of their "psychological dysfunction".[84]

In *Hickey*[85] the tension between circumstances and psychology is resolved in favour of a firm emphasis on the latter. The expert's treatment of the battered woman syndrome in this case goes beyond a description of how ordinary women in the process of surviving domestic violence might develop a unique perspective on their circumstances and a cluster of behavioural symptoms, as is the conventional wisdom demonstrated in the preceding two cases. He suggests that battered women are a category of people with a particular sort of mental and emotional makeup, one that is not only "inadequate" but that predates the violence itself and may therefore, by implication, be congenital or permanent.[86] He implies that battered women are the sort of people who are prone to enter into and possibly contribute to the creation of relationships characterised by violence.[87] He says that battered women:

> are normally quite dependant people, people if you like who initially when they get into the relationship place a great deal of emphasis on their mate, on the man, taking responsibility for their lives. This is when he starts to bash her.[88]

He recognises the accused as belonging to this category of people because of her "personality type".[89] He locates responsibility for the difficulties such women have in protecting themselves from violence or leaving the relationship in their personal inability to be anything other than passive or to survive life without their partner. He comments that they remain living with such abuse because, "They simply don't know how not to. They don't have the resources. There can't be assertion in a relationship."[90]

The expert's suggestion in *Hickey* that battered women have a psychological predisposition to dependency and helplessness means that, as well as failing to highlight the range of factors which might make women generally vulnerable to such abuse, the on-going and escalating violence itself is erased.

It is worth noting that the facts as they emerge from other witnesses' testimonies in *Hickey* make a psychological explanation of Hickey's inability to escape the violence she experienced unnecessary.[91] Instead these testimonies indicate the inadequacy of the external resources available to assist the accused in protecting herself. She was a young Aboriginal woman, marginalised by a racist society, who had little by way of job prospects and two dependant children. The accused was no physical match for her violent de facto husband and on those occasions when she stood up to him she was "bashed" by him. His violence towards herself and their children escalated when she left him, or attempted to do so, which she had done several times:

> I tried to leave him but if I left him he would bash me in the streets, drag me home and get into me again.[92]

There was evidence that the police and the criminal justice system had failed to provide her with any real protection. There was also a limit to the physical protection her family could offer her. The deceased was a strong man and had on occasions hit, stabbed and threatened various members of her family.

In *Woolsey* there are no details in the judgment of the deceased's violence towards the accused, the substance of the threats he made to her and action she had taken to protect herself and the children. The judge mentions that the accused had attempted to enlist police protection but comments that "the evidence is vague as to when it was that she had made complaints to the police". Instead the expert testified that:

> Due to her limited resources, she was not able to perceive any other alternative but to put up with his behaviour and it does seem that she had been somewhat dependant on him. This is rather inconsistent with her own statements about her dependency as she views herself as being a very independent person. However, she does not feel that she had any opportunity to leave her husband as he had threatened both her and the children. Rather than perceive that she would be able to get away, she then felt sufficiently threatened and therefore made no attempt to leave him.[93]

In *Spencer* no mention is made of the constraints that operate to prevent battered women from protecting themselves and their children by peaceable means. Instead the judge asks:

> why the prisoner did not terminate her relationship with the deceased if the situation was as bad as she painted, rather than remain with him with the devastating consequences which followed,[94]

and finds his answer in the psychology of women;

> It is not an unusual phenomenon for women, even women without children, to feel trapped in relationships and to lack the will or the capacity to escape from them. The prisoner has a very dependant personality. I accept that this personality trait played a major role in her remaining within this relationship, difficult and violent as it appears to have been.[95]

R v Gilbert signals a significant change in approach. In this case defence counsel not only relied on the battered woman syndrome but also succeeded in introducing a range of other evidence concerning the circumstances in which the accused woman had been living. An Aboriginal tribal elder was called who described the breakdown in Aboriginal law which has occurred in recent decades, one consequence of which was that:

> people like Miss Gilbert living in remote communities lost the protection of the checks and balances that were in existence in that Aboriginal custom and therefore had to turn to the non-Aboriginal institutions to protect her.[96]

Evidence was also given by this witness that people had tried to protect the accused against the deceased but because he was very strong and aggressive they were powerless to do so. He testified that the accused had sought help that was not available, that she was economically dependant on the deceased and that she had children to look after.

Other evidence indicated that a range of institutions had failed to respond to reports about the deceased's violence against the accused and their children. This failure occurred in the face of complaints to the police, the hospitalisation of the accused and the fact that the violence was general knowledge throughout the community. A retired Aboriginal police aide also testified to having witnessed an assault on the accused by the deceased for which she was hospitalised but in respect of which the police had not laid charges.

This evidence formed the basis for arguing that she had run out of realistic alternative means to protect herself at the time of the killing. The defence asked the jury to consider self-defence and provocation in the context of the deceased's past violence, his response to the accused's past efforts to protect herself and his threats as to what he would do if she left him, her lack of comparative size and strength, her economic dependence on him, the lack of support facilities or institutions both in the Aboriginal and the white community for people in her position (including a total lack of police assistance), and the fact that efforts by others to protect her had failed.

In addition to this description of the circumstances in which the accused found herself the defence called a psychologist, the same expert who had testified in *Hickey*. He gave evidence that the accused suffered from the battered woman syndrome and that, as a consequence of the repeated violence to which she had been subjected, her perceptions and responses were different to those of a normal person. He also gave evidence about a "trigger" which he testified could stir an otherwise depressed, dependant and passive woman into striking back.[97]

The tension between the evidence concerning the broader circumstances in which the accused found herself, and the psychological evidence introduced in this case shows in the unintentional irony of the judge's sentencing comments. He described a situation in which the accused was unable to escape the deceased in spite of her best attempts to do so:

> on the occasions when you had left him he had pursued you and virtually compelled you to return to him... You were extremely fearful of him and he was a very strong man, considerably stronger than you. Other people had been powerless to stop his continued violence towards you.[98]

In the next sentence he concluded that:

> as Mr Taylor expressed it, you had reached the stage of learned helplessness and apathy so that you were quite unable to resist the attacks upon you.[99]

With the benefit of hindsight counsel for the defence has commented to the authors that in his opinion battered woman syndrome evidence is inappropriate in a case like *Gilbert*. The accused's failure to leave the deceased over the years, and her inability to protect herself from his violence, can be readily explained by external circumstances. There is no need to talk about her psychology. To do so encourages the jury to think along the lines of provocation and tempts them to reach a compromise verdict of manslaughter.

The legal rules defining self-defence

As previously mentioned traditional self-defence doctrine embodies a range of concepts that are inappropriate to the circumstances and the manner in which women typically defend themselves or their children. In particular notions of imminence need to be challenged if self-defence is to be realistically available to battered women.

Both *Kontinnen* and *Hickey* were cases where self-defence arguably was successfully run in non-traditional circumstances. In *Kontinnen* the deceased was shot while he was sleeping after making threats. In *Hickey*[100] one possible and very damaging reading of the facts was that the accused's defensive force was pre-emptive, in the sense that she was not responding to an attack actually or almost underway. In spite of the success of self-defence in both these cases, neither case used the battered woman syndrome to directly challenge gender bias in the configuration of self-defence doctrine.[101] Unlike the judgment in *Lavallee*, there was no explicit acknowledgment in the cases that self-defence doctrine may be constructed in a manner which does not reflect women's experiences. Rather the focus was on the psychological consequences for a woman of enduring serious domestic violence. This approach has prompted the comment that the syndrome is being used to tack a new and stereotypical norm of the battered woman on to the old unchallenged male norms and experience embodied in the current application of self-defence doctrine.[102]

More disturbing are the recent cases of *R v Woolsey*[103] and *R v Taylor*.[104] Both cases lend themselves to interpretation as cases involving pre-emptive strikes according to traditional self-defence doctrine. In neither case was the battered woman syndrome run to challenge traditional legal doctrine and support self-defence. Instead it was run in mitigation of sentence after the accused had pleaded guilty to manslaughter.

Most disturbing of all is the suggestion that, as well as having to meet traditional male norms of self-defence, women are being subjected to an extra unwritten requirement, that is the requirement that they leave the violent relationship if they wish to qualify for self-defence. This is evident in the fact that in many of the cases where the battered woman syndrome is introduced it is used to explain why the accused had not terminated her relationship with the deceased. The focus on whether a woman had left the relationship implies that her description of the violence she was subjected to is not credible unless her failure to exit the situation is explained. In most cases the question of why a woman may have continued to live in a violent relationship is irrelevant to the legal issues raised by a strict application of self-defence doctrine.

Reasonableness

It has been argued that expert evidence concerning the battered woman syndrome, while purportedly demonstrating that the conduct of battered women might be reasonable within the circumstances in which they find themselves, in fact "reinforces notions of irrationality or disorder on the part of the woman".[105] The suggestion in *Hickey*[106] that battered women have an inability to cope with life that predates their experience of violence implies that the expert is not discussing the reasonableness of Hickey's beliefs but her personal inability to meet the reasonableness standard.

Elizabeth Schneider has argued on the basis of her considerable experience in the United States in working for the defence in cases using battered woman syndrome, that evidence of battered woman syndrome is often not understood by courts as demonstrating the reasonableness of a woman's belief that homicide was necessary to preserve her own life. Rather, Schneider believes that courts understand the evidence as a form of psychological defence or as evidence of an impaired mental state.[107]

MacCrimmon[108] criticises the battered woman syndrome for failing to challenge the prevailing assumption that choices women make on the basis of connectedness are irrational and blameworthy. Instead of explaining these choices as rational decisions within the framework of an alternative and equally valid set of moral norms it explains them as decisions women make from a determined and dysfunctional state of "learned helplessness" or dependency.

These points are illustrated in *Hickey*.[109] The fact that Hickey had voluntarily associated with the deceased on the night in question was viewed by her lawyer as being a serious weakness in her self-defence case. This was apparently because it destroyed her credibility both in saying that she feared serious harm when he attacked her and in claiming that defensive force was a reasonably necessary response. In order to counteract this perception, the expert explained Hickey's tendency to go back to the deceased over the previous years in terms of her dependency. Her decision to meet the accused on the night in question was also excused as an irrational choice prompted by her own inadequacy:

> *Miss Hickey is not able to explain why she agreed to meet Merv on the day that she did but said that she felt relatively safe as there would have been at least one other person, being Jodie. Also they were meeting in Jodie's home, which she felt would be relatively safe....It was probably because of her low level of ability but she did act naively in thinking she was going to be a lot safer than on previous occasions.[110]*

The choice Hickey had made over the preceding years to stay, which she explained in terms of love, and the choice she made to see the deceased on the night in question, which she explained as a decision to allow him to see the children, did not have to be constructed as helplessness or dependency. If such choices are at all relevant[111] then they are better explained in her own terms as decisions made on the basis of a sense of connectedness with others. The ethic of care which some have argued characterise women's decisions are reinforced in Hickey's case by the high importance given in Aboriginal communities to social and kinship obligations. A loyalty that is, in turn, reinforced by the racism of the broader community.

Stereotypes and dichotomies in legal thought

The battered woman syndrome has been criticised for being logically inconsistent. The concept of learned helplessness does not fit with either the woman's actions in killing her abuser or the agency displayed in the "help seeking behav-

iours of some women".[112] The expert's testimony in *Hickey*[113] graphically illustrates this argument. He was only able to avoid such an inconsistency by constructing a personality profile of the accused that downplayed or ignored all
her acts of agency. Hickey was constructed as being dependant, passive and
inadequate, a construction which seems at odds with the facts of the case.
Hickey had left the deceased on numerous occasions (and was separated from
him at the time in question), had gone to the police (demonstrating, given the
antipathy between the Aboriginal community in which she lived and the police,
a strong commitment to her personal safety), had obtained an Apprehended
Violence Order and had run the risk of aggravating him every time she had
attempted to stand up to him.

The acceptance of battered woman syndrome evidence by the Australian
courts may well be attributable to the fact that it has been used to reinforce,
and lend medical and professional credibility to, the very stereotypes about
women's passivity, masochism and responsibility for domestic violence that it
was developed in order to challenge. This is troublesome because it means that
women's self-defence claims, so long as they remain reliant on its use,[114] stand
on a precarious footing in Australia. If expert witnesses are unable to convincingly construct a helpless and dependent personality profile for a particular
woman in order to invoke the battered woman syndrome, then she will have to
establish imminence and necessity, and meet credibility standards on the intact
male terms.[115] It is also troublesome because the syndrome does not necessarily
describe the experiences of those women who can be constructed to fit within
the model provided by the syndrome. Many women reject the label of "battered
women" because they object to being represented as victims.[116] Their behaviours which are interpreted, by means of the syndrome, as self-denying and
compliant actually may be courageous and rational strategies for survival.[117]

The intersection of race and gender

The feminist critique of battered woman syndrome utilised above raises a number of significant concerns about the manner in which evidence concerning the
syndrome has been used in Australian cases. A further issue which has not been
adequately addressed in the literature is the concern that the syndrome has
been constructed from the experiences of white, middle class women, and may
misrepresent the experiences of other (Other) women.

Recent American literature suggests that the representation of battered
women as passive, helpless and dependent may be distorted and damaging for
women generally, but especially may be at odds with the experiences of Black
women whose lives do not readily conform to middle class gender role stereotypes.[118] There is no comparable Australian literature which examines battered
woman syndrome in the context of race,[119] and we cannot simply equate the

experiences of Aboriginal and Torres Strait Islander women in Australia[120] with those of African-American women. However, criticisms of the battered woman syndrome as constructed on white, middle class norms raise important questions about the manner in which the syndrome can be, and is applied in Australia with respect to Aboriginal and Torres Strait Islander women.[121]

The authors have argued elsewhere that it is crucial that the intersection of race and gender be addressed in locating the context in which an Aboriginal or Torres Strait Island woman defendant has acted.[122] Neither a feminist analysis nor anti-racist discourse alone offer the prospect of an adequate understanding of the specific context or life experiences of an Aboriginal or Torres Strait Island woman. [123]

There have been four cases identified to date in which an Aboriginal woman has been charged with murder, and in which the battered woman syndrome has been raised at some stage within the legal process—*Hickey*,[124] *Buzzacott*,[125] *Kina*[126] and *Gilbert*.[127] In reading those cases from a perspective attentive to the intersection of race and gender,[128] a number of problems emerge.

A disjunction between stereotypes of battered women and Aboriginal women's experiences

Stereotypes deny the diversity of women's experiences. Aboriginal and Torres Strait Islander women who have been the target of male violence confront two sets of stereotypes—those of battered women and those of Aboriginal women. Dominant representations of Aboriginal women have often distorted the role of Aboriginal women within Aboriginal communities, denying their leadership, political engagement, and their role in maintaining their culture. [129] As Jan Pettman has argued Aboriginal women are often presumed to be dependent on men, when in fact they

> are often heads of households, responsible for the financial as well as the emotional survival of their families as primary kin-keepers.[130]

This double designation of dependency, that is dependent as a battered woman and dependent as an Aboriginal woman, may render it very difficult for an Aboriginal woman's resort to lethal self-help to be understood and to be acknowledged as reasonable and necessary. Aboriginal women who are assertive, economically independent and who fight back against the violence that they experience may have difficulties in fitting the dominant stereotype of a battered woman as dependent.

In both *Hickey* and *Gilbert* the evidence presented to the Court is capable of being read as indicating survival against enormous odds. Both suffered extreme violence, and had made a number of attempts to seek protection from the police, and assistance from other Aboriginal and non-Aboriginal agencies. The

Courts seemed particularly unable to accommodate evidence which depicted the defendants as resourceful, and actively seeking aid whilst at the same time being the victim of life threatening violence. Instead evidence of their agency and survival was accorded less weight than that which conformed with the dominant construction of both Aboriginal women, and battered women, as dependent, apathetic and helpless.

In *Buzzacott* the defendant was said not to have been "battered enough" to satisfy the criteria for the battered woman syndrome. It is not clear what the judge's reasoning in this case was, nor what would constitute "enough". However, there is a concern amongst Aboriginal workers in the field of domestic violence that the myth that domestic violence is acceptable in traditional Aboriginal or Torres Strait Island cultures has been used to deny Aboriginal or Torres Strait Island women protection and justice.[131]

The failure to place Aboriginal women's behaviour in a broader context which includes the racism of the larger society

In *Hickey* the defendant's behaviour was not presented in the context of her experience as a young urban Aboriginal woman living in a racist society. Her experience as an early school leaver, with limited education and no experience in the paid workforce was presented as further evidence of her personal inadequacy, and was not located in the broader context of the limited educational and work opportunities available to Aboriginal women. These characteristics are not only personal to the defendant, but unfortunately reflect the position of a significant number of Aboriginal and Torres Strait Islander women in Australia. Hickey's connection with her family and her peers, was also presented by the expert witness in her case as evidence of her dependency and personal inadequacy. An alternative and more positive reading is one in which this affiliation with friends and family is characteristic of being a well functioning member of an Aboriginal community. Greater weight could also have been attached to Hickey's resort to the police, and attaining a domestic violence order, both of which were ineffective, in trying to deal with her ex-de facto's violence. In a small community in which relationships between Aboriginal people and the police have been hostile, this resort to criminal justice intervention shows a considerable resourcefulness on her part and a commitment to her own personal safety and that of her children.

By contrast with *Hickey*, the defence team in *Gilbert* went to great lengths to ensure that the context in which the defendant lived, and had killed her abusive partner, were put to the court. As described above, a tribal elder from the remote community in which the defendant lived gave evidence to the court, and the psychologist who was to present expert testimony about the battered woman syndrome was taken to that community to see at first hand how the defendant lived, and to meet other Aboriginal women from the community.

The cultural specificity of psychological testing

As argued above, Australian cases on battered woman syndrome have attached considerable weight to "learned helplessness" as a defining characteristic of the syndrome. Evidence has typically been given by a psychologist or psychiatrist often relying at least in part on IQ tests and/or diagnostic tests.[132] In *Hickey* the relevance of IQ to the battered woman syndrome was never made clear. Nor was there any acknowledgment of the extensive literature which argues that such tests are culturally specific, and that performance on the tests may be influenced by factors such as cultural variation in what constitutes "intelligence", the interaction between tester and the subject, familiarity with language and the danger of interpreting "outgroup" speech as inadequate, different cognitive styles and temporal sequences.[133]

Communication and the legal process

The *Kina* case has provided dramatic evidence of the injustices which can occur when Aboriginal women are unable to tell their stories, or are not heard. Profound "problems, difficulties and misunderstandings and mishaps" occurred in communication between Kina and her lawyers which resulted in certain evidence not being put before the court, and the defendant not giving or calling evidence at the trial.[134]

A reading of the transcript in *Hickey* also suggests that the Court was not attentive to the issue of appropriate forms of communication with Aboriginal English speaking witnesses.[135] The examination and cross examination of several key defence witnesses suggest fundamental misunderstandings occurred through the use of forms of questioning at odds with accepted speech forms for Aboriginal English speakers.[136]

Conclusion

When the battered woman syndrome first appeared in Australia we argued that it sat more comfortably with defences like diminished responsibility and provocation and might well end up being redirected into those areas.[137] Our concerns seem to have some foundation as evidenced by the number of cases in which the battered woman syndrome has been used to support a manslaughter conviction, or in mitigation of sentence in circumstances where a complete acquittal may have been more appropriate. There are few cases in which judges have given us any insight into the impact of testimony concerning the battered woman syndrome on their reasoning, and in the remaining cases we can but speculate as to what the outcome might have been in the absence of such evidence.[138] However, if the syndrome had presented a lasting challenge to patterns of gender (and race) bias informing the law of self-defence then arguably cases like *Gilbert*, *Woolsey* and *Taylor* would have been recognised as involving circumstances typical of women acting in self-defence. The development of battered woman syndrome in Australia seems in stark contrast to the fundamental challenges to traditional doctrine envisaged by Madame Justice Bertha Wilson in *Lavallee*.

Notes

1　Diminished responsibility is available as a defence to murder in New South Wales, Queensland, the Australian Capital Territory and the Northern Territory, but not in other Australian jurisdictions. See *The Laws of Australia: Homicide* (1992) at 192.

2　Lansdowne, R and Bacon, W, *Women Homicide Offenders in New South Wales* (1982).

3　The case of *The Queen v R* is an anomalous one in which a woman on re-trial following appeal offered a defence of provocation but was nonetheless acquitted by a jury, (1981) 28 SASR 321. See Brown, D, Farrier, D, Neal, D and Weisbrot, D, *Criminal Laws* (1990) at 747.

4　See Public Policy Research Centre, *Community Attitudes Towards Domestic Violence in Australia*, (Feb 1988). The report is summarised in Graycar, R and Morgan, J, *The Hidden Gender of Law* (1990) at 279-280. A New Zealand study has found that judges tend to continue this tradition by employing "family dysfunction" modes of analysing and understanding domestic violence, see Busch, this volume, and for the full report see Busch, R, Robertson, N and Lapsley, H, *Protection from Family Violence: A Study of Protection Orders under the Domestic Protection Act* (1992) at 153.

5　In New South Wales, for example, spousal killings amount to approximately one quarter of all homicides. Women are three times more likely to be killed by than to kill their spouses. A history of marital violence (almost exclusively male violence on women) is officially recorded in police files in at least 48 per cent of the spousal killings, 70 per cent of cases which involved wives killing their husbands and 40 per cent of cases where husbands killed their wives. Wallace, A, *Homicide: The Social Reality*, (1986); Bonney, R, *Homicide II* (1987).

6　Relegating past violence to the function of background information is also an inevitable result of the emphasis which self-defence doctrine gives to the immediate circumstances surrounding the particular killing; Tarrant, S, "Provocation and Self Defence: A Feminist Perspective" 15:4 (August 1990) *Legal Service Bulletin* 147.

7　Unreported Supreme Court of New South Wales, 5 April 1991.

8   Australian Law Reform Commission *Equality Before the Law: Women's Access to the Legal System* Report No 67 (Interim) ALRC Sydney.

9   Hatty, S, *Male Violence and the Police: An Australian Experience* (1988) at 184; McCulloch, J, "Police Response to Domestic Violence" in Hatty, S (ed), *Domestic Violence* (1985) at 523.

10   Stubbs, J and Powell, D, *Domestic Violence: Impact of Legal Reform in New South Wales* (1989); Stubbs, J and Wallace, A, "Protecting Victims of Domestic Violence?" in Findlay , M and Hogg, R (eds), *Understanding Crime and Criminal Justice* (1988) at 52.

11   Separation is considered by many to be the most dangerous time for the woman involved in a battering relationship. Not surprisingly some women cite fear as a major reason for not leaving the relationship. Nor does leaving guarantee an end to the violence. Wallace, above n16 at 98, found that 46 per cent of the spousal killings by men involved women who had either left or were in the process of leaving the relationship. Martha Mahoney has coined the term separation assault to refer to the fact that violence is a common response to a woman's attempt to separate from a relationship, and that some men use violence to intimidate women into remaining in a violent relationship; see Mahoney, M, "Legal Images of Battered Women: Redefining the Issue of Separation" (1991) 90 *Mich LR* 1.

12   Graycar, R, "Violence in the Home—A Legal Response: A Limited Solution", (1988) 26 (4) *Law Society Journal* 46.

13   Noesjirwan, J, *Evaluation of Women's Refuges 1985: Ten Years On* (1985) at 14.

14   Watson, S, *Accommodating Inequality: Gender and Housing* (1988).

15   Graycar, R, "Equal Rights Versus Father's Rights: The Child Custody Debate in Australia" in Smart , C and Sevenhuijsen, S (eds), *Child Custody and the Politics of Gender* (1989).

16   See, for example, the following cases in which the broader social and political factors would seem to have been relevant: *R v Collingburn* (1985) 18 A.Crim.R. 295; *R v Hill* (1981) 3 A.Crim.R. 397; *The Queen v R* (1981) 28 S.A.S.R. 321; *R v Cornick* (unreported) Tasmanian Court of Criminal Appeal, 1987; *R v Whalen* (unreported) Supreme Court of New South Wales, 14 April 1992; *R v Rose* (unreported) Supreme Court of Western Australia, August 1989.

17   Christine Boyle has suggested that a trier of fact should consider the following factors in assessing whether self-defence should be available:

(1) Were there realistic alternative means which the accused could have used to protect herself or other persons?

(2) (If relevant) with respect to (1), had the accused attempted alternatives in the past?

(2) Was she afraid of retaliation if she attempted any alternative?

(4) What was the accused's economic and psychological state?

(5) How did the accused and the person she killed or assaulted compare in size and strength?

(6) Was the accused's action reasonable, given her socialisation?

From Russell, J (ed), A Feminist Review of Criminal Law (1985) at 41.

18 This is hardly surprising given community explanations of domestic violence which stereotype the victim, blame her for contributing to the violence and diminish her credibility or attribute responsibility to her for not exiting the situation. See: Schuller, R, "The Impact of Battered Woman Syndrome Testimony on Jury Decision Making: *Lavallee v R* Considered" (1990) 10 *Windsor Yearbook of Access to Justice* 105 at 116; Walker, L, Thyfault, R and Browne, A, "Beyond the Jurors' Ken: Battered Women" (1982) 7 *Vermont LR* 1; Hatty, S, "Policing and Male Violence in Australia" in Hanmer, J, Radford, J and Stanko, E, *Women, Policing and Male Violence*(1989) at 70.

19 See; Lansdowne and Bacon, above n2; Bacon, W and Lansdowne, R, "Women Who Kill Husbands: The Battered Woman on Trial" in O'Donnell, C and Craney, J (eds), *Family Violence in Australia* (1992) at 67; Tolmie, J, "Provocation or Self-Defence for Battered Women Who Kill" in Yeo, S (ed), *Partial Excuses to Murder* (1990) at 61; Sheehy, E, Stubbs, J and Tolmie, J, "Defending Battered Women on Trial: The Battered Women Syndrome and its Limitations" (1992) 16:6 *Criminal LJ* 369.

20 Id at 374.

21 For a general discussion of the rule on hearsay see; Byrne, D and Heydon, J, *Cross on Evidence* (3rd edn,1986) at 727; Ligertwood, A, *Australian Evidence* (1988) at 332.

22 See *Lavallee*, (1990) 55 C.C.C. (3d) 97; Schneider, E, "Equal Rights to Trial for Women: Sex Bias in the Law of Self-Defense" (1980) 15 *Harv Civil Rights-Civil Liberties LR* 623; Kinports, K, "Defending Battered Women's Self-Defense Claims" (1988) 67 *Oregon LR* 391; P Crocker, "The Meaning of Equality for Battered Women Who Kill Men in Self-Defense" (1985) 8 *Harv Women's LJ* 121.

23 Wallace, above n5.

24 Wells, C, "Domestic Violence and Self-Defence" (1990) 140 *New LJ* 127; Sheehy, Stubbs, and Tolmie, above n19 at 12; O'Donovan, K, "Defences for Battered Women Who Kill" (1991) 18:2 *J of Law and Society* 219; Tarrant, above n6.

25 (1987) 71 ALR 641, 652

26 *The Queen v R*, above n3.

27 *Hill*, above n16.

28 *Cornick*, above n16.

29 In *Lavallee* Wilson J cites an American decision in which the judge found that a requirement for a battered woman to wait "until the physical assault is 'underway' before her apprehensions can be validated in law" would be "sentencing her to murder by instalment", see above n22 at 120.

30 Blackman, C, "Potential Uses for Expert Testimony: Ideas Towards the Representation of Battered Women Who Kill" (1986) 9 *Women's Rights Law Reporter* 227, 229.

31 Tarrant, above n6 at 149.

32 The test in Australia is whether or not the accused had reasonable grounds for her beliefs. See Sheehy, Stubbs and Tolmie, above n19 at 374.

33 *Lavallee*, above n22 at 114; Findley, L, "Breaking Women's Silence in Law: The Dilemma of the Gendered Nature of Legal Reasoning" (1989) 64 *Notre Dame LR* 886, 898.

34 MacCrimmon, M, "The Social Construction of Reality and the Rules of Evidence" (1991) 25 *UBCLR* 36, 48.

35 For a sensitive and complex discussion of the experiences and choices of women and the manner in which the concept of "exit" rewrites and obscures those choices see Mahoney, M, "Exit: Power and the Idea of Leaving in Love, Work and the Confirmation Hearings" (1992) 65 *Southern California LR* 1283; see also Leader-Elliot, I, "Battered But Not Beaten: Women Who Kill in Self Defence" (1993) 15 *Syd LR* 403.

36 Schneider, E, "Describing and Changing: Women's Self Defence Work and the Problem of Expert Testimony on Battering" (1986) 9 *Women's Rights Law Reporter* 195.

37 Although note *Winnett v Stephenson* below at n55.

38 Walker, L, *The Battered Woman Syndrome* (1984); Walker, L, "Battered Women, Psychology, and Public Policy" (1984) 29 *Am. Psychologist*; Ewing, C, *Battered Women Who Kill* (1987).

39 See Schneider, above n36.

40 Above n22: see Sheehy this volume for an analysis of the Canadian cases since *Lavallee*.

41 Above n22 at 115, 120, 124.

42 Id at 114.

43 Id at 113.

44 Id at 126.

45 Id at 123.

46 Id at 123.

47 Id at 124.

48 (1991) 53 A. Crim. R 362.

49 See Stubbs and Powell, above n10; Stubbs and Wallace, above n10; Graycar and Morgan, above n4 at 277.

50 King CJ was determining whether the law governing an admissibility of expert opinion permitted the introduction of testimony on the syndrome. Traditionally the courts had taken the view that experts are unable to assist triers of fact on the subject of human behaviour because this is a matter within their common knowledge. Magner, E, "Explaining the Construct: Opinion Evidence and the Battered Woman Syndrome" a presentation for *The Role of the Battered Woman Syndrome in Criminal Defences* (1992).

51 See, for example, Faigman, D, "The Battered Woman Syndrome and Self Defence: A legal and Empirical Dissent" (1986) 72 *Va LR* 619; Sheehy, Stubbs, and Tolmie, above n19; Stubbs, J, "The (Un)reasonable Battered Woman?: A Response to Easteal" 3:3 (1992) *Current Issues in Criminal Justice* 359; Leader-Elliot above n35.

52 See Martinson, D, Macrimmon, M, Grant, I and Boyle, C, "A Forum on *Lavallee*: Women and Self Defence" (1991) 25 *UBCLR* 23.

53 Above n48.

54 The defence was only partially successful. The appellant was acquitted of one count and convicted of another. Her appeal to the South Australian Court of Criminal Appeal was dismissed, unreported SA Court of Criminal Appeal 19 June 1992.

55 ACT Magistrates Court, unreported, 19 May 1993. The accused was charged with seven counts of imposing on the Commonwealth related to the receipt of unemployment benefits and rental assistance from the Department of Social Security in her maiden name while she was employed. The defence of duress was successful and the information dismissed and the defendant discharged by the magistrate. The case is noteworthy for two reasons. First, because the court, the ACT Magistrate's Court, accepted expert evidence concerning the battered woman syndrome from a criminologist, rather than from a psychiatrist or a psychologist which has been the usual practice in Australian courts. Secondly, the magistrate indicated explicitly that if not for evidence of the battered woman syndrome, he would have been sceptical about the accused's testimony; Easteal, P, Hughes, K and Easter, J, "Battered Women and Duress" (1993) 18 (3) *Alt LJ* 139.

56 *Kontinnen* unreported, S.A. Supreme Court, 30 March 1992.

57 Unreported, Supreme Court NSW 14 April 1992.

58 Unreported, Supreme Court NSW 8 September, 1992.

59 Unreported, New South Wales Court of Criminal Appeal, 4 March 1994.

60 Unreported, Supreme Court of Western Australia, 4 November 1993.

61 Unreported, Supreme Court of South Australia 12 July 1993; "Judge was insensitive, not wrong says A-G", and Editorial "A Hard Case for Justice Bollen", *Sydney Morning Herald*, 11 August 1993 at 12.

62 As quoted in the Editorial, ibid.

63 Unreported, Supreme Court of N.S.W. 19 August 1993.

64 Unreported, Supreme Court N.S.W. 18 December 1992.

65 The judge found that "It is a not unusual phenomenon for women, even women without children, to feel trapped in relationships and to lack the will or the capacity to escape from them. The prisoner has a very dependent personality. I accept that this personality trait played a major role in her remaining within this relationship, difficult and violent as it appears to have been." Whilst this is a marked departure from the manner in which battered woman syndrome is utilised in *Lavallee* it is consistent with the description offered in several Australian cases, most clearly *Hickey*.

66 Unreported, Supreme Court SA February 1994.

67 Unreported, Supreme Court of Tasmania 13 August 1992.

68 Conditional on the accused entering a good behaviour bond for a period of two years.

69 Unreported Supreme Court of South Australia 10 February 1993.

70 Reported in *Sydney Morning Herald*, 14 September 1993 at 1.

71 Conviction unreported Supreme Court of Queensland 5 September 1988; appeal unreported Court of Criminal Appeal of Queensland 23 November 1988; further appeal unreported Court of Appeal of Queensland 29 November 1993.

72 The judges called these "a number of cultural, psychological and personal factors".

73 *Kontinnen, Hickey* and *Winnett v Stephenson*.

74 See above n16.

75 With the exception of *The Queen v R*, see above n3.

76 This has occurred in some US jurisdictions and a campaign is currently underway in Canada to seek the *en bloc* review of comparable cases, see Noonan, S, "Strategies for survival: Exploring the limits of the battered woman syndrome" in Currie, C and Adelberg, E (eds), *Too Few to Count* (1993); see also Sheehy, this volume.

77 ALRC above n8.

78 See for example New South Wales Law Reform Commission *Provocation, Diminished Responsibility and Infanticide* Discussion Paper No 31 1993.

79 We recognise here the difficult strategic choices which face defence counsel in such matters. It seems that counsel prefer the relatively "safe" plea to manslaughter with the attendant possibility of a community based sanction rather than the plea of self-defence, carrying as it does the risk of a conviction for murder.

80 The focus on psychology at the expense of a recognition of the constraints imposed on a woman by the circumstances which she experienced is inherent in the nature of the "syndrome" and exacerbated by the manner in which the rules of evidence have interpreted "field of expertise" and who is qualified to be an expert for the purposes of the expert opinion evidence rule. Those whom the Australian courts initially considered competent to testify in this area were psychologists and psychiatrists. Obviously *Winnett v Stephenson* makes some inroads into that position. That was the first case in which expert evidence of the battered woman syndrome was given by a criminologist. See; Byrne, D and Heydon, J, above n21 at 710; Brown, R, "Limitations on Expert Testimony on the Battered Woman Syndrome in Homicide Cases: The Return of the Ultimate Issue Rule" (1990) 32 *Arizona LR* 665.

81 Above n48.

82 Above n56.

83 In *Runjanjic and Kontinnen*, above n48 at 368, King CJ accepted syndrome evidence in support of a plea of duress because such evidence was concerned;
    with what could be expected of women generally, that is to say women of reasonable firmness who should find themselves in a domestic situation such as that in which the appellants were.

In *Kontinnen*, above n56, syndrome evidence was introduced to explain why the accused might have had reasonable grounds, on the facts of that case, for believing that her circumstances necessitated fatal self-defence. Legoe J was careful to emphasise that the syndrome was not evidence which suggested a "psychological or psychiatric illness" on the part of the accused but instead a "cumulated attitude of mind", featuring "symptoms" such as learned helplessness, chronic fear, dependency and low self-esteem. The typical result of being "brought...down...both physically and mentally" by the circumstances of a "long history of battering".

84 Above n56 at 52-4.

85 Above n57.

86 He details the category of people he labels the "battered wife" as being people who are different from other women in that they are dependant unassertive people in relationships. Their distinguishing features are that they have "learned helplessness" and are "passive in a situation". When describing learned helplessness, he neglects to link the learning component to the violence such women receive during the relationship. One can spell out an implication that it is part of the dependency he describes them bringing to relationships.

87 He comes dangerously close to suggesting that the violence in the particular accused's relationship with the deceased was a reflection of her own personality deficiencies when he comments that:
    is sensitive to the demands others make on her and yet is relatively insensitive with regard to the needs of others. Because of her lack of insight a good deal of conflict is likely to occur in her relationships.

    Above n57 at 120.

88 Id at 123.

89 Which he goes to considerable lengths to describe in his initial testimony. Her dependency, her low level of intelligence, her immaturity and her limited abilities to cope with life are mentioned.

90 Above n57 at 124. And that "She can't get away. She hasn't got the resources to cope herself therefore they remain in the situation being repeatedly bashed." He uses the word "resources" in these statements in a psychological rather than a material sense.

91 In fairness to the expert in *Hickey* he does refer to the inadequacy of the domestic violence order and some of the difficulties the accused faced in exiting her relationship with the deceased when expressing his opinion that "there seems to be a strong element of defence in what she did as she had no other means of protecting herself". However his mention of these factors

is brief compared to his detailed testimony about the psychological characteristics of both her and battered women in general. These factors are also mentioned in the context of relaying her subjective beliefs and narrative and do not form part of his professional assessment of why battered women are unable to protect themselves in violent relationships. He also alludes to the violence of the deceased but does not discuss the failures of the police to provide the accused with adequate protection.

92 Above n57 at 108.

93 Above n63 at 8.

94 Above n64 at 10.

95 Id at 11.

96 Above n60.

97 In correspondence received by the authors, counsel indicated that they had been concerned that evidence about a trigger would inspire the jury to reach a compromise verdict of manslaughter on the basis of provocation. As it transpired this fear was not unfounded.

98 Above n60 at 36.

99 Ibid.

100 Above n57.

101 Ibid. The judgment in *Kontinnen,* above n56, fails to problematise the operation of the legal doctrines giving shape to self defence in respect of battered women, and these are similarly unchallenged by the expert evidence in *Hickey.*

102 Sheehy, Stubbs and Tolmie, above n19.

103 In *Woolsey* the accused left the room to get a knife to "scare him off" and then stabbed her violent husband. He had threatened to kill her son who had barricaded himself in his bedroom and was trying to leave via the bedroom window to seek help. The deceased had then attacked her. The judge commented that "the facts of the matter do not amount to a situation where I believe that, as the law now stands, the prisoner could have successfully claimed that she acted in self defence of either herself or her son."

104 In *Taylor* the judge said to the accused; "He punched, kicked and half-strangled you. Leaving you lying on the floor in a state of considerable distress, he then sat down and ate his dinner. Having finished his dinner, he again beat you and then, having done so, simply sat down to resume drinking and watch television." It was at this stage that the accused got a rifle from the bedroom and shot her husband in the head. The Crown contended that there was not enough violence to qualify the accused for the battered woman syndrome and that the deceased was asleep in front of the television when he was shot and did not pose an immediate threat.

105 Schneider, above n36; Sheehy, Stubbs and Tolmie, above n19 at 384. Schuller, above n18 at 115, notes that in the experiments she conducted, "jurors in a number of the juries in the expert conditions spontaneously stated that the defense should have used the defense of temporary insanity".

106 Above n57. If the syndrome evidence in *Runjanjic and Kontinnen*, above n48, and *Kontinnen,* above n56, is to be taken as explaining why it is understandable for battered women to be so psychologically affected by violence per se as to develop an unrealistic perception of the circumstances in which they find themselves, then it is apparent that both have failed to convincingly demonstrate how the offender's perceptions and reactions could be reasonable in those circumstances.

107 Schneider, above n36 at 197.

108 Above n34. See also Mahoney, above n35.

109 Above n57 at 124. The expert in that case dealt obliquely with the accused's claim that she loved the deceased by saying that:
Most if not all [battered women] depend but certainly most are not aware of it. They simply feel that they are part of a committed relationship and the other person should be committed too. They cannot perceive the extreme dependency they form...very often you might see a couple and assume they are very much in love because the women may have hold of him.

110 Id at 123.

111 On the assumption that Hickey's inability to leave her relationship is relevant to her self-defence case and that her failure to do so cannot be adequately explained in terms of the structural obstacles she faced as a young Aboriginal women with two dependant children.

112 Sheehy, Stubbs and Tolmie, above n19 at 384. For evidence of battered women's resistance see Gordon, L, *Heroes of their Own Lives: The Politics and History of Family Violence, Boston 1880-1960* (1988).

113 Above n57.

114 Unreported, August 19 1992 Supreme Court of Queensland. Dagma Stephenson was acquitted of murder on the basis of self-defence. The solicitor instructing in her case was the co-ordinator of the Brisbane Women's Legal Service and chairperson of the Queensland Domestic Violence Council. The defence team chose not to tender evidence of the battered woman syndrome. See Fletcher, K, "Domestic Violence: How the Law Fails Women" (9 Sept 1992) *Green Left Review*; Rathus, Z, *Rougher than Usual Handling: Women and the Criminal Justice System* (1993) at 96-7.

115 Martinson et al, above n52 at 54. The authors cite *State v Anaya* (456 A 2d. 1255 Me. 1983) and *State v Griffiths* (101 Idaho 163, 610 P 2d. 522 1980) as cases in which women were deemed not to fit the profile of a battered woman, in the first instance because she had attempted to escape from her husband and thus was not seen as helpless, and in the second because the woman had only experienced the cycle of violence once, not twice as is necessary according to Lenore Walker's definition of battered woman. See also Crocker, above n30, at 146.

116 Schneider, E, "Particularity and Generality: Challenges of Feminist Theory and Practice in Work on Woman-Abuse" (1992) 67 *NYULR* 520 at 530.

117 Gordon, above n112.

118 See Schneider, above n36 and Mahoney above n11.

119 Although see Stubbs, J and Tolmie, J, "Women Out of Context: Battered Woman Syndrome and the Australia Experience" (forthcoming) *Canadian J of Women and the L.*

120 Nor should we deny the diversity among Aboriginal and Torres Strait Islander peoples.

121 The significance of an analysis which recognises the intersection of race and gender is not confined to Aboriginal and Torres Strait Islander women. It is also true that other intersections, such as those between gender and class are worthy of analysis. However, for the purposes of this paper we have chosen to focus on the intersection between race and gender with respect to Aboriginal and Torres Strait Islander women, since there have been four cases involving Aboriginal and Torres Strait Islander women and the battered woman syndrome. The large number of Aboriginal and Torres Strait Island women serving sentences in Australian gaols for killing violent men suggests that such an analysis is overdue, see O'Donoghue, L, "Setting the Scene" in *Part of the Solution: Aboriginal and Torres Strait Islander Women National Conference* (1992).

122 Ibid.

123 See Behrendt, L, "Aboriginal Women and the White Lies of Feminism: Implications for Aboriginal Women in Rights Discourse" (1993) 1 *Aust Feminist LJ* 27. See also in the American context Crenshaw, K, "A Black Feminist Critique of Antidiscrimination Law and Politics" in Kairys, D (ed), *The Politics of Law: A Progressive Critique* (1990); Matsuda, M, "Affirmative Action and Legal Knowledge: Planting Seeds in Plowed up Ground" (1988) 11 *Harv Women's LJ* 1; Harris, A, "Race and Essentialism in Feminist Legal Theory" (1990) 42 .*Stanford LR* 581.

124 Above n57.

125 Above n61.

126 Above n71.

127 Above n60.

128 In presenting one reading of these cases from a perspective informed by the intersection of race and gender, we do not intend to imply that this is the only possible reading, nor do we deny that their are important differences in experiences among and between Aboriginal and Torres Strait Islander women.

129 Scutt, J, "Invisible Women? Projecting White Cultural Invisibility on Black Women" (1990) 2(46) *Aboriginal Law Bulletin* 4.

130 Pettman, J, *Living in the Margins: Racism, Sexism and Feminism in Australia* (1992) at 65.

131 Atkinson, J, "Violence in Aboriginal Australia: Part 2" (1990) September *Aboriginal and Islander Health Worker J* 5; Payne, S, "Aboriginal Women and the Law" in Cunneen, C (ed), *Aboriginal Perspectives on Criminal Justice* (1992).

132 In *Hickey* the expert witness described conducting the Weschler Adult Intelligence Scale test, the MMPI and the Jessness inventory.

133 Kearins, J, "A Quotient of Awareness" (1983) 18 *Educ News* 18; Michael, R, "Intelligence Testing in Australian Aboriginals" (1984) 20(3) *Comparative Educ* 371; see also Budrikis, K, "Note on *Hickey*: The Problems with a Psychological Approach to Domestic Violence" (1993) 15 *Sydney LR* 365.

134 *Kina* above n71.

135 See Eades, D, *Aboriginal English and the Law* (1992).

136 Ibid; see also Stubbs and Tolmie above n119.

137 This is because it explains the aberrant and irrational (although understandably so) psyche of the particular offender rather than her circumstances. See the English experience in *R v Ahluwalia* [1992] 4 All E.R. 889.

138 In a recent case *R v Stephenson* the defence chose not to introduce evidence of the battered woman syndrome. The accused was acquitted. See above n114.

Appendix 1

Declaration on the elimination of violence against women

Adopted by the United Nations General Assembly on 20 December 1993, GA Res 48/104

The General Assembly,

Recognizing the urgent need for the universal application to women of the rights and principles with regard to equality, security, liberty, integrity and dignity of all human persons,

Noting that those rights and principles are enshrined in international instruments, including the Universal Declaration of Human Rights, the International Covenant on Civil and Political Rights, the International Covenant on Economic, Social and Cultural Rights, the Convention on the Elimination of All Forms of Discrimination against Women, and the Convention against Torture and Other Cruel, Inhuman or Degrading Treatment or Punishment,

Recognizing that the effective implementation of the Convention on the Elimination of All Forms of Discrimination against Women would contribute to the elimination of violence against women and that the Declaration on the Elimination of Violence against Women, annexed to the present resolution, will strengthen and complement that process,

Concerned that violence against women is an obstacle to the achievement of equality, development and peace, as recognized in the Nairobi Forward-looking Strategies for the Advancement of Women, which recommend a set of measures to combat violence against women, and to the full implementation of the Convention on the Elimination of All Forms of Discrimination against Women,

Affirming that violence against women both violates and impairs or nullifies the enjoyment by women of human rights and fundamental freedoms, and concerned about the long-standing failure to protect and promote those rights and freedoms in relation to violence against women,

Recognizing that violence against women is a manifestation of historically unequal power relations between men and women, which have led to domination over and discrimination against women by men and to the prevention of their full advancement, and that violence against women is one of the crucial social mechanisms by which women are forced into a subordinate position compared with men,

Concerned that some groups of women, such as women belonging to minority groups, indigenous women, refugee women, migrant women,

women living in rural or remote communities, destitute women, women in institutions or in detention, female children, women with disabilities, elderly women and women in situations of armed conflict, are especially vulnerable to violence,

Recalling Economic and Social Council resolution 1990/15 of 24 May 1990, in the annex to which it was recognized that violence against women in the family and society was pervasive and cut across lines of income, class and culture, and had to be matched by urgent and effective steps to eliminate its incidence,

Recalling also Economic and Social Council resolution 1991/18 of 30 May 1991, in which the Council recommended the development of a framework for an international instrument that would address explicitly the issue of violence against women,

Welcoming the role that women's movements have played in drawing increasing attention to the nature, severity and magnitude of the problem of violence against women,

Alarmed that women's opportunities to achieve legal, social, political and economic equality in society are limited, *inter alia*, by continuing and endemic violence,

Convinced that in the light of the above there is a need for a clear and comprehensive definition of violence against women, a clear statement of the rights to be applied to ensure the elimination of violence against women in all its forms, a commitment by States in respect of their responsibilities, and a commitment by the international community at large towards the elimination of violence against women,

Solemnly proclaims the following Declaration on the Elimination of Violence against Women and urges that every effort be made so that it becomes generally known and respected:

Article 1

For the purposes of this Declaration, the term 'violence against women' means any act of gender-based violence that results in, or is likely to result in, physical, sexual or psychological harm or suffering to women, including threats of such acts, coercion or arbitrary deprivation of liberty, whether occurring in public or in private life.

Article 2

Violence against women shall be understood to encompass, but not be limited to, the following:
(a) Physical, sexual and psychological violence occurring in the family, including battering, sexual abuse of female children in the household, dowry-related violence, marital rape, female genital mutilation and other traditional

practices harmful to women, non-spousal violence and violence related to exploitation;

(b) Physical, sexual and psychological violence occurring within the general community, including rape, sexual abuse, sexual harassment and intimidation at work, in educational institutions and elsewhere, trafficking in women and forced prostitution;

(c) Physical, sexual and psychological violence perpetrated or condoned by the State, wherever it occurs.

Article 3

Women are entitled to the equal enjoyment and protection of all human rights and fundamental freedoms in the political, economic, social, cultural, civil or any other field. These rights include, *inter alia*:

(a) The right to life;

(b) The right to equality;

(c) The right to liberty and security of person;

(d) The right to equal protection under the law;

(e) The right to be free from all forms of discrimination;

(f) The right to the highest standard attainable of physical and mental health;

(g) The right to just and favourable conditions of work;

(h) The right not to be subjected to torture, or other cruel, inhuman or degrading treatment or punishment.

Article 4

States should condemn violence against women and should not invoke any custom, tradition or religious consideration to avoid their obligations with respect to its elimination.

States should pursue by all appropriate means and without delay a policy of eliminating violence against women and, to this end, should:

(a) Consider, where they have not yet done so, ratifying or acceding to the Convention on the Elimination of All Forms of Discrimination against Women or withdrawing reservations to that Convention;

(b) Refrain from engaging in violence against women;

(c) Exercise due diligence to prevent, investigate and, in accordance with national legislation, punish acts of violence against women, whether those acts are perpetrated by the State or by private persons;

(d) Develop penal, civil, labour and administrative sanctions in domestic legislation to punish and redress the wrongs caused to women who are subjected to violence; women who are subjected to violence should be provided with access to the mechanisms of justice and, as provided for by national legislation, to just and effective remedies for the harm that they have suffered;

States should also inform women of their rights in seeking redress through such mechanisms;

(e) Consider the possibility of developing national plans of action to promote the protection of women against any form of violence, or to include provisions for this purpose in plans already existing, taking into account, as appropriate, such cooperation as can be provided by non-governmental organizations, particularly those concerned
with this subject;

(f) Develop, in a comprehensive way, preventive approaches and all those measures of a legal, political, administrative and cultural nature that promote the protection of women against any form of violence, and ensure that the re-victimization of women does not occur because of gender insensitive laws, enforcement practices or other interventions;

(g) Work to ensure, to the maximum extent feasible in the light of their available resources and, where needed, within the framework of international cooperation, that women subjected to violence and, where appropriate, their children have specialized assistance, such as rehabilitation, assistance in child care and maintenance, treatment, counselling, health and social services, facilities and programmes, as well as support structures, and should take all other appropriate measures to promote their safety and physical and psychological rehabilitation;

(h) Include in government budgets adequate resources for their activities related to the elimination of violence against women;

(i) Take measures to ensure that law enforcement officers and public officials responsible for implementing policies to prevent, investigate and punish violence against women receive training to sensitize them to the needs of women;

(j) Adopt all appropriate measures, especially in the field of education, to modify the social and cultural patterns of conduct of men and women and to eliminate prejudices, customary practices and all other practices based on the idea of the inferiority or superiority of either of the sexes and on stereotyped roles for men and women;

(k) Promote research, collect data and compile statistics, especially concerning domestic violence, relating to the prevalence of different forms of violence against women and encourage research on the causes, nature, seriousness and consequences of violence against women and on the effectiveness of measures implemented to prevent and redress violence against women; those statistics and findings of the research will be made public;

(l) Adopt measures directed to the elimination of violence against women who are especially vulnerable to violence;

(m) Include, in submitting reports as required under relevant human rights instruments of the United Nations, information pertaining to violence against women and measures taken to implement the present Declaration;

(n) Encourage the development of appropriate guidelines to assist in the implementation of the principles set forth in the present Declaration;

(o) Recognize the important role of the women's movement and non-governmental organizations world wide in raising awareness and alleviating the problem of violence against women;

(p) Facilitate and enhance the work of the women's movement and non-governmental organizations and cooperate with them at local, national and regional levels;

(q) Encourage intergovernmental regional organizations of which they are members to include the elimination of violence against women in their programmes, as appropriate.

Article 5

The organs and specialized agencies of the United Nations system should, within their respective fields of competence, contribute to the recognition and realization of the rights and the principles set forth in the present Declaration, and to this end should, *inter alia*:

(a) Foster international and regional cooperation with a view to defining regional strategies for combating violence, exchanging experiences and financing programmes relating to the elimination of violence against women;

(b) Promote meetings and seminars with the aim of creating and raising awareness among all persons the issue of the elimination of violence against women;

(c) Foster coordination and exchange within the United Nations system between human rights treaty bodies to address the matter effectively;

(d) Include in analyses prepared by organizations and bodies of the United Nations system of social trends and problems, such as the periodic reports on the world social situation, examination of trends in violence against women;

(e) Encourage coordination between organizations and bodies of the United Nations system to incorporate the issue of violence against women into ongoing programmes, especially with reference to groups of women particularly vulnerable to violence;

(f) Promote the formulation of guidelines or manuals relating to violence against women, taking into account the measures mentioned herein;

(g) Consider the issue of the elimination of violence against women, as appropriate, in fulfilling their mandates with respect to the implementation of human rights instruments;

(h) Cooperate with non-governmental organizations in addressing violence against women.

Article 6

Nothing in the present Declaration shall affect any provision that is more conducive to the elimination of violence against women that may be contained in the legislation of a State or in any international convention, treaty or other instrument in force in a State.

Resolution 217 A (III).

Resolution 2200 A (XXI), annex.

Resolution 2200 A (XXI), annex.

Resolution 34/180, annex.

Resolution 39/46, annex.

Report of the World Conference to review and Appraise the Achievements of the United Nations Decade for Women: Equality. Development and Peace, Nairobi. 15-26 July 1985 (United Nations publication, Sales No. E.85.IV.10), chap. I, sect. A.

Universal Declaration of Human Rights, article 3; and International Covenant on Civil and Political Rights, article 6.

International Covenant on Civil and Political Rights, article 26.

Universal Declaration of Human Rights, article 3; and

International Covenant on Civil and Political Rights, article 9.

International Covenant on Civil and Political Rights, article 26.

International Covenant on Civil and Political Rights, article 26.

International Covenant on Economic, Social and Cultural Rights, article 12.

Universal Declaration of Human Rights, article 23; and

International Covenant on Economic, Social and Cultural Rights, articles 6 and 7.

Universal Declaration of Human Rights, article 5;

International Covenant on Civil and Political Rights, article 7; and

Convention against Torture and Other Cruel, Inhuman or Degrading Treatment or Punishment.

Appendix 2

The power and control wheel

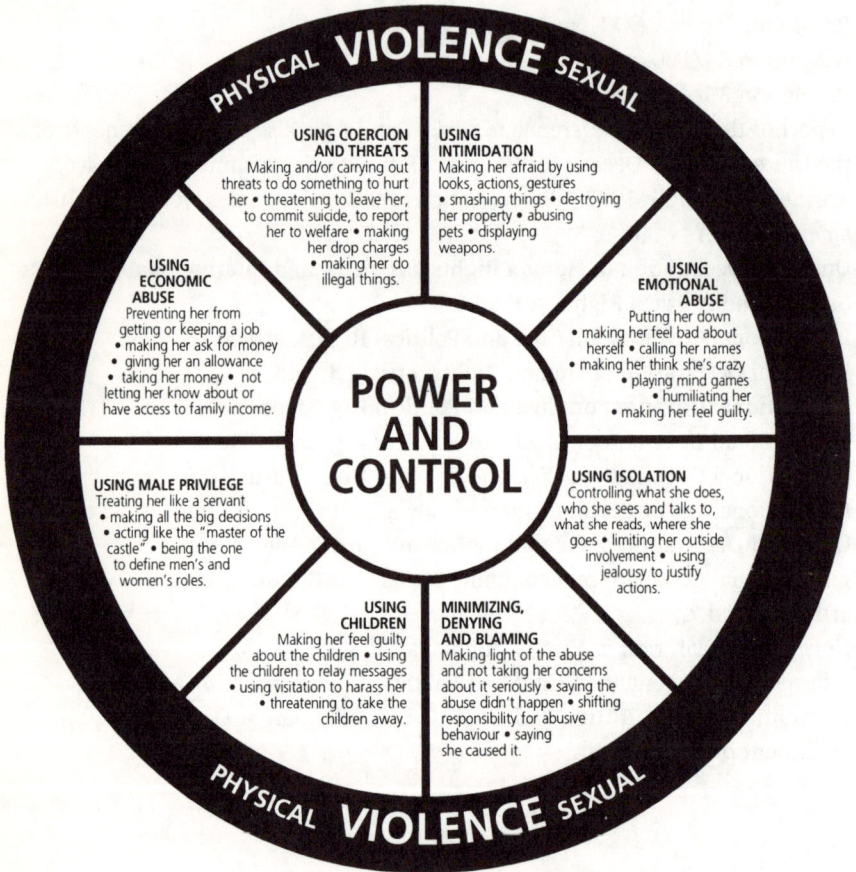

PHYSICAL VIOLENCE SEXUAL

USING COERCION AND THREATS
Making and/or carrying out threats to do something to hurt her • threatening to leave her, to commit suicide, to report her to welfare • making her drop charges • making her do illegal things.

USING INTIMIDATION
Making her afraid by using looks, actions, gestures • smashing things • destroying her property • abusing pets • displaying weapons.

USING ECONOMIC ABUSE
Preventing her from getting or keeping a job • making her ask for money • giving her an allowance • taking her money • not letting her know about or have access to family income.

USING EMOTIONAL ABUSE
Putting her down • making her feel bad about herself • calling her names • making her think she's crazy • playing mind games • humiliating her • making her feel guilty.

POWER AND CONTROL

USING MALE PRIVILEGE
Treating her like a servant • making all the big decisions • acting like the "master of the castle" • being the one to define men's and women's roles.

USING ISOLATION
Controlling what she does, who she sees and talks to, what she reads, where she goes • limiting her outside involvement • using jealousy to justify actions.

USING CHILDREN
Making her feel guilty about the children • using the children to relay messages • using visitation to harass her • threatening to take the children away.

MINIMIZING, DENYING AND BLAMING
Making light of the abuse and not taking her concerns about it seriously • saying the abuse didn't happen • shifting responsibility for abusive behaviour • saying she caused it.

PHYSICAL VIOLENCE SEXUAL

Figure 1: The Power and Control Wheel

Source: Reprinted with permission from Minnesota Program Development, Inc., Domestic Abuse Intervention Project, 206 W. 4th Street, Duluth, MN 55806.

Statutes

Australia

Family Law Act 1975 (Cth)

New Zealand

Crimes Act 1961
Criminal Justice Act 1985
Domestic Protection Act 1982
Family Proceedings Act 1980
Guardianship Act 1968
Summary Offences Act 1981

United States

Massachusetts Abuse Prevention Act 1978

International Instruments, Treaties and other Documents

1945 *Statute of the International Court of Justice*
1966 *International Covenant on Civil and Political Rights* (ICCPR)
1966 *International Covenant on Economic, Social and Cultural Rights*
(ICESCR)
1979 *Convention on the Elimination of All Forms of Discrimination
Against Women* (the Women's Convention)
1993 *United Nations Declaration on the Elimination of Violence
Against Women*

Cases

Australia

Buzzacott ....unreported, Supreme Court of S.A., 12 July 1993.

Collingburn ....(1985) 18 A.Crim. 295.

Cornick ....unreported, Court of Criminal Appeal of Tas.,
  27 July 1987.

Gilbert ....unreported, Supreme Court of W.A., 4 November 1993.

Gunnarsson

Weiner ....unreported, Supreme Court of Tas., 13 August 1992.

Hickey ....unreported, Supreme Court of N.S.W., 14 April 1992.

Hill ....(1981) 3 A.Crim.R. 397.

Kina........................unreported, Supreme Court of Qld., 5 September 1988
  (trial).
  unreported, Court of Criminal Appeal of Qld., 23
  November 1988.
  unreported, Court of Appeal of Qld., 29 November 1993
  (further appeal).

Kontinnen ....unreported, Supreme Court of S.A., 30 March 1992.

Muy Ky Chhay ....unreported, Supreme court of N.S.W., 8 September 1992
  unreported, Court of Criminal Appeal of N.S.W.,
  4 March 1994.

R...............................(1981) 28 S.A.S.R. 321.

Rose ....unreported, Supreme Court of W.A., August 1989.

Runjanjic and

Kontinnen ....(1991) 53 A.Crim.R.362 (appeal).
  unreported, Supreme Court of S.A., 10 February 1993
  (sentencing subsequent to appeal).

Spencer ....unreported, Supreme Court of N.S.W.,
  18 December 1992.

Stephenson ....unreported, Supreme Court of Qld., 19 August 1992.

Taylor ....unreported, Supreme Court of S.A., February 1994.

Webb ....unreported, Court of Criminal Appeal of S.A.,
  19 June 1992.

Whalen ....unreported, Supreme Court of N.S.W, 5 April 1991.

Winnett v

Stephenson ....unreported, Magistrates Court of A.C.T., 19 May 1993.

Woolsey..................unreported, Supreme Court of N.S.W., 19 August 1993.

Zecevic ....(1987) 71 ALR 641, 162 CLR 645.

Canada

Bennett [no.1] ....[unreported] (Ont. Prov. Ct) (Ottawa, 28 January 1993).
Bennett [no.2] ....[1993] O.J. No.892 (Ont.Prov.Ct.).
Bradbury ....[1992] N.W.T.J. No.178 (N.W.T. Terr. Ct.).
Catholique ....[1990] N.W.T.J. No.164 (N.W.T. Sup. Ct.).
Dunlap ....(1991) 101 N.S.R.(2d) 263 (S.Ct. App.Div.).
Eagles ....[1991] Y. J. No. 147 (Yukon Terr. Ct.).
Eyapaise..................(1993) 20 C.R.(4th) 246 (Alta.Q.B.).
Howard ....(1992) 8 B.C.A.C. 241 (C.A.)
                  (1992) 8 B.C.A.C. 249 (C.A).
Lavallee ....[1990] 4 W.W.R. 1 (Man.C.A.).
                  (1990) 55 C.C.C. (3d) 97 (S.C.C.).
Phillips ....[1992] O.J. 2716 (Ont.Ct.J. Gen.Div.).
Robins ....(1982) 66 C.C.C.(2d) 550 (Que.C.A.).
Urbanovitch and
Brown ....(1985) 19 C.C.C.(3d) 43 (Man.C.A.).
Whitten ....(1992) 110 N.S.R.(2d) 149 (S.Ct. T.Div.).
Whynot(Stafford).....(1983) 37 C.R.(3d) 198 (N.S.S.Ct.).

England

Ahluwalia ....[1992] 4 All E.R. 899.

International

Velasquez Rodriguez
v Honduras ....(1989) 28 ILM 294 (Inter-American Court of
                  Human Rights, 29 July 1988).
X and Y v
The Netherlands ......(1985) European Court of Human Rights, 26 March 1985
                  Series A, No. 91; (1985) 8 E.H.R.R. 235.
Airey v Ireland ....(1979) European Court of Human Rights,
                  9 October 1979 Series A,
                  No. 32; (1979) 2 E.H.R.R. 305.

New Zealand

Chambers ....unreported, Hamilton District Court,
CRN 3019008149251, 12 May 1993.

D v N ....unreported, Napier Family Court,
FP 041/277/92, 22 March 1993.

Descatoires ....unreported, Hamilton District Court,
CRN 3019010743, 13 May 1993.

G v G ....unreported, Wellington Family Court,
FP 085/1127/83, 8 October 1986.

Harris ....unreported, High Court, New Plymouth Registry,
AP 15/91, 2 July 1991.

Kelly ....unreported, High Court, Rotorua Registry,
AP 29/91, 15 May 1991.

Lynch ....unreported, High Court, Auckland, A.P. 16/86.

Manihera ....unreported, Hamilton District Court,
CRN 3019010032, 3 May 1993.

Martens ....unreported, High Court, Tauranga Registry,
AP 14/9, 24 June 1991.

N ....(1984) 1 FRNZ 156.

N v N ....(1986) 2 FRNZ 534.

Newlands ....unreported, High Court, Timaru Registry,
AP 30/90, 6 July 1990.
[1992] NZFLR 74.

P-W v P-W ....unreported, Napier Family Court,
FP 041/079/90, 16 May 1990.

Paki ....unreported, High Court, Rotorua Registry,
AP 23/93, 17 May 1993.

Panoa-Masina ....unreported, Court of Appeal,
7 October 1991 (CA 309/91).

Redward v Redward .(1988) 4 NZFLR 528.

Shortland ....(1989) 4 CRNZ 155.

T ....unreported, High Court, Dunedin Registry,
AP 94/91, 13 September 1991.

Teinatoa ....unreported, High Court, Wellington Registry,
T 16/93, 4 June 1993.

Thomas ....unreported, High Court, Wellington,
13 November 1991 AP.222/91.

Titter v Titter ....[1992] NZFLR 79.

W v W ....(1985) 1 FRNZ 554.

Wilson ....unreported, Hamilton District Court,
CRN 3019013810, 4 August (1991).

Wright v Saunders....(1990) 5 CRNZ 234.

United States

Anaya ....456 A 2d. 1255 Me. (1983).
Griffiths ....101 Idaho 163, 610 P 2d. 522 (1980).

Bibliography

Abell, J and Sheehy, E (eds), *Criminal Law & Procedure: Cases, Context, Critique,* North York: Captus Press, 1993.

Aboriginal Women's Legal Issues Group, *Aboriginal Women's Legal Issues Conference Report,* (no date or publisher provided).

Abrams, K, "Hearing the Call of Stories" (1991) 79 *Calif LR* 971.

Acker, J, Barry, K and Esseveld, J, "Objectivity and Truth: Problems in Doing Feminist Research" in Fonow M and Cook, J (eds), *Beyond Methodology: Feminist Scholarship as Lived Research,* Bloomington: Indiana University Press, 1991.

Adams, D, "Counselling Men who Batter: A Profeminist Analysis of Five Treatment Models" in Yllo, K and Bograd, M (eds), *Feminist Perspectives on Wife Abuse,* Newbury Park, CA: Sage, 1988.

Addelson, K P, "The Man of Professional Wisdom" in Fonow, M and Cook, J (eds), *Beyond Methodology: Feminist Scholarship as Lived Research,* Bloomington: Indiana University Press, 1991.

Allen, J, "The Masculinity of Criminality and Criminology: Interrogating some Impasses" in Findlay, M and Hogg, R (eds), *Understanding Crime and Criminal Justice,* Sydney: Law Book Company, 1988.

Alston, P (ed), *The United Nations and Human Rights: A Critical Appraisal,* Oxford: Clarendon Press, 1992.

Americas Watch, *Criminal Justice: Violence Against Women in Brazil,* New York: Human Rights Watch, 1991.

Amnesty International, *Bosnia-Herzegovina, Rape and Sexual Abuse by Armed Forces,* New York: Amnesty International Publications, 1993.

Amnesty International, *Women in the Front Line: Human Rights Violations Against Women,* London: Amnesty International Publications, 1991.

Ashworth, G, *Of Violence and Violation: Women and Human Rights,* London: Change Publications, 1986.

Astor, H, *Position Paper on Mediation,* Canberra: Office of the Status of Women, 1991.

Astor, H, "Feminist Issues in ADR" (1991) 65 *Law Inst J* 69.

Astor, H, "Mediation of Family Disputes in Australia" in Stark, B (ed), *Family Law and Gender Bias: Comparative Perspectives* (1992) 4 *International Review of Comparative Public Policy* 107.

Astor, H, *Women and Mediation: Information About Mediation for Women,* Canberra: Office for the Status of Women, 1992.

Astor, H, *Guidelines for Use if Mediating in Cases Involving Violence Against Women,* Canberra: Office for the Status of Women, 1992.

Astor, H, "Violence and Family Mediation Policy" (1994) *Aust J Family Law* (forthcoming).

Astor, H and Chinkin, C, "Dispute Resolution as Part of Legal Education" (1990) 1 *Aust Dispute Resolution J* 208.

Astor, H and Chinkin, C, *Dispute Resolution in Australia*, Sydney: Butterworths, 1992.

Atkinson, J, "Violence in Aboriginal Australia: Colonisation and Gender (Part I)" (1990) 14 (2) *Aboriginal and Islander Health Worker J* 5.

Atkinson, J, "Violence in Aboriginal Australia (Part II)" (1990) 14 (3) *Aboriginal and Islander Health Worker J* 4.

Atkinson, J, "Violence Against Aboriginal Women: Reconstitution of Community Law - The Way Forward" (1990) 2 (46) *Aboriginal Law Bulletin* 6.

Atkinson, J, and Morton-Robinson, A, "Violence is Contagious: Gender Relations in Aboriginal Communities in Queensland", unpublished paper, 1991.

Australian Law Reform Commission, *Equality Before the Law: Women's Access to the Legal System* Report No 67, Sydney: Australian Law Reform Commission, 1994.

Avery, J, *Police-Force or Service?*, Sydney: Butterworths,1981.

Bacon,W and Lansdowne, R, "Women Who Kill Husbands: The Battered Woman on Trial" in O'Donnell, C and Craney, J (eds), *Family Violence in Australia*, Melbourne: Longman Cheshire, 1992.

Bailey, M, "Unpacking the Rational Alternative: A Critical Review of the Family Mediation Movement Claims" (1989) 8 *Canadian J Family Law* 61.

Barber, G J, Punt, J and Albers, J, "Alcohol and Power on Palm Island" (1990) 23 (2) *Aust J of Social Issues* 87.

Barry, K, "Female Sexual Slavery: Understanding the International Dimensions of Women's Oppression" (1981) 3 *Human Rights Q* 44.

Bartlett, K, "Feminist Legal Methods" (1990) 103 *Harv LR* 829.

Beasley, M E, *Punishing the Victim: Rape and Mistreatment of Asian Maids in Kuwait*, New York: Middle East Watch, 1992.

Behrendt, L, "Aboriginal Women and the White Lies of Feminism: Implications for Aboriginal Women in Rights Discourse" (1993) 1 *Aust Feminist LJ* 27.

Benjamin, M and Irving, H, "Towards a Feminist-Informed Model of Therapeutic Family Mediation" (1992) 10 *Mediation Q* 129.

Bennett, C, "Ordinary Madness" *The Guardian*, Second Front 2/3, 20 January 1993.

Blackman, C, "Potential Uses for Expert Testimony: Ideas Towards the Representation of Battered Women Who Kill" (1986) 9 *Women's Rights Law Reporter* 227.

Blanchfield, M, "Millar Convicted of Manslaughter" *The Ottawa Citizen*, 30 October 1992.

Bolger, A, *Aboriginal Women and Violence,* Darwin: Australian National University, North Australia Research Unit, 1991.

Bone, P, "Crying Out for Justice" *The Age,* 11 February 1994.

Bonney, R, *Homicide II,* Sydney: New South Wales Bureau of Crime Statistics and Research, 1988.

Boshier, P, *The Review of the Family Court: A Report for the Principal Family Court Judge,* New Zealand, April 1993.

Bowker, L H, Arbitell, M and McFerron, J R , "On the Relationship Between Wife Beating and Child Abuse", in Yllo, K and Bograd, M (eds), *Feminist Perspectives on Wife Abuse,* Newbury Park: Sage, 1988.

Bowles, G and Klein, R D (eds), *Theories of Women's Studies,* London: Routledge, 1983.

Brown, D, Farrier, D, Neal, D and Weisbrot, D, *Criminal Laws,* Sydney: Federation Press, 1990.

Brown, R, "Limitations on Expert Testimony on the Battered Woman Syndrome in Homicide Cases: The Return of the Ultimate Issue Rule" (1990) 32 *Arizona LR* 665.

Browne, C, "Dispute Resolution Services: Family Court of Australia" in Fisher, L (ed), *Dispute Resolution in the 90's, Proceedings of the Conference of the Australian Dispute Resolution Association,* Turramurra: Australian Dispute Resolution Association, 1990.

Brygger, M P and Edleson, J , "The Domestic Abuse Project: A Multisystems Intervention in Woman Battering" (1987) 2 (3) *J of Interpersonal Violence* 326.

Budrikis, K, "Note on *Hickey*: The Problems with a Psychological Approach to Domestic Violence" (1993) 15 *Sydney LR* 365.

Bunch, C, "Women's Rights as Human Rights: Towards a Revision of Human Rights" (1990) 12 *Human Rights Q* 486.

Busch, R, Robertson, N and Lapsley, H, *Protection From Family Violence: A Study of Protection Orders Under the Domestic Protection Act,* Wellington: Victims Task Force, 1992.

Busch, R and Robertson, N, "What's Love Got to Do with It? An Analysis of An Intervention Approach to Domestic Violence" (1993) 1 *Waikato LR* 109.

Butler, J and Scott, J (eds), *Feminists Theorize the Political,* New York: Routledge, 1992.

Buzawa, E S and Buzawa, C G, *Domestic Violence: The Criminal Justice Response,* Newbury Park: Sage, 1990.

Byrne, D and Heydon, J, *Cross on Evidence,* Sydney: Butterworths, (3rd edn) 1986.

Byrnes, A, "The 'Other' Human Rights Treaty Body: The Work of the Committee on the Elimination of Discrimination Against Women" (1989) 14 *Yale J Int'l L* 1.

Cahn, N R, "Innovative Approaches to the Prosecution of Domestic Violence Crimes: An Overview" in Buzawa, E S and Buzawa, C G (eds), *Domestic Violence: The Changing Criminal Justice Response*, Westport: Auburn House, 1992.

Cain, P A, "Teaching Feminist Theory at Texas: Listening to Difference and Exploring Connection" (1988) 38 *J Leg Educ* 165.

Cain, P A, "Feminist Jurisprudence: Grounding the Theories" (1989) 4 *Berkeley Women's LJ* 191.

Cannon, L W, Higgenbotham, E and Leung, M L A, "Race and Class Bias in Qualitative Research on Women" in Fonow, M and Cook, J (eds), *Beyond Methodology: Feminist Scholarship as Lived Research*, Bloomington: Indiana University Press, 1991.

Carillo, R, *Battered Dreams: Violence Against Women as an Obstacle to Development*, New York: United Nations Development Fund for Women, 1992.

Carrington, K, "Feminist Readings of Female Delinquency" (1990) 8 (2) *Law in Context* 5.

Charlesworth, H, Chinkin, C, and Wright, S, "Feminist Approaches to International Law" (1991) 85 *Am J Int'l L* 613.

Charlesworth, H, and Chinkin, C, "The Gender of Jus Cogens" (1993) 15 *Human Rights Q* 63.

Charlesworth, S, Turner, J and Foreman, L, *Lawyers, Social Workers and Families*, Sydney: Federation Press, 1990.

Chinkin, C, "Women and Peace: Militarism and Oppression", in Mahoney, K and Mahoney, P (eds), *Human Rights in the 21st Century*, Boston: M. Nijhoff Publications, 1993.

Chinkin, C, and Werksman, K, *CEDAW No. 12, Report of the Twelfth Session of the Committee on the Elimination of All Forms of Discrimination Against Women,* Minneapolis: Hubert H. Humphrey Institute of Public Affairs, University of Minnesota, 1993.

Chinkin, C, "Rape And Sexual Abuse Of Women In International Law" (1994) *Eur J Int'l L* (forthcoming).

Chisholm, R, "Mediation Services for the Family Court: Something New Under the Sun" *(1991) 5 Aust J Family Law* 277.

Church, J and Church, D, *Listen to Me Please: The Legal Needs of Domestic Violence Victims*, Christchurch: Battered Women's Support Group, 1981.

Clark, B, "The Vienna Conventions Regime and the Convention on Discrimination Against Women" (1991) 85 *Am J Int'l L* 281.

Cobourg Daily Star, "Taunted Husband Lashes Out At Wife", 22 July 1993.

Coddington, B, "Mediation in Private Legal Practice" in Fisher, L (ed), *Dispute Resolution in the 90's: Proceedings of the Conference of the Australian Dispute Resolution Association*, Turramurra: Australian Dispute Resolution Association, 1991.

Community Justice Centres, *Annual Report 1988-9*, Sydney: Government Printer, 1989.

Connors, J, *Violence Against Women in the Family*, New York: United Nations, 1989.

Cook, R, "Accountability in International Law for Violations of Women's Rights by Non-state Actors" in Dallmeyer, D (ed), *Reconceiving Reality: Women and International Law*, Washington: American Society of International Law, 1993.

Cook, R, "Reservations to the Convention on the Elimination of All Forms of Discrimination Against Women" (1990) 30 *Va J Int'l L* 643.

Coomaraswamy, R, "Of Kali Born: Women, Violence and the Law in Sri Lanka", in Schuler, M, (ed), *Freedom from Violence: Women's Strategies from Around the World*, New York: OEF International, 1992.

Cox, E, "Costs of Domestic Violence" in New South Wales Domestic Violence Committee (ed), *Local Domestic Violence Committees Conference: Papers and Proceedings*, New South Wales: Women's Coordination Unit, 1992.

Crenshaw, K, "A Black Feminist Critique of Antidiscrimination Law and Politics" in Kairys, D (ed), *The Politics of Law: A Progressive Critique*, New York: Pantheon Books, (2nd edn) 1990.

Crenshaw, K, "Mapping the Margins: Intersectionality, Identity Politics, and Violence Against Women of Color" (1991) 43 *Stanford LR* 1241.

Crocker, P, "The Meaning of Equality for Battered Women Who Kill Men in Self-Defense" (1985) 8 *Harv Women's LJ* 121.

Culliton, K, "Finding a Mechanism to Enforce Women's Right to State Protection from Domestic Violence in the Americas" (1993) 34 *Harv Int'l LJ* 507.

Davis, A and Salem, R, "Dealing With Power Imbalances in the Mediation of Interpersonal Disputes" (1984) 6 *Mediation Q* 17.

Davis, G, *Partisans and Mediators: The Resolution of Divorce Disputes*, New York: Clarendon Press, 1988.

Deaux, K and Wrightsman, L S, *Social Psychology*, Pacific Grove: Brooks Cole, (5th edn) 1988.

De Biasi, F, "Children's Rights and Children's Participation in Litigation and ADR" (1992) 6 *ADRA Newsletter* 8.

Department of Justice, *Submission to the Committee of Inquiry into Violence*, Wellington: Department of Justice, 1986.

Dobash, R and Dobash, R P, *Women, Violence & Social Change*, New York: Routledge, 1992.

Dobash, R and Dobash, R P, *Violence Against Wives: A Case Against the Patriarchy*, New York: Free Press, 1979.

Donnelly, L, "Establishing an Alternative Dispute Resolution Centre with a Community Based Philosophy" in Mugford, J (ed), *Alternative Dispute Resolution, Seminar Proceedings No 15*, Canberra: Australian Institute of Criminology, 1986.

Eades, D, *Aboriginal English and the Law*, Brisbane: Queensland University Law Society, 1992.

Easteal, P, "Battered Woman Syndrome: What is Reasonable?" (1992) 17 *Alt LJ* 220.

Easteal, P, "Battered Woman Syndrome Misunderstood?" (1992) 3 *Current Issues in Criminal Justice* 356.

Easteal, P, Hughes, K and Easter, J, "Battered Women and Duress" (1993) 18 *Alt LJ* 139.

Edwards, S, "Violence Against Women: Feminism and the Law" in Gelsthorpe, L and Morris, A (eds), *Feminist Perspectives in Criminology*, Milton Keynes: Open University Press, 1990.

Ehrlich, S, *Lisa, Hedda & Joel*, New York: St Martin's Press 1989.

Eisenstein, H, *Gender Shock: Practising Feminism on Two Continents*, North Sydney: Allen and Unwin, 1991.

Eisikovits, Z C and Edelson, J L, "Intervening with Men who Batter: A Critical Review of the Literature" (1989) *Social Services Review* 384.

Elshtain, J, *Public Man, Private Woman: Women in Social and Political Thought*, Oxford: Robertson Press, 1981.

European Community Investigative Mission into the Treatment of Muslim Women in the Former Yugoslavia, Warburton Report, E/CN 4/1993/92, United Nations publication.

Ewing, C, *Battered Women Who Kill: Psychological Self-Defense as Legal Justification*, Massachusetts: Lexington Books, 1987.

Executive Committee of the High Commissioner's Programme, *Note on Certain Aspects of Sexual Violence Against Refugee Women*, unpublished United Nations Document, EC/1993/SCP/CRP 2, 29 April 1993.

Faigman, D, "The Battered Woman Syndrome and Self Defence: A Legal and Empirical Dissent" (1986) 72 *Va LR* 619.

Family Law Council, *Family Mediation Report*, Canberra: Australian Government Publishing Service, 1992.

Family Violence Co-ordinating Committee, *Attitudes to Family Violence- A Study Across Cultures*, Wellington: Family Violence Prevention Co-Ordinating Committee, 1988.

Family Violence Professional Education Taskforce, *Family Violence: Everybody's Business, Somebody's Life*, Sydney: Federation Press, 1991.

Family Violence Project, *Domestic Violence Is Crime*, San Francisco: Family Violence Project, (no date).

Fanslow, J, *The OASIS Protocol: Guidelines for Identifying, Treating and Referring Abused Women*, Auckland: Injury Prevention Research Centre, Department of Com-munity Health, University of Auckland, 1993.

Fanslow, J L , Chalmers, D J and Langley, J D, *Injury from Assault: A Public Health Problem*, Dunedin: Injury Prevention Research Unit, Dunedin Occasional Report Series, 1991.

Farina, C R, "Getting From Here to There" [1991] *Duke LJ* 689.

Findlay, M and Hogg, R (eds), *Understanding Crime and Criminal Justice*, Sydney: Law Books, 1988.

Findley, L, "Breaking Women's Silence in Law: The dilemma of the gendered nature of legal reasoning" (1989) 64 *Notre Dame LR* 886.

Fine, S, "Woman Seeks To Use Coercion As Abuse Defence" *The [Toronto] Globe and Mail*, 31 December 1992.

Fineman, M, "Dominant Discourse, Professional Language, and Legal Change in Child Custody Decisionmaking" (1988) 101 *Harv LR* 727.

Fineman, M and Opie, A, "The Uses of Social Science Data in Legal Policymaking: Custody Determinations at Divorce" [1987] *Wisc LR* 107.

Finlay, H and Bailey-Harris, R, *Family Law In Australia*, Sydney: Butterworths, (4th edn) 1989.

Fisher, L and Blondel, M, *Couples Mediation: A Forum and a Framework*, Lane Cove: Marriage Guidance New South Wales, 1993.

Fletcher, K, "Domestic Violence: How the Law Fails Women" (9 Sept. 1992) *Green Left Review*.

Folberg, J and Taylor, A, *Mediation: A Comprehensive Guide to Resolving Conflict*, San Francisco: Jossey-Bass, 1984.

Fonow, M and Cook, J (eds), *Beyond Methodology: Feminist Scholarship as Lived Research*, Bloomington: Indiana University Press, 1991.

Ford, G, *Research Project on Domestic Disputes: Final Report*, Wellington: Police Psychological Services, 1986.

Foster, B and Bicehouse, T, "Principles of Practice" in Hart, B J (ed), *Accountability: Program Standards for Batterer Intervention Services*, Reading: Pennsylvania Coalition Against Domestic Violence, 1992.

Fownes, N, "Woman Pleads Guilty To Not Reporting Abuse" *The [Halifax] Chronicle Herald*, 1 October 1993.

Fraser, A, and Kazantsis M, *CEDAW No 11, the Committee on the Elimination of Discrimination Against Women, Convention on the Elimination of All Forms of Discrimination Against Women, and Violence Against Women*, Minneapolis: University of Minnesota, 1992.

Fraser, N, "Apologia for Academic Radicals" in *Unruly Practices: Power, Discourse and Gender in Contemporary Social Theory*, Oxford: Polity Press, 1989.

Freire, P, *Pedagogy of the Oppressed*, New York: Herder and Herder, 1970.

Freire, P, *Education for Critical Consciousness*, New York: Seabury Press, 1973.

Furness, J A, "From a Woman's Perspective: A Multiple Case Study Evaluation of an Education Programme for Abusers", unpublished M.Soc.Sci. thesis, New Zealand: University of Waikato, 1993.

Gagnon, A, "Ending Mandatory Divorce Mediation for Battered Women" (1992) 15 *Harv Women's LJ* 272.

Garmanikow, E, et al (eds), *The Public and The Private*, London: Heinemann,1983.

Germane, C, Johnson, M and Lemon, N, "Mandatory Custody Mediation and Joint Custody Orders in California: The Danger for Victims of Domestic Violence" (1985) 1 *Berkeley Women's LJ* 175.

Gibson, J, *Non-custodial Fathers and Access Patterns*, Australia: Family Court of Australia Research Report No 10, 1992.

Goldfarb, P, "A Theory Practice Spiral: The Ethics of Feminism and Clinical Education" (1991) 75 *Minn LR* 1599.

Goldman, A, *The Group Depth Interview: Principles and Practice*, Englewood Cliffs: Prentice Hall, 1987.

Gondolf, E, *Men Who Batter: An Integrated Approach for Stopping Wife Abuse*, Florida: Learning Publications, 1985.

Gondolf, E W, "The Effect of Batterer Counselling on Shelter Outcome" (1988) 3 *J of Interpersonal Violence* 275.

Gordon, L, *Heroes Of Their Own Lives: The Politics and History of Family Violence, Boston 1880-1960*, New York: Viking, 1988.

Gore, J, *The Struggle for Pedagogies: Critical and Feminist Discourses*, New York: Routledge, 1993.

Graham, D L R, Rawlings, E and Rimini, N, "Survivors of Terror: Battered Women, Hostages and the Stockholm Syndrome " in Yllo, K and Bograd, M (eds), *Feminist Perspectives on Wife Abuse*, Newbury Park: Sage, 1988.

Graycar, R, "Violence in the Home- A Legal Response: A Limited Solution" (1988) 26 (4) *Law Soc J* 46.

Graycar, R, "Equal Rights Versus Father's Rights: The Child Custody Debate in Australia" in Smart, C and Sevenhuijsen, S (eds), *Child Custody and the Politics of Gender*, London: Routledge, 1989.

Graycar, R and Morgan, J, *The Hidden Gender of Law*, Sydney: Federation Press, 1990.

Greatbatch, D and Dingwall, R, "Selective Facilitation: Some Observations on a Strategy Used by Divorce Mediators" (1989) 23 *Law and Soc Review* 613.

Gribben, S, "Mediation of Family Disputes" (1992) 6 *Aust J Family Law* 126.

Grillo T, "The Mediation Alternative: Process Dangers for Women" (1991) 100 *Yale LJ* 1545.

The [Halifax] Chronicle Herald, "An Inexplicable Double Standard", 28 September 1993.

Haraway, D J, *Simians, Cyborgs, and Women: The Reinvention of Nature*, New York: Routledge, 1991.

Harding, S, *Feminism and Methodology: Social Science Issues*, Bloomington: Indiana University Press, 1987.

Harris, A, "Race and Essentialism in Feminist Legal Theory" (1990) 42 *Stanford LR* 581.

Hart, B J, "Gentle Jeopardy: The Further Endangerment of Battered Women and Children in Custody Mediation" (1990) 7 *Mediation Q* 317.

Hart, B, "Assessing Whether Batterers Will Kill" in Hart, B J (ed), *Accountability: Program Standards for Batterer Intervention Services*, Reading: Pennsylvania Coalition Against Domestic Violence, 1992.

Hatty, S, *Male Violence and the Police: An Australian Experience*, Sydney: N.S.W. University School of Social Work, 1988.

Hatty, S, "Policing and Male Violence in Australia" in Hanmer, J, Radford, J and Stanko, E, *Women, Policing and Male Violence*, London: Routledge, 1989.

Hawthorn, F, "Interviews With Four Battered Women At The Prison For Women Who Are Serving Life Sentences For Murder", unpublished paper, Canada, 1992.

Hekman, S, *Gender and Knowledge: Elements of a Postmodern Feminism*, Oxford: Polity Press, 1990.

Herman, J L, *Trauma and Recovery*, New York: Basic Books,1992.

Hilton, N Z, "Mediating Wife Assault: Battered Women and the New Family'" (1991) 9 *Canadian J Family Law* 29.

Hogg, R, "Perspectives on the Criminal Justice System" in Findlay, M, Egger, S and Sutton, J, *Issues in Criminal Justice Administration*, Sydney: George Allen and Unwin, 1983.

hooks, b, *Talking Back: Thinking Feminist, Thinking Black*, Boston: South End Press, 1989.

Hurston, Z N, *I Love Myself When I Am Laughing...And Then Again When I Am Looking Mean and Impressive* , Old Westbury: Feminist Press, 1979.

Human Rights and Equal Opportunity Commission, *Racist Violence* Canberra: Australian Government Publishing Service, 1991.

Ingleby, R, *In the Ball Park: Alternative Dispute Resolution and the Courts*, Carlton: Australian Institute of Judicial Administration, 1991.

International Law Commission,"Draft Articles on State Responsibility", (1980) 2 *Year Book Int'l Law Commission.*

Irving, H and Benjamin, M, *Family Mediation: Theory and Practice of Dispute Resolution*, Toronto: Carswell, 1987.

Jackson, M, *The Maori and the Criminal Justice System: a new perspective- He Whaipaanga Hou*, (Parts 1 and 2), Wellington: Department of Justice Studies Series 18, 1988.

Jang, D, Lee, D and Morello-Frosch, R, "Domestic Violence in Immigrant and Refugee Communities: Responding to the Needs of Immigrant Women" (1991) 13 *Response* No. 4.

Jayaratne, T and Stewart, A, "Quantitative and Qualitative Methods in The Social Sciences: Current Feminist Issues and Practical Strategies" in Fonow, M and Cook, J (eds), *Beyond Methodology: Feminist Scholarship as Lived Research*, Bloomington: Indiana University Press, 1991.

Joint Select Committee on Certain Aspects of the Operation and Interpretation of the Family Law Act, *The Family Law Act 1975: Aspects of its Operation and Interpretation: Report*, Canberra: Australian Government Publishing Service, 1992.

Kearins, J, "A Quotient of Awareness" (1983) 18 *Educ News* 18.

Kelly, J, "Mediated and Adversarial Divorce Resolution Processes: A Comparison of Post Divorce Outcomes" (1991) 21 *Family Law* 382.

Kinports, K, "Defending Battered Women's Self-Defense Claims" (1988) 67 *Oregon LR* 391.

Kirk, R, *Untold Terror: Violence Against Women in Peru's Armed Conflict*, New York: Human Rights Watch, 1992.

Kline, M, "Race, Racism and Feminist Legal Theory" (1989) 12 *Harv Women's LJ* 115.

Kressel, K, "Clinical Implications of Existing Research on Divorce Mediation" (1987) 15 *Am J Family Therapy* 69.

Kurz, D, "Battering and the Criminal Justice System: A Feminist View" in Buzawa, E S and Buzawa C G (eds), *Domestic Violence: The Changing Criminal Justice Response*, Westport: Auburn House, 1992.

Lahey, K A, "'...Until Women Themselves Have Told All That They Have To Tell...'" (1985) 23 *Osgoode Hall LJ* 525.

Landau, B, Bartoletti, M and Mesbur, R, *Family Mediation Handbook*, Toronto: Butterworths, 1987.

Langton, M," Feminism: What Do Aboriginal Women Gain?" (1989) 2 *Broadside* 3.

Langton, M, "Aborigines and Policing: Aboriginal Solutions from Northern Territory Communities" (1992) 2 *Australian Aboriginal Studies 14*.

Langton, M, *Well I Heard It On the Radio and I Saw It On the Television*, Sydney: Australian Film Commission, 1993.

Lansdowne, R and Bacon W, *Women Homicide Offenders in New South Wales*, Sydney: Feminist Legal Action Group, 1982.

Lapsley, H, Robertson, N and Busch, R, "Family Court Counselling, Part I" (March 1993) 3 *Butterworths Family Law Bulletin* 152.

Lapsley, H, Robertson, N and Busch, R, "Family Court Counselling, Part II" (June 1993) 1 *Butterworths Family LJ* 9.

Lather, P, *Getting Smart: Feminist Research and Pedagogy With/in the Postmodern*, New York: Routledge,1991.

[The] Laws of Australia: Homicide, Sydney: Law Book Company, 1992.

Leader-Elliot, I , "Battered But Not Beaten: Women Who Kill in Self Defence" (1993) 15 *Syd LR* 403.

Lerman, L, "Mediation of Wife Abuse Cases: The Adverse Impact of Informal Dispute Settlement on Women" (1984) 7 *Harv Women's LJ* 57.

Levinger, G, "Sources of Marital Dissatisfaction Amongst Applicants for Divorce" 26 *Am J Orthopsychiatry* 803, reprinted in Straus, M and Steinmetz, S, *Violence in the Family*, New York: Dodd Mead, 1974.

Ligertwood, A, *Australian Evidence*, Sydney: Butterworths, 1988.

Littleton, C A, "Feminist Jurisprudence: The Difference Method Makes" (1989) 41 *Stan LR* 751.

Lorde, A, "The Master's Tools Will Never Dismantle the Master's House" and "Age, Race, Class and Sex: Women Redefining Difference" in Lorde, A, *Sister Outsider*, NewYork: Crossing Press, 1984.

MacCrimmon, M, "The Social Construction of Reality and the Rules of Evidence" (1991) 25 *UBCLR* 36.

MacDonald, P (ed), *Settling Up: Property and Income Distribution on Divorce in Australia*, Sydney: Prentice Hall, 1986.

MacKinnon, C, "From Practice to Theory or What is a White Woman Anyway?" (1991) 4 *Yale J of Law and Feminism* 13.

MacQueen, K, "Justifiable Homicide" *The Ottawa Citizen*, 3 May 1991.

Magner, E, "Explaining the Construct: Opinion, Evidence and the Battered Woman Syndrome" in Continuing Legal Education Seminar, *The Role of the Battered Woman Syndrome in Criminal Defences*, Sydney: Committee for Postgraduate Studies in the Department of Law Sydney University, 1992 .

Maguire, P, *Doing Participatory Research: A Feminist Approach*, Amherst: Centre for International Education, University of Massachusetts, 1987.

Mahoney, M, "Legal Images of Battered Women: Redefining the Issue of Separation" (1991) 90 *Mich LR* 1.

Mahoney, M, "Exit: Power and the Idea of Leaving in Love, Work and the Confirmation Hearings" (1992) 65 *Southern Calif LR* 1283.

Maloney, L, "Beyond Custody and Access: Post-Separation Parenting in the Nineties", (1993) 34 *Family Matters* 11.

Marthaler, D, "Successful Mediation With Abusive Couples" (1989) 23 *Mediation Q* 53.

Martinson, D, Macrimmon, M, Grant, I and Boyle, C, "A Forum on *Lavallee*: Women and Self-Defence" (1991) 25 *UBCLR* 23.

Matsuda, M, "Affirmative Action and Legal Knowledge: Planting Seeds in Plowed-Up Ground" (1988) 11 *Harv Women's LJ* 1.

Mayer, B, "The Dynamics of Power in Mediation and Negotiation" (1987) 16 *Mediation Q* 75.

Mazowiecki, T, Special Rapporteur of the Commission on Human Rights, *Report Pursuant to Commission Resolution 1992/S-1/1 of 14 August 1992*, E/CN.4/1993/50 (10 February 1993), United Nations publication.

McCulloch, J, "Police Response to Domestic Violence", in Hatty, S (ed), *National Conference on Domestic Violence*, Canberra: Australian Institute of Criminology, 1986.

McDonald, M, *Children's Perceptions of Access and their Adjustment in the Post-Separation Period*, Australia: Family Court of Australia Research Report No 9, 1990.

McFerren, L, "Interpretation of a Frontline State: Australian Women's Refuges and the State" in Watson, S (ed), *Playing the State: Australian Feminist Interventions*, Sydney: Allen and Unwin, 1990.

McGregor, H and Hopkins, A, *Working For Change: The Movement Against Domestic Violence*, North Sydney: Allen and Unwin, 1991.

McLaren, K, "Programmes to Reduce Domestic Violence: Draft of a Literature Review", unpublished paper, Wellington: Penal Policy Division of the Department of Justice, 1992.

McLaren, P and Leonard, P (eds), *Paulo Freire: A Critical Encounter*, New York: Routledge, 1993.

Melamed, J, "Attorneys and Mediation: From Threat to Opportunity" (1989) 23 *Mediation Q* 13.

Micka, C, "From Litigator to Mediator" (1989) 23 *Mediation Q* 85.

Middle East Watch, *A Victory Turned Sour: Human Rights in Kuwait Since Liberation*, New York: Human Rights Watch, 1991.

Minister of Justice, written reply, Order Paper 8/8/91 as cited in *The Capital Letter*, Vol 14, no. 32.

Minow, M, "Feminist Reason: Getting It and Losing It" (1988) 38 *J Leg Educ* 47.

Minow, M, "Words and the Door to the Land of Change: Law, Language and Family Violence" (1990) 43 *Vanderbilt LR* 1665.

Minnesota Program Development, *In Our Best Interests: A Process for Personal and Social Change*, Duluth: Minnesota Program Development Inc., (no date).

Moore, C, *The Mediation Process: Practical Strategies for Resolving Conflict*, San Francisco: Jossey-Bass, 1986.

Moore, J M, "Is a Non-Molestation Order Enough? Women's Experiences of the Family Court", unpublished Master of Arts (Applied) in Social Work thesis, Wellington: Victoria University, 1989.

Mossman, M J, "Gender Equality and Legal Aid Services: A Research Agenda for Institutional Change" (1993) 15 *Syd LR* 30.

National Committee on Violence *Violence: Directions for Australia*, Canberra: Australian Institute of Criminology, 1990

National Committee on Violence Against Women, *Position Paper*, Canberra: Australian Government Publishing Service, 1991.

New South Wales Law Reform Commission, *Provocation, Diminished Responsibility and Infanticide* Discussion Paper 31, Sydney: New South Wales Law Reform Commission, 1993.

New York Times , "Clemency Granted to 25 Women Convicted for Assault or Murder", 22 December 1990.

Newman, F, and Weissbrodt, D, *International Human Rights: Law, Policy, and Process*, Cincinnati: Anderson Publications Company, 1990.

Noesjirwan, J, *Evaluation of Women's Refuges 1985: Ten Years On*, Sydney: New South Wales Refuges Evaluation Steering Committee, 1985.

Noonan, S, "Strategies of Survival: Exploring the Limits of the Battered Woman Syndrome" in Currie, C and Adelberg, E, *Too Few To Count*, Vancouver: Press Gang, (3rd edn) 1993.

Oakley, A,"Interviewing Women: A Contradiction in Terms" in Roberts, H (ed), *Doing Feminist Research*, London: Routledge and Kegan Paul, 1981.

O'Donoghue, L, "Setting the Scene" in *Part of the Solution: Aboriginal and Torres Strait Islander Women's National Conference*, Canberra: Aboriginal and Torres Strait Islander Commission, 1992.

O'Donovan, K, *Sexual Divisions in Law*, London: Weidenfeld and Nicolson, 1985.

O'Donovan, K "Defences for Battered Women Who Kill" (1991) 18 *J of Law and Soc* 219.

Olsen, F, "The Family and the Market: A Study of Ideology and Legal Reform" (1983) 96 *Harv LR* 1497.

O'Shane, P, "Report on Aboriginal Women and Domestic Violence" in *Report of the New South Wales Task Force on Domestic Violence* Volume 2, Sydney: New South Wales Women's Co-ordination Unit, 1981.

Pateman, C, "Feminist Critiques of the Public/Private Dichotomy" in Benn, S, and Gaus, G, (eds), *Public and Private in Social Life*, London: Croom Helm St. Martin's Press, 1983.

Patton, M, *Qualitative Evaluation and Research Methods* , Newbury Park: Sage, (2nd edn) 1990.

Payne, S, "Aboriginal Women and the Law" in Cunneen, C (ed), *Aboriginal Perspectives on Criminal Justice*, Sydney: Institute of Criminology, 1992.

Pears, G, *Beyond Dispute: Alternative Dispute Resolution in Australia*, Edgecliffe: Corporate Impacts, 1989.

Penal Policy Review Committee, *Report to the Minister of Justice*, Wellington: Government Printer, 1981.

Pence, E and Paymer, M, *Power and Control: Tactics of Men Who Batter: An Educational Curriculum*, Duluth: Minnesota Program Development Inc., 1986.

Pence, E, *The Justice System's Response to Domestic Assault Cases: A Guide for Policy Development*, Duluth: Minnesota Program Development Inc., 1986.

Personal Narratives Group, *Interpreting Women's Lives: Feminist Theory and Personal Narrative*, Bloomington: Indiana University Press, 1989.

Pettman, J, *Living in the Margins: Racism, Sexism and Feminism in Australia*, Sydney: Allen & Unwin, 1992.

Pettman, J, "Gendered Knowledges" in Attwood, B and Arnold, J (eds), *Power, Knowledge and Aborigines*, Melbourne: LaTrobe University Press (special issue, (1992) 35 *J of Australian Studies*).

Police Commissioner, *Commissioner Circular 1987/11*, Wellington: Police National Headquarters, 1987.

Police Commissioner, *Commissioner Circular 1992/07*, Wellington: Police National Headquarters, 1992.

Ptacek J, "Why Do Men Batter Their Wives" in Yllo, K and Bograd, M (eds), *Feminist Perspectives on Wife Abuse*, Newbury Park: Sage, 1988.

Public Policy Research Centre, *Community Attitudes Towards Domestic Violence in Australia*, Canberra: Australian Government Office of the Status of Women, 1988.

Queensland Domestic Violence Task Force, *Beyond These Walls: Report of the Queensland Domestic Violence Task Force*, Brisbane: Department of Family Services, 1988.

Rasche, C, "Minority Women and Domestic Violence: The Unique Dilemmas of Battered Women of Color" (1986) 4 *J of Contemporary Criminal Justice* 150.

Rathus, Z, *Rougher Than Usual Handling: Women and the Criminal Justice System*, Brisbane: Women's Legal Service, 1993.

Ray, M, "Divorce Settlements: Comparing the Outcomes of Three Different Dispute Resolution Mechanisms", unpublished doctoral dissertation, New York State: Cornell University, 1988.

Reanda, L, "The Commission on the Status of Women" in Alston, P (ed), *The United Nations and Human Rights: A Critical Appraisal*, Oxford: Clarendon Press, 1992.

Report of the World Conference of the International Women's Year, Mexico City, 19 June - 2 July 1975, New York: United Nations, 1976.

Report of the United Nations Mid-Decade for Women Conference, Copenhagen 14 to 30 July 1980, New York: United Nations Publications, 1980.

Report of the World Conference to Review and Appraise the Achievements of the United Nations Decade for Women: Equality, Development and Peace, Nairobi, Kenya 15-26 July 1985, Jakarta: Office of the Minister of State for the Role of Women, 1985.

Rhoodie, E M, *Discrimination Against Women: A Global Survey of the Economic, Educational, Social and Political Status of Women*, Jefferson: McFarland, 1989.

Roberts, H (ed), *Doing Feminist Research*, London: Routledge and Kegan Paul, 1981.

Robertson, N, Busch, R, Glover, M and Furness, J, *Hamilton Abuse Intervention Project: The First Year*, Wellington: Family Violence Prevention Co-ordinating Com-mittee, 1992.

Robertson, N and Busch, R, *Hamilton Abuse Intervention Pilot Project Report no. 2: Six Month Evaluation Report*, Wellington: Family Violence Prevention Co-ordinating Committee, 1992.

Robertson, N and Busch, R, *Hamilton Abuse Intervention Pilot Project Report No. 5: The Two Year Review*, Wellington: Family Violence Prevention Co-ordinating Commit-tee, 1993.

Rosaldo, M, "Women, Culture and Society: A Theoretical Overview" in Rosaldo, M and Lamphere, L (eds), *Women, Culture and Society*, California: Stanford University Press, 1974.

Ross, M, "Intelligence Testing in Australian Aboriginals" (1984) 20 (3) *Comparative Educ* 371.

Royal Commission into Aboriginal Deaths in Custody, Research Paper No. 11, Canberra: Australian Government Publishing Service, 1989.

Royal Commission into Aboriginal Deaths in Custody, National Report Volume 2, Canberra: Australian Government Publishing Service, 1991.

Russell, J (ed), *A Feminist Review of Criminal Law*, Ottawa: Minister of Supply and Services, 1985.

Russell, D and Van de Ven, N (eds), *Crimes Against Women: Proceedings of the International Tribunal*, California: Les Femmes Publications, 1976.

Sam, M, *Through Black Eyes:A Handbook of Family Violence in Aboriginal and Torres Strait Islander Communities*, Melbourne: Secretariat of National Aboriginal and Islander Child Care, (2nd edn) 1992.

Schneider, E, "Equal Rights to Trial for Women: Sex Bias in the Law of Self-Defense" (1980) 15 *Harv Civil Rights-Civil Liberties LR* 623.

Schneider, E, "Describing And Changing: Women's Self-Defence Work and the Problem of Expert Testimony on Battering" (1986) 9 *Women's Rights Law Reporter* 195.

Schneider, E M, "The Dialectic of Rights and Politics: Perspectives from the Women's Movement" (1986) 61 *NYULR* 589.

Schneider, E, "Particularity and Generality: Challenges of Feminist Theory and Practice in Work on Woman-Abuse" (1992) 67 *NYULR* 520.

Schneider, E, "Violence Against Women and Legal Education: An Essay for Mary Joe Frug" (1992) 26 *New England LJ* 843.

Schuler, M (ed), *Freedom from Violence: Women's Strategies from Around the World,* New York: OEF International, 1992.

Schuler, M, "Violence Against Women: An International Perspective" in Schuler, M, *Freedom from Violence: Women's Strategies from Around the World,* New York: OEF International, 1992.

Schuller, R, "The Impact of Battered Woman Syndrome Testimony on Jury Decision Making: *Lavallee v R* Considered" (1990) 10 *Windsor Yearbook of Access to Justice* 105.

Scott, J, "Experience" in Butler, J and Scott, J (eds), *Feminists Theorize the Political,* New York: Routledge, 1992.

Scutt, J, "Invisible Women? Projecting White Cultural Invisibility On Black Women" (1990) 2 (46) *Aboriginal Law Bulletin* 4.

Seddon, N, *Domestic Violence in Australia: The Legal Response,* Sydney: Federation Press, 1993.

Sheehy, E, Stubbs, J and Tolmie, J, "Defending Battered Women on Trial: The Battered Woman Syndrome and its Limitations" (1992) 16 *Crim LJ* 369.

Silbey, S and Sarat, A, "Dispute Processing in Law and Legal Scholarship: From Institutional Critique to the Reconstruction of the Juridical Subject" (1989) 66 *Denver ULR* 437.

Sinclair, J, "A Presentation to the Western Workshop of the Western Judicial Education Centre" in Abell, J and Sheehy, E (eds), *Criminal Law & Procedure: Cases, Context, Critique,* North York: Captus Press, 1993.

Smart, C, *Feminism and the Power of Law,* London: Routledge, 1989.

Smith, D E, *The Everyday World As Problematic: A Feminist Sociology,* Milton Keynes: Open University Press, 1988.

Smith, S and Williams, S, "Remaking the Connections: An Aboriginal Response to Domestic Violence in Australian Aboriginal Communities" 1992 (16) 6 *Aboriginal and Islander Health Worker J* 6.

Spender, D, *Invisible Women: The Schooling Scandal,* London: Writers and Readers, 1982.

Stallone, D, "Decriminalisation of Violence in the Home: Mediation in Wife Battering Cases" (1984) 2 *Law and Inequality* 493.

Stanley, L (ed), *Feminist Praxis,* New York: Routledge, 1990.

Stanley, L and Wise, S, *Breaking Out: Feminist Consciousness and Feminist Research,* London: Routledge and Kegan Paul, 1983.

Stanley, L and Wise, S, "Method, Methodology and Epistemology in Feminist Research" in Stanley, L (ed), *Feminist Praxis,* New York: Routledge, 1990.

Stevenson, E, "The Use of Community Mediation in the Family Mediation Centre (NSW)" (1990) 1 *Aust Dispute Resolution J* 24.

Strang, H, *Homicides in Australia 1990-91,* Canberra: Australian Institute of Criminology, 1992.

Straus, M, Gelles, R and Steinmetz, S, *Behind Closed Doors: Violence and the American Family*, Newbury Park: Sage, 1988.

Stubbs, J, "The (Un) reasonable Battered Woman?: A Response to Easteal" (1992) 3:3 *Current Issues in Criminal Justice* 359.

Stubbs, J and Egger, S, *The Effectiveness of Protection Orders in Australian Jurisdictions*, Canberra: Australian Government Printing Service, 1993.

Stubbs, J and Powell, D, *Domestic Violence: Impact of Legal Reform in New South Wales*, Sydney: New South Wales Bureau of Crime Statistics and Research, Attorney General's Department, 1989.

Stubbs, J and Tolmie, J, "Women Out Of Context: Battered Woman Syndrome and the Australian Experience" (1994) 8 *Canadian J Women and Law* (forthcoming).

Stubbs, J and Wallace, A, "Protecting Victims of Domestic Violence?" in Findlay, M and Hogg, R (eds), *Understanding Crime and Criminal Justice*, Sydney: Law Books, 1988.

Sugar, F and Fox, L, "Nistum Peyako Seht'wawin Iskwewak: Breaking Chains" (1989-90) 3 *Canadian J Women and Law* 465.

Sun, M and Woods, L, *A Mediator's Guide to Domestic Abuse*, New York: National Centre on Women and Family Law, 1989.

Sydney Morning Herald, "A Hard Case for Justice Bollen", 11 August 1993.

Tarrant, S, "Provocation and Self-Defence: A Feminist Perspective" (1990) 15:4 *Legal Service Bulletin* 147.

Te Awekotuku, N, "He Tikanga Whakaaro: Research Ethics in the Maori Community", unpublished paper, Auckland, Manatu Maori, 1991.

Thomas, C, *Report On Consultations with Aboriginal Communities* in NSW *Domestic Violence Strategic Plan Report No. 2*, Sydney: Women's Co-ordination Unit, 1991.

Thomas, D and Beasley, M, "Domestic Violence as a Human Rights Issue" (1993) 15 *Human Rights Q* 36.

Thornhill, E, "Focus on Black Women!" (1985) 1 *Canadian J of Women and Law* 153.

Thornton, M, "Feminism and the Contradictions of Law Reform" (1991) 19 *International J of the Sociology of Law* 453.

Tolman, R M and Bennett, L W, "A Review of Quantitative Research on Men Who Batter" (1990) *J of Interpersonal Violence* 87.

Tolmie, J, "Provocation or Self Defence for Battered Women Who Kill" in Yeo, S (ed), *Partial Excuses to Murder*, Sydney: Federation Press, 1991.

Tomasevski, K, *Women and Human Rights*, London: Zed Books, 1993.

Twaddle, A J, and Wasey, J F, *Hamilton Abuse Intervention Pilot Project (HAIPP)*, unpublished paper, Wellington: Family Court Judges' Conference, April 1993.

UNIFEM, "Calling for Change: International Strategies to End Violence Against Women", The Hague, 6-9 June 1993.

United Nations, *1989 World Survey on the Role of Women in Development*, New York: Centre for Social Development and Humanitarian Affairs, 1989.

United Nations, *Women, Challenges to the Year 2000*, New York: United Nations Publications, 1991.

United Nations, *The World's Women 1970-1990: Trends and Statistics*, New York: United Nations Publications, 1991.

Wade, J, "Lawyers and Mediators: Learning from and about Each Other" (1991) 2 *Aust Dispute Resolution J* 159.

Walker, L, *The Battered Woman Syndrome*, New York: Springer Publishing Company, 1984.

Walker, L, "Battered Women, Psychology, and Public Policy" (1984) 29 *Am Psychologist* 1178.

Walker, L, "Psychology and Violence Against Women" (1989) 44 *Am Psychologist* 695.

Walker, L, Thyfault, R and Browne, A, "Beyond the Jurors' Ken: Battered Women" (1982) 7 *Vermont LR* 1.

Wallace, A, *Homicide: The Social Reality*, Sydney: New South Wales Bureau of Crime Statistics and Research, 1986.

Wallerstein, J and Blakeslee, S, *Second Chances: Men, Women and Children a Decade after Divorce*, New York: Ticknor and Fields, 1989.

Watson, S, *Accommodating Inequality: Gender and Housing*, Sydney: Allen and Unwin, 1988.

Watson, S (ed), *Playing the State: Australian Feminist Interventions,* Sydney: Allen and Unwin, 1990.

Weitzman, L J, *The Divorce Revolution: The Unexpected Social and Economic Consequences for Women and Children in America*, New York: Free Press,1985.

Wells, C, "Domestic Violence and Self-Defence" (1990) 140 *New LJ* 127.

Wilson, P, *Black Death: White Hands,* Sydney: George Allen and Unwin, 1982.

Women's Legal Resources Centre, *Women Out West* Sydney: Women's Legal Resources Centre, 1994.

Women Living under Muslim Laws, Compilation of Informations on Crimes of War Against Women in Ex-Yugoslavia (3 December 1992, updated 11 January 1993, available International Solidarity Network, PO Box 23-34790 Grabels, Montpellier, France.

Women's Rights Project and Asia Watch, *Double Jeopardy: Police Abuse of Women in Pakistan*, New York: Human Rights Watch, 1992.

Women's Rights Project, *Token Gestures,* Washington, DC: International Human Rights Law Group, 1993.

Young, W, *Rape Study: A Discussion of Law and Practice (Volume 1),* Wellington: Department of Justice, 1983.

Index